THE ROAR
OF THE CROWD

JAMES J. CORBETT

THE ROAR
OF THE CROWD

THE RISE AND FALL
OF A CHAMPION

•

by
JAMES J. CORBETT

with a foreword by
JOHN ARLOTT

PHOENIX HOUSE LTD

LONDON

Printed in Great Britain by
The Aldine Press of Letchworth for
Phoenix House Ltd, 38 William IV Street,
Charing Cross, W.C.2
First published in this edition
1954

FOREWORD

by John Arlott

JUST as James J. Corbett was one of the builders of modern boxing technique, so his book, *The Roar of the Crowd*, was one of the first of the now established form of sporting 'life-story'.

It was first issued in 1925, with a foreword by Robert Gordon Anderson, in the course of which occurs the phrase 'his story, as he told it to me', which may be taken as indication that the book was, in fact, written by Anderson from Corbett's conversation.

This single passage seems to me to absolve both Corbett and Anderson from the major offence committed by the 'name' and writer of the average 'ghosted' book – in that they do not claim that the boxer is also a writer.

Secondly, there is no doubt that this was a genuine collaboration. The 'ghosted' reminiscences of the present day are all too often – and only too clearly – made up from scrap-books and newspaper cuttings, so that they lack authenticity of quality and character.

The Roar of the Crowd, however, emerges to the reasonable reader as a book in the line of, say, Nyren's *The Cricketers of My Time*, which was, admittedly, 'collected and edited by Charles Cowden Clarke'. There is no certainty that the man of action is also a good writer: in fact, the reverse is always likely to be true, for writing is, by and large, a full-time occupation. Yet that is no reason why the world should be deprived of the man of action's life-story. Thus, with the man of letters to set out his memories in assimilable form, our practising sportsman may earn our gratitude – provided he gives us the first guarantee of the honesty of the book by stating clearly who wrote it.

Here, as in Clarke's version of Nyren's story, the writer obviously sat diligently taking notes at the feet of the story-teller.

While some of the text is written in the manner which was later to emerge as the now widely admired American sports-reporting style, even more of it is convincingly Corbett's own story in his own words. The dialogue frequently comes to real life. Here, we can believe, are the words – or as near as maybe – which one great boxer spoke to another. That quality is enough to convince us that we are being taken genuinely behind the scenes of the first days of the 'big fight game'.

Corbett himself was not a roughneck. He was brought up in a good home, where religion, music, ethical standards of business, formed the normal atmosphere.

Against that background the world of boxing was a strange place where the young man moved with a naïve wonderment.

His story is of the lad who 'rose' to become a bank clerk and then, establishing himself as a first-class amateur boxer, failed to find the man round the corner who could knock him out. He became a professional, and nowhere has the story been better told of the gradual dawning of the realization that the teller is, in fact, the champion boxer of the world.

Boxing's best modern historian – Nat Fleischer – says of him: 'Corbett had one thing very few professional fighters ever won. That was universal respect.' He was known as 'Gentleman Jim', and he toured both America and – with great success – England in the play *Gentleman Jack*.

In the boxing ring and on the stage he found his stake of glory, but it did not spoil him. He made one of the few admirable attempts – though not quite a successful one – to 'come back' and regain the title he had lost to Fitzsimmons, and then retired with decent grace – and a reputation which has endured.

There is good reason to suppose that he was proud of his book. James Stephens, the poet, once told me how he treasured the copy of it that Corbett gave him, inscribed 'From one Champion of Ireland to another'. They had met on board ship, crossing the Atlantic, and the poet found the boxer good and intelligent company.

In short, the man who told this story was an intelligent, decent chap – and Champion of the World: the man who set it down for him was an experienced journalist with a genuine admiration for his principal, and with no hackneyed form of sporting reminiscence to inhibit him. That his book should have been copied is a compliment to him, but the copies do not invalidate – rather they emphasize – the honesty and interest of the very readable book which the collaboration produced.

CONTENTS

ILLUSTRATIONS

*These photographs are reproduced by
permission of 'Picture Post' Library*

THE ROAR
OF THE CROWD

I

My First Fight and how I wanted to run away – Expulsion
from School – Father's Livery Stable and what happened in a
Box Stall – Blackbeard and the Boxing Instructor – My First
Dose of Smelling-salts.

FROM my first fight I started to run away. This scrap came at an
early age, when I was about twelve years old. I was attending
St Ignatius College in San Francisco, and at noon and recess
periods was confined to what they called the 'Little Yard'. Up
to a certain grade you were in the Little Yard with the smaller
youngsters, and when you were promoted out of the Little Yard
you could go in the 'Big Yard' with the big boys; but I was
always large for my age and looked much older than I really was,
so I would go to the picnics and they would have prizes for boys
under twelve years old and they never would let me try for
them, and I felt rather out of it and often lonely, so whenever I
could I would sneak in the Big Yard at lunch times to play hand
ball and prisoners' base with the older boys.

The bully of the Big Yard was a boy called 'Fatty' Carney,
but I had never been warned about him. Now about this time I
struck up an acquaintance with a fellow by the name of Hopkins.
We used to bring our own lunches, as we lived quite a distance
from the school, and this Hopkins boy, whose folks were well-
to-do, brought all the finest kinds of cakes and sandwiches. Perhaps this was one of the attractions of the friendship. Anyway,
I used to go in and play with him and get some of his lunch,
which was much finer than anything I had ever had. In playing
prisoners' base one day I happened to chase him, and Fatty
Carney, the bully I have just spoken of, was running after someone else, and Hopkins ran into Fatty and Carney promptly hit
him. Of course I took Hopkins's part, as he was my pal, and
grabbed Carney's arms and started to fight him then and there,
but the other boys interfered and a Brother of the College came
and ordered me back to the Little Yard where I belonged, but
not before Carney had said : 'I'll get you after school!' Someone

was then kind enough to inform me that I was up against the roughest fellow in the school.

When school was dismissed that afternoon one of the boys whispered to me, as we marched out in line, that Carney was waiting for me outside. My first intention was to run away. There were two exits and I was trying to decide which was the safer, when it suddenly occurred to me that if I ran away all the boys would laugh at me and I would be looked upon as a coward. I kept thinking it over while I was marching, but my pride was now aroused and I said to myself: 'I will go out and get licked.' And out I marched on the street and there was Carney with a bunch of fellows surrounding him, waiting. I was only a kid then, but that afternoon an idea came to me that has since stood me in good stead – to avoid trouble, if possible, but if it lay ahead of me, to be the aggressor and not let the other fellow think I was at all afraid. In my heart I was afraid of Carney then, but I marched right over to him, scared as I was, and said: 'Are you waiting for me?' He said 'Yes'.

We went around to a lot opposite the United States Mint, called the 'Mint Yard', and the whole school followed. We started to fight. He was a big, strong fellow – if we had been men and in a regular ring, they would have called him the slugger, and me a panther, terms much used in descriptions of fights those days.

I had never had a boxing lesson, but occasionally had watched my older brother box. He was six years older than I and I remembered a few of his tricks, such as looking at the stomach and hitting in the face – just the crude principles of the boxing art.

Fatty started to rush me, and as he was stronger and older than I, I began to jump out of his way, trying to make him miss. Then I'd jab at him and jump away – instinctively using my head even at that age, though I didn't realize it myself. After a few minutes the police came and scattered us, but by that time I was sure I could whip Fatty, and when we ran away from the police I ran in the same direction that he took, as I wanted to have it out with him. He made for his home, and we came to the Circus Lot, used for the circus performances in those days. I had no supporters with me, just two or three of the boys of my own neighbourhood who had followed me, while Fatty had his whole gang at his back. We started fighting in this lot and I was getting

4

the better of him and he realized it, so he grabbed hold of me and started to wrestle and, being much stronger than I, threw me down and proceeded to punch me while I lay underneath him. An old gentleman with a cane stood near, watching us. He took the cane in his hand and stepped in and hit Fatty on the back with it and told him he ought to fight boys of his own age and size. I went home with a black eye.

My father, an old-fashioned Irishman, discovered this little souvenir of the fight. Pointing at it, he asked sternly: 'Where did you get this?'

I explained the circumstances to him and told him it had been a case of either fighting or running away and being called a coward. I didn't realize at the time that my father was really proud of me because I had not chosen the other entrance of the school. He asked me who it was I had fought with and I told him Fatty Carney.

'Carney down on Howard Street?' he asked.

In those days San Francisco wasn't as big as it is now and everybody knew everybody else, and he repeated: 'Carney down on Howard Street? H'm! What d'ye think uv that!' He seemed surprised to think that I had been fighting with this big Carney boy and couldn't understand it.

I returned to school the next day; so did Carney. Then the older boys in the Big Yard came around, making a fuss over me, and I could hear the boys talking and saying to each other: 'Why, you ought to have seen him yesterday! This kid was shifting and using judgment just the way professionals do.'

I was surprised and pleased, but the wind was taken out of my sails when the head of the College appeared and put us both out of school. He did not suspend us, but expelled us for good. Anyway, this fight grew to be a legend, a sort of historical event in the school and was talked of long afterwards, so the boys told me.

From that fight I learned a lesson that has lasted me all my life – that the size of a man does not count, and that by using my head and feet I could lick a man much stronger than myself.

I don't think that I really proved that I had what I call *real* courage in that first fight. After all, it was merely a question of my pride. As a matter of fact, I do not think I had my courage tested until eight years afterwards when I fought Choinyski. Then I found out what it means to keep on going in the face of a

5

terrible beating, when defeat stares you in the face; but more of this later.

The next year I attended Sacred Heart College. Two incidents of that year stand out in my mind. There was a boy from my neighbourhood who went to this school and who was subject to epileptic fits. He used to look on me as a protector. When one of these attacks would come on the teacher would say: 'Corbett, take him out into the yard.' Out we would go, and when the attack subsided we would have a real good time together. This gave me a bright idea, and finally one day I tried it. I leaned over to my epileptic friend and whispered: 'Tim, can you throw a fit for me?'

Being grateful for all my trouble, he did this promptly as a little act of friendship. The teacher yelled: 'Corbett, take him out!' and we had a wonderful time, fooling around, playing knife and telling stories, and stayed out in the yard about an hour. This worked so splendidly that we tried it at least once a week and got many an unearned recess thereby.

During this period I had some fights. I think I can truthfully say that I never started one. In fact I have tried to follow such a policy all my life; but after the first fight with Carney, through the confidence gained in it, I never took any 'back talk' from any boy, no matter what his size.

The second incident that I recall most vividly was quite dramatic and was also the cause of my being expelled from Sacred Heart College.

One of the boys sitting behind me was constantly whispering slurs at me. This I of course resented. The Brother in charge of the classroom called me forward, broke a window pole in half, told me to hold out my hand, and gave me one of the most terrific blows I have ever had in my life. The pain was intense, and when he said 'Hold out your other hand', for once I didn't obey, and turned and walked back to my seat.

When the class was dismissed I started to go out with the other boys but was ordered by this kind-hearted Brother to remain behind the rest. I caught a glimpse of the big stick under his gown, and lit out of the door. This happened to be on the fourth floor, and the school was so built that there were four galleries circling an open court. Around each successive gallery I ran, pursued by the Brother with this stick, then on the third floor by two more of the order, on the second by another group, until I came to the bottom where a seventh lay in wait – a big fat fellow looking like Friar Tuck. I have heard since of the 'solar plexus blow'. It was not then known, but I delivered it – with my head – in the fat Brother's stomach, and over we went, rolling on the floor and out into the street. This valedictory ended my schooldays, though not my education.

School over, work was ahead. My father kept a livery stable and among his customers was the cashier of the Nevada Bank of San Francisco, J. S. Angus. One of the owners of this bank was John W. Mackay, father of the well-known Clarence H. Mackay. Mr Angus got me a job as messenger boy and I worked there for six years, rising at last to the post of assistant receiving teller.

During this period – from 1879 to 1886 – I used to box frequently. With my father's consent I kept boxing-gloves in the stable, and the boys of the neighbourhood would come around in the evenings after supper, and we had many informal bouts.

However, the form of athletics that seemed to appeal to me most at this time was baseball. In fact I think I may say that I was headed for the Big League, for our team, 'The Alcazars', played against clubs that had on their roster such players as Ed Morris and Fred Carroll, later a famous battery of the Pittsburgh Nationals, George Van Haltren, for many years centre-fielder of the Giants, Tom Brown of the Washingtons, and many others that figured in the box scores of the '80s and '90s. With those whose names I have just mentioned, and others who later became famous, I was really being groomed by the baseball magnates of the Coast for a baseball career.

There is a famous story called 'A Piece of String', which tells of a man who stooped down to pick up this little article and so had his whole career changed. Well, that is what a simple thing like a liner did for me – it split my hand between the little and third fingers so badly that I had to leave the diamond, and thereafter devoted more time to boxing.

Just before this accident occurred I had been asked by the officers of the famous Olympic Athletic Club of San Francisco to play second base for their team. Unfortunately I never did, because of the mishap just referred to, but it brought me within the walls of this club, famous in all sporting annals, and there I began to take up boxing in a more serious way.

7

At this time I had a pal named Lew Harding who was interested in boxing and still more so in wrestling. In his father's cellar he had boxing-gloves and a wrestling pad, and twice a week we went to this favourite haunt at night. Now his ideas about training were not as helpful as his ideas of wrestling. As soon as we arrived, as first part of our routine, we would freeze four quarts of ice-cream. When that was hard, we would wrestle half an hour, then eat a quart of cream, following this up with boxing for an hour; after which strenuous exercise we would eat up the remainder of the cream. It was enough to kill any ordinary individual and I would not advise anyone seriously considering taking up boxing adopting this course.

I did not really know that I had any natural boxing ability, although I had tried to remember and put in practice certain things I had seen professionals do; however, Lew saw in me things that I didn't see in myself – quickness of eye and feet, and a natural understanding of and instinct for the game. So without telling me that he was putting me through a course of stunts for any purpose, he began to take me around to various places where I must 'mix it' with the toughest characters in town.

For instance, on Wednesday nights he would lead me, an unconscious victim, to the fire-engine house where the roughest young fellows of the town used to congregate, and on Friday nights to a blacksmith shop where the crowd was even worse. I had a good many fights at each of these places – some of them pretty tough ones, for, as I said, the gangs were composed of noted scrappers of the town. When I first came there they used to sneer at me and look upon me as a dude, for, being a bank clerk, I naturally took pains with my personal appearance. However, I fought myself into their estimation and soon they forgot to call me this withering name and made no more remarks about my white collar or kid gloves, although many compliments were paid me about my use of those of another sort.

By and by, having licked all the regular frequenters of the place, they began to scout around along the shore front, 'The Barbary Coast', and all the low dives of the underworld to secure the roughest talent they could. I found the road pretty tough going for a while, but stuck it out, never losing a single bout. All these were earned without any real boxing instruction, which was to come later; but here I feel I developed resourcefulness, generalship, and ability to size up all kinds of men. Of course, my antagonists were all of the brutal slugging type, and used no judgment at all; but it was undoubtedly a great experience for me.

When I joined the Olympic Club it happened that their building had just burned down and the members were using the Turn Verein, which had an open gymnasium, a gallery, and a running track. The first day after I had signed up, being very confident of my ability, through my victories in the engine house and blacksmith shop, I went up to the boxing instructor to 'take him on'. He asked me if I had ever boxed and I replied, with a great deal of pride: 'Oh, yes, hundreds of times!' He said: 'Box with me awhile', and then proceeded to show me up.

It seems that in the gallery were several German friends of his and he tried to make a 'monkey' out of this fresh 'kid' to their great delight. Every time my head went back from one of his blows they would roar over their steins until the rafters rang. He hit me so often that I thought there was a shower of boxing-gloves like big hailstones coming through the air. Although I had always managed to keep good control of my temper, I felt that afternoon that he, with his skill, was taking advantage of a youngster in rather a mean way and 'showing off' before his German friends. I 'saw red' and began to rough it with him, scuffling around, and he threatened to report me and have my privileges at the club rescinded. So that ended our relations.

The next day my friend Harding and I went to the club again and I saw a fellow with an immense black beard like a Russian's or the ones the bearded miners wore in '48. (There were still some left around Frisco.) Blackbeard was boxing with a friend and he must have been fooling with him, but I didn't know this at the time. He had a magnificent torso, like Jeffries', but I didn't take note of it just then; all I could see were those black whiskers, and I said to myself: 'A fellow who would wear a beard like that cannot box.'

Then I leaned over to my friend Harding and suggested that he 'fix it up for me'. Harding went over to the Professor and asked him to arrange a few rounds with the black-bearded man. The Professor smiled, seeing revenge ahead, as this fellow, although I did not know it, was the heavyweight champion of the club, weighed 215 pounds, and was a terrific hitter.

The gloves once on, I struck out for the Blackbeard – for still

9

all I could see were those whiskers. In the next second I was sitting in a chair and they were throwing water over me, rubbing my legs and holding smelling salts to my nose. I had been 'knocked dead cold', but even then didn't realize it.

I got up and, in a groggy way, said 'Come on, let's box', but 'Blackbeard' replied:

'No, you have had enough for today.'

To show them that I was all right and had not been hurt I started to circle the running track, which ran around the room, the centre being occupied by the apparatus. Somehow I couldn't keep to the track and before I had lurched three yards was reeling into the centre of the room and banging into the apparatus, still very groggy and in danger of other knock-out blows – from the parallel bars and flying rings.

Lew led me from the gymnasium down to the dressing-room, and then it began to dawn on me that I had really been knocked out and for the first time in my life; and I think it was one of the greatest blows to my pride I have ever experienced. I saw then that I needed boxing instruction.

About twelve months after this incident the beautiful new Olympic Club was opened and a boxing instructor, Walter Watson, was imported from England. On the first day of his appearance a man named Eiseman, who happened to be the middleweight champion of the club, asked Watson for a bout, and in front of his (Eiseman's) friends tried to put the finishing touch on the new teacher, a 'grand stand' and very mean trick, also decidedly unethical, as Eiseman was a younger man than Watson and the latter was not in condition and was simply engaged to teach the members points. There followed a terrific fight which was later stopped, and Watson, resenting the unfairness of it, shook his fist in Eiseman's face and said: 'In three months I will develop some youngster from this club who will give you the worst licking you ever had in your life.'

The next day, I, being sixth on the list for the boxing lesson, waited my turn with the instructor. Meantime, I watched the other men and noticed that they all seemed afraid of Watson and didn't 'open up'. This caution – or respect – rather annoyed him, I also noticed, because he was anxious to find out how much they knew and what material he had to work with. When it came to my turn he asked me: 'Have you ever boxed?'

'A good many times,' I told him.

He said: 'Open up; I want you to show me what you have.'

Feeling a little impressed by this man, who was quite noted for his skill, I looked at him, puzzled, and inquired: 'Do you really mean it?'

'Of course,' he replied, impatiently.

'Open up with all I have and hit you as hard as I want to?' I asked, to make sure.

He smiled. 'That's what I want.'

So off I started, like a runaway horse, and showered blows at him from all directions. In about a minute he held up his hand and said: 'Is there any Irish blood in you, by any chance?'

'Yes, sir, my father and mother are Irish,' I answered.

He grinned. 'In three months you will lick any man in this club.'

His confidence somehow seemed to stimulate me as no other words had ever done. Every spare moment I could get I practised feints and shifts, even trying them before my mirror at night, and in the morning would study my own action, which furnished considerable amusement for my other brothers who looked through the door. Meanwhile the instructor took particular pains with me from then on and I became his favourite pupil.

After I had taken my second boxing lesson I approached my brother Harry, who was next to the oldest of the ten children in our family, and asked him to put on the gloves with me. Having always been able to cuff me about as he liked, he laughed at me, but I persisted and finally, giving in, he went out to the box stall in the livery stable.

A little patronizingly he put up his hands, but before he knew it I had hit him so quickly that he was jolted hard up against the sides of the stall. This was a new experience for him and he grew angry and started to rush me; but I had benefited by my lessons and shifted and ducked this way and that under his arm so he couldn't land a glove on me. I tried one or two more blows on him; then he suddenly stopped and said, with a mischievous grin: 'Wait, I'll get Frank!'

Now Frank was my oldest brother and had always had a wonderful time chasing me about and was considered the star scrapper of the family. Harry found him and he came into the box stall, all confidence and prepared to give me the punishment earned by my freshness and impudence. Like Harry he put his hands up, but before he had time even to lead I had landed at least ten blows on him in such rapid succession that he was quite as stunned as Harry had been. I was under him and back of him and all around; he might as well have been chasing a shadow, and then I turned to and slammed him all over the place. He tore off the gloves and went into the office of the livery stable where my father sat, busy at his accounts.

'Dad,' said Frank, 'you better look out for that fellow.'

Watching by the window, I heard Dad reply, without discontinuing his work: 'What fellow?'

'Jim.'

Then he looked up.

'Why, what has he done?'

'Done!' exclaimed Frank, 'why he's just knocked Harry and me all over the box stall out there and he'll turn into a prizefighter if you don't look out, he's getting so chesty!'

The old gentleman laughed and thought it was a great joke, but of course didn't take it seriously.

As you may have guessed, we were a very united family, but naturally, like all others, had our troubles, and one of the things that impressed me most, even as a boy, was hearing my father and mother, who were quite thrifty, talking about that mortgage of $6,000 on their San Francisco home and the stable property. You see that although he worked hard, his livery stable business could not bring many luxuries to a family of twelve.

During the time I held the position in the bank, I used to keep his books at night to help him out and realized just how he stood and was early impressed with his financial hardships. Seeing him worry about the feed bill and all such little details brought this home, and then and there, even as a boy, I determined if I ever got hold of any big sum of money, the first thing I would do would be to pay off that mortgage. Then, if there was anything left, I planned to send them to the old country to see their childhood home. Often they used to talk about the place and say: 'Oh, if we could only see Ireland again before we die!'

A fellow never had better or more affectionate parents than I. Perhaps they were a little too lenient with us sometimes, but I think on the whole they were just. Honestly, I cannot think, as

I look back over the years, of a single mistake they ever made, except perhaps in being too open-hearted. For instance, I can now remember how once, after I became champion and was playing in San Francisco, my mother insisted on having the whole company of forty people out to see her, simply because 'they were friends of Jim's'. And I know they never tasted a better supper, and after it was over my sister went to the piano and accompanied my mother singing 'Annie Laurie' in her sweet old voice. When the song was over father and mother, in response to a unanimous demand, danced an Irish jig. She was a beautiful waltzer, too – so light on her feet, although she was plump. I have never danced with a finer, it seems to me.

That there was harmony in our family, and respect paid to our parents, is evident from the fact that for the six years I was a bank clerk I gave my monthly salary to my mother each pay day. Afterwards I would ask my father for what I needed from time to time. When my mother died they found in her bureau a bank-book in my name with the entries of my salary, the first of each month, showing the raises as they came along.

Their plans for me may seem amusing to some of my friends, for earlier in life they had determined upon my being a priest – perhaps because a brother of my father's, who was born after father left Ireland and whom he had never seen, the uncle for whom I was named, was a priest.

2

A Feud Fight in which I was an Innocent Victim – 'The Sailor Lad' – The Sacred Egg – The Famous 'Nonpareil' – Maurice Barrymore and Camille.

DURING the months following Walter Watson's taking charge at the Olympic Club, I took lessons from him three times a week, but was so enthusiastic that I used to go on the days between to watch the others box and pick up what I could as a spectator. I guess I must have been developing pretty fast, although I did not know it at the time.

Watson took an unusual interest in me, not merely because of any actual talent I may have been fortunate enough to possess but because of the old grudge between him and Eiseman, the middle-weight champion of the club, who had treated him so roughly at his first appearance. The bad feeling between these two had grown with each day and they did not speak to each other. Every member in the club knew of this bitterness and it was common gossip that Watson was grooming me for his own personal revenge on the other man; but so absorbed was I in the game itself and all it opened up to me in the way of science that I was ignorant of any trouble brewing and of the role I had been picked to play in the event that was later to be staged.

I suppose my lack of observation was also partly due to my youth, for I was only a kid sixteen years old, and stood too much in awe of the famous amateurs and well-known bankers and business men of the city who were interested in sports and frequented the place, to think of any intrigue or feuds going on in such distinguished company.

Meantime I was coming along at a much faster clip than I knew, and Watson must have been watching my progress with pleasure. About six months after the start of the trouble with Eiseman, Professor Watson staged his first 'boxing night' at the club. In this exhibition he hoped to prove to the satisfaction of the members and directors the progress made by all the boys whom he had himself developed, and he hoped that they would show up favourably in comparison with the older men who had been trained by a former instructor.

This was really more than an exhibition, it was really the climax of the feud I have described; and every man in the club that night knew that the real event of the evening was to be the bout between Eiseman and myself, which I thought was merely a friendly exhibition and not at all for blood. So I was surprised when, in my dressing-room, Watson approached me and said: 'Boy, from the call of "Time" you go for that fellow with all you've got!'

'What!' I replied, a little puzzled. 'You want me to try to knock him out? I thought this was just an exhibition.'

'Never mind the exhibition part,' he returned. 'He is going to try to knock you out, and you'd better get him first.'

It was a wonderful night for me, being my first public appearance, not only before the famous Olympic Club, but in the city. Hitherto my fights had been such as those described, at the engine house and blacksmith shop, or in my father's stable.

The place was packed to the rafters with leading men of San Francisco. But after the first thrill over my audience, I tried to forget them, and keep but one thought in mind, that implanted there a few minutes before by my instructor, and so, as directed, from the call of 'Time' I went after Eiseman with all I had. Now although I was ignorant of the real purpose of the fight, he knew it well, and he stood up to me and we slugged it toe to toe for the three minutes without stopping or budging scarcely an inch from the spot in the ring where we met.

At once the big room was in an uproar. Never had the Olympic Club staged so thrilling a fight, so they told me afterwards. If I had had time to think about it I would have been surprised at doing so well, but although I was still, because of my early experience, somewhat of a slugger, I had natural quickness, which my friends used to like to call 'panther-like'; and Watson had added at least some rudiments of science.

It is hard to tell in whose favour this round ended, but it must have been even. At any rate, the spectators got the full worth of a year's membership in those three minutes, and one thing I was glad to see, as I rested, was that the pace had begun to tell on Eiseman.

During this intermission, as he worked over me, Watson said: 'No matter how tired you feel, remember the other fellow is worse off than you are and that the pace is killing him.'

Up we came at the call of 'Time' – for in those days at the club the beginning and the end of a round were announced by the timekeeper, there being no gong – and again we went at it hammer and tongs, he plainly weakening under the terrific bombardment.

All of a sudden, to my surprise, a right-hander, without any aim or timing, landed on the point of his jaw, and Mr Eiseman went through the ropes, à la Dempsey-Firpo, to sit in somebody's lap.

Then for the first time I heard officially the count of that sacred number 'Ten', and the whole crowd made a rush for the ring as one man, and lifted me on their shoulders – bankers, lawyers, merchants, for once forgetting their dignity! Some even going so far as to kiss me on the cheek. And all the time Walter Watson hovered over me and patted me like a little pet dog who ad done something well he had been told to do.

From that time on until my entrance into the professio al ring, four years later, I reigned, first as middleweight and then s heavyweight champion of the club.[1]

During this time many other exhibitions were held and I ha taken to the work so well and advanced so far that they had t call in professionals to meet me in the final and star bouts of the evening – they of course receiving pay, but I no reward except the honour.

One of those selected was Mike Brennan, the Port Costa giant, a recognized heavyweight of the Coast; but probably the most prominent I met was the famous Jack Burke, 'the Irish Lad', then very generally considered the most skilful boxer in the world. Some idea of his ability may be gained from the fact that when Sullivan, then at his prime, was knocking out men right and left in four rounds, Burke stood up eight against him without being knocked out. He also fought Charley Mitchell in some nine or ten limited contests, eight of which, I think, were draws.

My bosses at the bank took a great interest in this fight that was scheduled, and on hearing that Burke was to receive $100 a round, I nothing, decided that the least they could do was to allow me a week's vacation for training.

I took this very seriously, though I really did not know very much about the principles of conditioning oneself for a fight. Watson did give me some excellent advice, but in my youthful enthusiasm, like the man who, ordered by the doctor to take one teaspoonful, takes four, thinking he will get well four times as quick, I increased the dose.

I had read somewhere that getting up at five o'clock in the morning and taking a raw egg and sherry on rising would make a man very strong. So, wanting to become a mighty man, followed this recipe and managed the first few nights of that critical week not to sleep at all through fear I wouldn't wake up

[1] It is interesting to learn from old-time members of the club that the new champion outclassed all the rest of the talent so far that at the last boxing tournament held at the Olympic all other heavyweights entered withdrew, and he himself was persuaded by the management to withdraw in turn and let the others fight it out among themselves. A medal was given to the winner of this contest, and another was struck off for Mr Corbett in recognition not only of his sacrifice, but of the indisputability of his title. R. G. A.

at the exact minute. I impressed Joe, the brother who later played in the National League, but then about ten years old, into service as trainer. He acted as alarm clock for me so that I should not oversleep and would steal on tiptoe into my room in the grey of the morning, shake me by the shoulder, and whisper in my ear: 'Jim, hustle! It's time to get up!'

Then I would rise, half drowsily, and draw on my trousers, while he was bringing the magical egg and sherry. This gulped down, I would descend the stairs, shoes in hand so as not to waken the old folks, then slip out to the street.

The next part of this vigorous training was to run miles, at top speed, until I almost dropped, exhausting the strength I should have saved for the fight.

But one morning Joe woke me up with some terrible news. 'Jim,' he said, as he stood by my bed with a woebegone face, 'there's no egg!'

Now, without an egg and sherry I felt I couldn't run or fight a lick – that drink was the secret of success!

What to do was the question. Well, we spent fifteen valuable minutes looking through the kitchen cupboards for a stray egg – I say *valuable* fifteen minutes, because not only was I convinced of the magic of the egg and sherry, but also of the hour, and felt I must start precisely on schedule or else all the good of the road work would be lost!

We had no luck; but as I looked through the kitchen window and saw the chicken-house of our next-door neighbour, a bright idea occurred to me.

'Joe,' I said, 'there ought to be a couple over there'; and he, being a dutiful younger brother, and almost ready to commit murder if it would help me win the fight, replied: 'Sure'; which reply meant more than mere assent to my statement. So, feeling with all the dignity of eighteen that if he were caught it would only be considered a small boy's prank, while it would be very serious for me, a bank clerk! to be discovered robbing a hen roost, I let Joe do it, and off he went over the fence and crept safely into the darkness of the coop.

There was a moment of breathless silence while I watched, but all of a sudden one old mother hen flew out with a most alarming squawk. Twenty-four of her female relatives joined in the hubbub, to say nothing of the gentlemen of the family.

They made so much noise I didn't think there were so many chickens in the world! Up went the windows, all the neighbours sticking out their heads, and through the back door rushed the owner of the hen-coop with a cane in his hand, stuffing his nightshirt into his trousers as he ran. But Joe was game and came back with the egg.

By this time my oldest sister, whose executive ability made her the head of the house, had arrived on the scene; also my father, and naturally he wanted to know what was the matter. I think the lecture I got then was worse than the fight. However, we stood by our guns, got the tumbler and started to break the egg – but – it was a nest-egg – and china!

With hanging head I went out on the road at half my usual pace, feeling that the fight was hopelessly lost. When I came back to the porch there sat little Joe, with his head in his hands, thinking hard. All of a sudden he jumped up, and clapping me on the shoulder cried: 'I'll tell you what, Joe. To make it up I'll give you two eggs to-morrow morning.' So again came a gleam of hope and we felt that we still had a chance.

I really think that this incident was more interesting than the fight itself; there was nothing so exciting in it as the theft of the egg. I stood up eight rounds against the famous Burke, without a decision, by the way, as he had insisted upon this condition before agreeing to box with me. But in spite of my crude ideas of training I felt that I had held my own.

Years afterwards, when I was fighting as a professional, I learned I had done more than that, for on meeting Otto Floto, who acted as second to Burke that evening, I was told by the former: 'If you hadn't been such a "kid" and had had more experience, you could have knocked him cold. You hit him more than once very hard and hurt him; but he covered up and "kidded" you out of it.'

It was also during these amateur days that the original Jack Dempsey, the famous 'Nonpareil', whose name should live for ever as one of the real masters of the game, came to San Francisco and was given guest privileges at the Olympic Club and frequently exercised there. With him was Mike Cleary, heavyweight, and one of the hardest hitters that ever lived, as the records will show.

Cleary worked with me several times, but always insisted on

18

going upstairs, above the 'gym', with the excuse that it was not so crowded there. After several set-tos, he said to me: 'Boy, you're a "comer". You are going to be a great boxer some day.'

I felt rather sheepish and embarrassed, and replied: 'Thank you, Mr Cleary; that's very kind of you.'

'Kind? Not at all!' he assured me. 'It's God's own truth. You get away from a right-handed punch better than anybody I ever fought.'

Though naturally I was pleased, I could hardly accept the compliment. It seemed an exaggeration made to encourage me to train harder.

The following afternoon, Dempsey appeared at the boxing room downstairs, in tights, and wanted Cleary to box with him. The latter, having a sore mouth, begged to be excused. I was standing a little distance away, with my back towards Cleary, and I heard him say: 'There's a young fellow over there, named Corbett. He'll box with you.'

'Hell!' said Dempsey. 'I want a sweat!'

That was an awful shock to me, to feel that I couldn't even give him practice!

But my confidence returned a little when I heard Cleary reply: 'Oh, he'll give you a sweat all right!'

His interest aroused, Dempsey turned in my direction – not knowing that I had overheard the conversation – and clapping me on the back said: 'Young fellow, put on the gloves with me, will you?'

I, for my part, felt not only pleased at the opportunity, but honoured and rather impressed, for I had long been an ardent admirer of Dempsey's, who at that time was considered the greatest middleweight in the world and is still held to be one of the greatest fighters of his weight that ever lived.

It will be interesting, and will probably be surprising, not only to the public but to many of the sporting writers to learn that Dempsey's fighting weight at his prime was only 144 pounds with tights on; also that he was no bigger than Benny Leonard is today. Can you imagine Benny Leonard fighting with Bob Fitzsimmons? That will give you an idea of what a wonderful fighter he was, if you read the list of the big men he met.

One of the best in his bag of tricks was feinting – which is, sad to say, practically a lost art now. And the first thing he did with me was to feint. Usually his opponent, unless he were a seasoned ring man, would shut his eyes or retreat, or would show some sign of fear.

I had watched Dempsey box before and had myself practised his feinting with many of his other tricks. So I did not budge, having gauged the distance perfectly. Again and again he feinted, but each time I knew by the distance between us that he couldn't touch me. He looked at me in surprise and I could read him enough to know that he was thinking: 'Is this boy really clever, or just plain dumb?'

The next time he feinted, he advanced a little, and I stepped back a corresponding distance, still gauging it perfectly, he wondering meanwhile whether this accuracy were due to judgment or merely lucky accident. For three minutes this sort of thing kept up without a blow being struck, he doing his best to disconcert me before starting to work on me with his blows. Several times he left himself open and I knew that I could hit him, but I had too great respect for him and felt it a sort of discourtesy to so famous a champion to strike the first blow. I wanted him to do that, then I could begin.

The next time he stepped up I said to myself: 'Boy, it's up to you to give Mr Dempsey a sweat – that's what he wanted.' So this time I didn't back, and took the blow. It landed – a smart left-hand hook on my face. That started me, and a little later, when I saw another opening, I let fly and hit Dempsey flush on the nose. We exchanged blows for a few minutes, neither having the advantage. If he landed on me, I landed in return, and vice versa. Finally it began to get really serious, the famous 'Nonpareil' feeling that an unknown youngster had held his own with him long enough, and he promptly proceeded to try and stop me.

Then there was a furious battle. We slugged with each other all around that place, and soon word went through the club that Dempsey and Corbett were hot at it! Billiard cues slammed down on the floors, cards were scattered all over the tables, waiters dropped their steins, and in a moment the room was crowded.

We had started at six o'clock, and without the usual intermission of rounds were still fighting at six-thirty. The climax came in a clinch. As we were breaking away Dempsey used one of the smart professional tricks of which I knew very little, and hit me with his wrist across the nose, giving me the first nose-bleed I ever had had in my life.

At this my temper flared up, and I started after him, but he stopped me by holding up his glove and said: 'Boy, that's enough for to-day.'

He put his arm around me and grew quite friendly, even taking me into the wash-room, where he examined my nose, finding nothing broken. Then, to my bewilderment, he took me upstairs to the scales and weighed me. The arrow stopped at 160 pounds and I asked him, in turn, what he weighed? He jumped on the scales and I saw with my own eyes his weight 144, which is my reason for making the statement in the paragraph above about this most remarkable man.

Then he looked me over, felt my shoulders, and after a minute or two of quiet thought, inquired: 'What did you say your name is?'

'Jim Corbett.'

Then he slapped me on the back and said: 'If I was as big as you, I'd lick any man in the world!'

As he left, he called over his shoulder: 'Boy, I'll see you again.'

I had a confirmation of this flattering opinion – which, to tell the truth, I could not in my heart believe and felt was just uttered in kindness – when, on my way downstairs I met an acquaintance, a real estate man of the town, by the name of Jones. He made up to me and said, determinedly: 'Boy, I'll bet ten thousands dollars on you if you'll fight Jack Dempsey.'

'You're jollying,' I replied – and meant it.

'No,' he assured me, 'I mean it. There's a cool ten thousand waiting for you to sign.'

But I shook my head. 'Now, Mr Jones, you're trying to get me into trouble. I'm going to stick to business and haven't any idea of going into the fighting game.'

I had further evidence of the impression I must have made on Dempsey, the following night, when I went to a minstrel show. As I was handing the ticket-taker my ticket he grabbed me by the shoulder. 'Are you "Jim" Corbett of the Olympic Club?' he asked, a little bit excited. As I nodded, he called over his shoulder: 'Hey, Bill, this is the "kid" who boxed Dempsey yesterday!'

There was a general shout from the bar, and in a minute I

was in there and being generally shaken by the hand. 'This is the fellow Dempsey said he had the tough go with at the Olympic Club yesterday,' was their enlightening way of introducing me.

It seems Dempsey had also admitted that it was one of the toughest 'goes' he had ever had, and entirely unexpected, and he predicted great things for me. This good word undoubtedly had considerable influence later on my choice of a career; but for the time being I felt sufficient satisfaction in having given Mr Dempsey his 'sweat'.

I can also say that my theatrical career began at this time.

There was an actor named 'Nick' Long, in San Francisco, a member of a stock company there, and a great favourite with theatregoers of the town. He had broken his leg and it looked as if he would never be able to appear on the stage again. Accordingly a benefit was arranged for him by the two theatrical companies in San Francisco at the time – one, with Willie Collier, May Irwin, and Charley Reed in the cast, was presenting *The City Directory*. The other was Tony Palmer's great stock company and had Maurice Barrymore and Agnes Booth at the head.

A burlesque of *Camille* had been decided on for the closing act of this benefit, May Irwin to play *Camille*, Willie Collier, *Gaston*, Charley Reed, *Armand*, and Maurice Barrymore, the *Count*. It was the latter who suggested that some popular San Franciscan join the cast, to give it local colour, and as I had many friends in town they picked on me.

Feeling quite thrilled, I did my best at the rehearsals, and one night I went to Barrymore's dressing-room and asked for some suggestions as to my make-up.

Looking me up and down, he asked: 'Have you ever been on the stage before?'

'No,' I assured him, quite truthfully, 'I've never been on the stage in my life.'

'H'm – let me think,' he went on, looking very serious. 'Yes, that's it. All the others will have on burlesque make-up, you see, so you go out in full evening dress and play the Count just as I would if I were playing with Modjeska. Be very serious. Stalk out on the stage and *try* to act, and you'll be so rotten you'll be the hit of the show!'

I was!

22

3

ABOUT this time I met a man who proved to be a great influence in my career and whom I have always held to be a mighty good friend. This was 'Billy' Delaney, one of the wisest trainers in the world – later famous for bringing out James J. Jeffries; also as one of the shrewdest counsellors of men in the ring, being chief man in the corner for Jack Johnson when he defeated Jeffries.

Delaney at this time kept a little saloon, with a couple of back rooms, at Oakland, just across the bay from San Francisco. It was a queer sort of place, not much better than the sawdust variety you find along the water fronts. He had a wide and varied acquaintance, was on good terms with many of the solid citizens of the city, yet knew well the picturesque characters of the Coast underworld.

He was a curious-looking individual, with rather womanish features and a look of the keenest intelligence which a cold, poker face could not wholly mask. Coolness under all circumstances was a matter of pride with him, as a little incident of our later career together will show.

While training to fight Peter Jackson I purchased a ferocious bulldog, a big brindled fellow. We were sitting in the little country hotel where we were training, one day, reading our papers, when a stranger came in the door with another bull in tow. The two dogs looked at each other and, in a second, flew at each other's throats. A most terrible fight followed, and all in the lobby were standing on chairs or looking for the nearest exits, but through it all, even while the dogs were tearing at each other right under his very chair and round his feet, Billy Delaney continued to read the paper, never even looking around the edges to see the result! Such tactics as these were probably deliberately adopted and certainly increased his reputation for being cool under fire.

It was about this time too that, like most boys of my age, I grew foolish enough to think it was smart to dissipate a little. I couldn't resist the temptations which were many, even more in San Francisco those days than they are now. The boys would say: 'Come, Jim, and have a drink', or else: 'Let's go to such and such place', and I, feeling it was unmanly to refuse, and wanting to be popular, would consent. I became quite well acquainted with whisky punches, though I never liked them, and did lots of other things just to be a 'good fellow' and a 'good sport'.

Sometimes parties of us would go over to Billy Delaney's across the bay, for his place was open to us and we could do about as we pleased. I caught him, studying me, several times, with his cold eye and poker face, and I guess I was hitting it up pretty fast. Anyway, he called me aside, and talked things over with me.

'Jim,' Delaney would say, 'it's against my interests to tell you so, for I can't make any money by this kind of advice; but I am interested in you and would like to see you make something out of yourself. I've watched you in your bouts and you're a good boy. You can go a long ways, but lushing like this will ruin your constitution and never get you anywhere. Remember, you're not developed yet, you're only a kid.'

What he said, of course, stuck in my craw. I laughed at him, but suddenly one day I found he was right, when boxing with a man I had always easily defeated. I managed to get through the bout that afternoon, but found myself pretty weak towards the end, although I covered up so my antagonist did not recognize my condition. So I began to realize that I wasn't any different from anyone else; that drinking, losing sleep, putting one's stomach out of commission, and indulging in all other sorts of dissipation wouldn't help a man box or do any sort of athletic work.

I began to cut it out a little, but I guess I only made a half-hearted try at it. I'd go along pretty straight for a while, then some 'good fellow' would start me off again for a night. Still, my batting average was better, and on looking back I can now see I was gaining all the time. But it was really one of the toughest fights I ever had – this struggle to say: 'No, I don't drink', and come out with that flat.

It just occurs to me that I haven't mentioned the name of the man I fought more often than anyone else, Joe Choinyski – in my estimation one of the gamest and best fighters that ever lived, though a little bit too light for the heavyweight class. He was really as good as most champions I have seen, and this statement covers a period of nearly fifty years.

The first fray took place about the time I entered the Olympic Club. My older brother Frank had a job at the City Hall, working alongside of another chap in the auditor's department. Something started them boasting about the fighting ability of their younger brothers and at lunch time they almost got to fighting themselves, in arguing over the question as to which kid brother was the better. Finally Frank arranged with the older Choinyski boy to bring Joe, whom I had never seen, to my father's livery stable the following night. I was introduced to him – a magnificent-looking fellow with a blond head and great strength. We had only been fighting for a minute or two when I knocked him cold. However, the argument between the two older brothers continued, and for nearly a year, Frank crowing over Herbert Choinyski, the latter getting back at him with: 'Even if Jim did lick him with the gloves, Joe can knock the "daylights" out of him with bare fists.'

Accordingly another fight was arranged between us two and scheduled for a Sunday afternoon, in a quarry on the outskirts of San Francisco. In some way, my father got wind of it and calling me into the office of the livery stable, protested. 'Jim,' he said, 'what's this I hear about your scrapping with the Choinyski boy today?'

'Dad,' I said, trying to put the best light on it, 'I haven't any grudge against him, but he's been threatening me and you wouldn't have me back out, would you?'

My father replied: 'Jim, my boy, you know how proud I am of your working in the bank. Your mother and your sisters are, too. Boxing at the club's all right, but the bank people won't like fighting in the street and I wouldn't have you lose that job for anything in the world.'

'All right, Dad,' I said, 'if you feel that way about it I won't fight. I'll go up to Choinyski's house like a man and tell him I can't.' I did not mention my brother's part in the affair, you see, not wanting to drag him in.

'Fine, my boy,' my father replied, much pleased. 'You know where they live?'

'Up on Golden Gate Avenue,' I said; and off I went to explain my reasons for getting out of the fight.

'Chauncey,' another of the Choinyski boys, met me at the door and I asked for Joe. He wouldn't let me see him or explain anything, and began to insult me, saying: 'You wait until this afternoon, you'll see him then, all right. He'll knock you all over the lot.'

One word led to another, until I grew mad. 'Bring him out now, and I'll show you,' I told him.

Sure enough, he brought Joe out, and the five of us walked three or four miles to the sandhills beyond the limits of the town, stopping at a little hollow, where we peeled to the waist. The only spectator was a man out for his Sunday afternoon walk with a baby in his arms, and there he sat, enjoying this free entertainment, little realizing, I suppose, that of those two slugging kids one was later to be a near champion, the other champion heavyweight of the world!

After our first set-to at the barn, Joe Choinyski had joined the Golden Gate Club, another well-known organization of the city, where he had taken boxing lessons and he now showed the benefit of these lessons in a way that surprised me.

In about ten seconds he landed a terrific blow on the ear, which staggered me. However, I got full revenge for this, a few seconds later, by knocking him down and almost out. After that I also had the satisfaction of putting out for the count his older brother, who was much bigger and stronger than I.

Then I hurried back to the house and, dodging the folks, slipped up to my room to clean up the marks of the battle; but the two boys with me were so excited over the outcome that they rushed into the stable and told my father I had whipped Choinyski. He came up to my room and said, rather sadly: 'Jim, is it true that you had a fight with Choinyski, after what you promised me?'

'Yes, Dad,' I confessed, 'but I couldn't help it. If you had only heard the names they called me you'd have fought too. If I had backed out I would have been a coward. I licked him and his brother too.'

'What!' retorted Dad, 'not only Joe, but that big fellow who goes past the door every morning?'

'Yes, Dad, the two of them.'

26

Turning quickly, he went to the door and called to my mother, very excitedly: 'Kate, Kate, come up quick! Jim's after licking two of the Choinyski boys!'

My mother came up, smiling a little at first, through pride, but suddenly the smile faded. 'Suppose they hear of this at the bank!' she exclaimed.

My father scratched his head for a minute reflectively.

'That's so,' he said, 'they *might* hear of it.'

Then he looked at me again and an Irish grin broke all over his face. He seemed to be considering the facts for a minute, then he said: 'You licked the *two* of them – the *two* Choinyski boys? Aah! To hell with the bank!'

The greatest fight I had during those four years was – but I am getting ahead of my story. It's worth telling here, I think, although it occurred a little before the Choinyski fight and before I became well known as a boxer.

One night I was calling on a young lady of whom I was quite fond, when the doorbell rang and another chap, whom she knew fairly well, came with a message asking us to join a party of eight couples who were going out to a place called the Fourteen-Mile House for supper and a dance. After we had started she regretted accepting the invitation, for most of the people turned out to be of a different sort from what she had expected, and on the way out the passage was rather rough.

There was one fellow, I noticed particularly, who was continually putting a whisky bottle to his mouth and accompanying this gesture with rather rough language. I soon observed that he always made a show of drinking in the dark parts of the road, where the dim light obscured his actions, and finally discovered that he never really drank at all, and I immediately classed him as a 'bluff', trying to appear 'hard-boiled'.

At supper this same fellow made some insulting remark to the girl I was escorting and I promptly 'called him' for it. For a moment it looked as if there would be a fight then and there, for all the others, with the exception of the girl I was with and one other young woman who seemed well brought up, took the rowdy's part. For the rest of the evening I was an outcast.

Soon they cooked up a new dodge and started coming to me between dances and asking for money in addition to the tickets which had already been settled for, and I knew they were just doing this to humiliate me. I had but five dollars with me and when he asked me for 'Five', I handed him this lonely bill; and that left me flat.

After a repetition of this manœuvre I realized their intentions and turned to this fellow and said: 'Have you five?' as if I wanted change. He held out the five dollars I had given him and taking it, I put it in my pocket and said: 'Now you won't get a thing!'

This sort of funny work continued all evening, I being on the outside looking in. Finally the driver, a friend of my father's, took me aside and cautioned me. 'Jim,' he said, 'don't fight. You haven't a chance, for the gang will jump you if you do.'

When we came to start back home their leader, the one who had tried to appear so 'hard-boiled' and who had started the trouble, came up and announced rather nastily: 'You don't ride', and I, wanting to save the young lady from notoriety and unpleasantness, for she was of a very good family, tried to patch matters up. 'Give me your name,' I suggested, 'and I'll send the money to you this week.'

This chap who had annoyed us owned a little drug store in a part of the town distant from where I lived, and someone must have posted him, the day following, telling him that he had seen me boxing at the Olympic Club.

Well, anyway, I started for the drug store one night not long after, but took precautions to have a friend with me so that if the neighbourhood gang rushed me I would have some support. This friend was a wonderful character, with the magnificent name of Gallagher, 'Blub' Gallagher. He admired me solely because of my fighting ability and considered my position at the bank the most useless thing in the world. There could, as Bunker Bean used to say, 'be nothing of less consequence'. Fighting was what counted.

'Hey, Blub,' I said, 'want to go down to Blank Street? I've got to beat up a fellow who insulted a lady and they may rush me.'

He gave his famous grin, like a darkey seeing a slice of watermelon before him, and exclaimed: 'Where is it, kid? Lead me to it!'

I found the drug store and planted Blub on the opposite corner, where he sat on a hydrant, his elbows on his knees, looking up and down the streets, praying in his heart for the gang to come along! He didn't want it to be a private fight – he'd rather have the whole neighbourhood jump me, than to be left out of it! I can see him still, sitting there with that hope written all over his face.

Then I crossed over and found the fellow who had insulted the girl, alone at his counter. He almost fainted when he saw me, having been posted, as I say. His fingers trembled, he turned white and he called me 'Mr Corbett' as if I were a judge who had the power to send him to the electric chair!

I went up to him and, looking him square in the face, declared: 'I promised to pay you and here I am, but I'm going to pay you with these', holding up my 'dukes'.

Well, you never saw a more scared man in your life. His knees came together so that he almost sank below the counter, and he begged me, for the sake of his business, his reputation, his old mother – he said nothing about his face! – to let him alone. His cowardice was such that I actually felt sorry for him and couldn't even think of hitting him.

At last I agreed to let him off if he would write a letter to the girl, apologizing for his ungentlemanly conduct and also saying – for I wanted this satisfaction – that I had come down and ordered him to write it. He promised me this and then pushed a box of cigars in front of me. When I refused it, he plunged his fingers in the box, stuffed my pockets full of the cigars, then handed me a five-pound box of candy to take to the girl, thoroughly embarrassing me with his cringing and his attentions!

To wind it all up, the climax came when he grabbed me by the arm and, to the consternation of Mr Blub Gallagher sitting across the street fairly thirsting for a scrap, sat me down on a stool in front of the soda fountain and proceeded to treat me to ice-cream soda! To his dying day Blub never forgot that sight! He had come all that way for a 'free-for-all', and here I was, sitting on a stool, with the man I had come to lick, a box of candy under my arm for my best girl, my pockets full of cigars, and licking up an ice-cream soda!

Poor old Blub! He was a good sort.

4

A Fight for Two Brides – I am mistaken for Charley Mitchell –
An Audience with Guns on their Hips – The Papers egg
Choinyski and myself into Battle.

No young fellow's life is complete without a love affair, and I
didn't escape. A pal of mine at this time, Herman Eppinger, now
a steady and successful business man in San Francisco, had a love
affair too; and it happened that our young ladies had also long
been chums; so one rash night we decided we would all run
away and get married.

We had about five hundred dollars between us and in our
ignorance thought that this magnificent sum would keep us for
about five or ten years, since two could live more cheaply than
one, therefore four more cheaply than two; so the double knot
was tied by the Justice of the Peace. Like many too youthful
marriages (we were all of us under age) ours was later annulled;
but we didn't foresee anything but an unclouded life then. We
two boys threw up our jobs; and we all took the train for Salt
Lake where for a while we lived a care-free irresponsible
existence.

Our week's rent we had to pay in advance, on each Monday.
After about six weeks, we suddenly decided that this five
hundred dollars was *not* going to last out the five or ten
years after all. In fact, we just had enough to pay our next
week's rent.

Thus the worries of my life began. 'What are we going to do
week after next?' I asked myself; and responsibility sat heavily
on me.

One morning, while puzzling over this question, my eye
lighted on a paragraph in a newspaper – a challenge issued broad-
cast to any pugilist in the territory of Utah. It was signed
'Frank Smith'. After reading it over twice, I decided that by
taking a licking I could earn money enough to stay on at the
cottage for a while. This plan was no sooner thought of than
decided on. 'Ep,' said I to my friend, 'sit down, and we'll write
out an acceptance at once. I'll probably get a terrible lacing, but
I'll take on Mr Frank Smith.'

'But Jim,' he protested, 'you've been loafing, you're in no condition to fight.'

'It doesn't make any difference,' I replied, 'my mind's made up. We *must* get some money!'

So we wrote out the acceptance with great pains and I signed it 'Jim Dillon'; and Eppinger taking on himself the duties of manager, we went down to the office of the newspaper that had printed the challenge and gave the acceptance to the sporting editor.

On the following evening as we were sitting, all a little blue, in the parlour of the cottage, the doorbell rang. I went to the door and opened it, and four of the toughest looking customers I ever saw in my life stood before me. The fellow nearest me – one of those typical little 'hick' fight managers you see in the 'bushes' – said: 'Does Jim Dillon live here?'

'Yes, sir,' said I, a little relieved at the prospect of action, 'I'm Mr Dillon.'

'I'm managing Frank Smith,' he informed me, 'the heavy-weight champion of Utah.' Then he added, to make sure: 'You're the guy who accepted his challenge?'

'Yes, sir,' I said, all business now, 'come right in, gentlemen!'

So they entered and we sat down in the little parlour from which the ladies had retired. 'Which one is Smith?' I asked, and he jerked his thumb toward a great, big burly fellow weighing about 200 pounds, a tough-looking customer.

We shook hands and I thought he'd break my hand when he tried the old trick of crushing it.

'Well, gentlemen,' I began, trying to appear unconcerned, and not to betray that this was my first real fight we were to discuss, 'we can fight any way you like fifty-fifty or sixty-five-thirty-five.' (You see I was afraid they might offer the loser only twenty-five per cent and I expected to lose because I knew I was quite out of training and in no condition to fight anybody at that time, so I wanted to be sure of at least thirty-five for the loser's end. All that worried me then was that board bill!)

After discussing and practically settling all the details, the little 'hick' manager inquired: 'When do you want to fight?'

'A week from Friday,' I told him boldly.

'My God!' Smith broke in, 'I want six weeks to train!'

'It's impossible for me to be here after next week,' I replied, looking him straight in the eye. 'After next Friday I'll be on my way to Denver.'

He wouldn't stand for that at first, but I always had a breezy way about me and the indifferent manner in which I treated the challenger made him think I was perfectly at ease.

'Well,' I finally proposed, 'if you'll agree to that date, I'll tell what I'll do, gentlemen. I've been down to the skating rink and gotten acquainted with the manager. What's the matter with us letting him in on it? We'll stage the fight in the rink and get him to manage it. He'll advertise it and do the printing and give us the hall – we won't have to put up any money at all – just go down there, the night of the fight, and take our end of the receipts without putting up anything.' So I saved myself the embarrassment of admitting I had no money at all in my jeans and no way to raise it.

The proposition appealed to him and it was settled that I was to see the manager of the rink, Smith agreeing to fight on the night I had named, if the former accepted our proposition.

As it turned out the rink-man was delighted. 'Why,' he said, 'you know you'd really be quite a drawing card here! People all over the city have been wondering who all you people are.' (The four of us dressed well and looked like ladies and gentlemen and the skating-rink manager had himself thought that we were on the stage.) 'When they find out you're a boxer,' he added, 'we'll have a full house.'

For the next ten days, in fact up to the fight, the four of us in the 'honeymoon cottage' did nothing but worry. The girls were of course frightened to death, for they had seen this big brute Smith as he was leaving the house, and pictured me being brought home in an ambulance. I thought they were not so far wrong.

Finally Friday night came and the burdens of the world weighted my shoulders as I went down to the rink to fight Mr Frank Smith! We were to start at about ten o'clock – I was in the dressing-room at 7.30! And there I stayed, walking up and down like a panther in a cage, and losing, I suppose, a pound the half-hour from worry and fretting!

The preliminary bouts were started, nine o'clock came, but Smith did not show up.

Suddenly a timid knock sounded on my dressing-room door, and although it was very faint I was startled by the sound.

However, I opened the door bravely, and in sneaked a fellow who looked around the room very mysteriously like some sleuth in a burlesque, before he said a word. Seeing no one there who might overhear what he had to say, he approached me stealthily and whispered in my ear: 'Mr Dillon, Smith wants to see you.'

I could not understand the reason for all this secrecy, and was further disturbed when, looking over his shoulder again he mumbled: 'He's down at the corner; he wants to see you *private*.'

I began to wonder if Mr Smith wanted to beat me up out there in the dark, and, knowing that I was in such bad fighting condition, I wasn't at all anxious to go. However, that board bill must be paid somehow, so I put on my clothes over my trunks and sneaked down to the corner.

'He's up there under that tree,' said my mysterious guide, pointing to a tree about a quarter of a block away, and left me as suddenly as he had come.

Well, I walked up, trying to put on as brave a front as possible, and, sure enough, there was Smith hiding in the darkest shadow he could find.

I said, very sternly: 'Do you want to see me?'

'Yes,' he replied, like the other fellow, looking around to make sure no one was within hearing.

'What's the matter?' I demanded.

For reply he gave me a sickly grin and patted me timidly on the elbow. 'I'm "on" to you, Charley,' he whispered, trying to look wise.

'"You're 'on' to me, *Charley*?"' I replied, bewildered.

'Yes,' he said, 'I know who you are.'

'*You know who I am?* What do you mean?'

He raised his hands as if to stop what he thought was mere bluffing. 'That's all right. I know you're Charley Mitchell. You can't fool me!'

Now this was an unexpected compliment as well as something of a shock, since Charley Mitchell was one of the greatest fighters in the world at that time, having fought John L. Sullivan a draw at Chantilly, France, not long before. It was true that Mitchell was travelling through America at this very time. Furthermore he was known as 'the gentleman pugilist', always dressing well, which fact probably helped along Smith's delusion, for I had taken much pains with my personal appearance since entering the position at the bank.

He had knocked me flat and, unable yet to take advantage of his conviction, I repeated incredulously: '*Me Charley Mitchell?*'

'Yes, you are,' he insisted, 'and I don't want to get my head knocked off!'

I couldn't believe it! To see this fellow so afraid of me was laughable! What seemed funniest of all, as I thought it over, was my worry of the last ten days.

Finally I took a deep breath, threw out my chest, and re-assured him: 'That's all right, my boy,' I said patronizingly, 'as long as you know I am Mitchell and don't breathe it to a soul, I won't hurt a hair of your head!'

'You might forget,' he hedged, 'I don't want to go in there.'

'Now be sensible,' I argued. 'You're in the business for money and we'll just split the receipts, and all you will have to do is to go in there and stop any time you like.'

'What do you mean?'

'Why, you just make the best showing you can for a while, and in the second or third round' (I knew I hadn't strength for more than that) 'if you want to stop, you can. We might as well pick up the money.'

'Will you promise you won't hurt me?' he asked, looking horribly afraid.

'Sure! Just pick the round you want to flop in. Second or third, I don't care. I won't hurt you up until that time; but if you go on after the round agreed on you'd better look out for yourself, I won't pull a single punch then.'

'Well,' he growled, 'I'll stop in the second round.'

'All right,' I answered, trying to appear indifferent, 'I promise I won't hurt you the first two, but if you come up for the third, don't look for any mercy from me!'

Once more he begged me not to hurt him and it made me ashamed of my kind to see this great big fellow wilt like that! But, Lord! what a load it had taken off my mind!

The discussion over, we went to our dressing-rooms, put on our togs, and entered the ring. The preliminaries were ended, 'Time' was called, and we started.

It was funny, very funny, for, being forced to make an impression on this fellow at the beginning, I hit him often and absolutely as hard as I could, *and he thought I was pulling my punches*! All he was thinking of was how hard Charley Mitchell really could hit when he once let loose.

Of course, to put the show over, I made considerable display of footwork and flashed some science, having learned a good deal about boxing during the previous two years. This 'grandstand' effort pleased the crowd, which is never really wise, you know, nor 'on to things', and covered up my real lack of hitting power. I hit him so often in that first round that he thought someone in the audience was throwing boxing-gloves at him, and he ducked and dodged like those darkies at the county fair who stick their heads out of holes in canvas for the crowd to throw baseballs at. But I was not hurting him at all, making absolutely no impression on him, except through fear.

At the end of the round I went to my corner feeling more tired and ill than ever I had in all my life. Actually, I could hardly get up for the second. Still, I had to make the bluff. This was the round he was to stop in, and victory was near!

So I pulled myself together, called on all the speed left in my carcass, and dashed at him, looking as ferocious and ugly as I could, to frighten him – as much as to say: 'Now, you big coward, if you don't stop as you agreed, you're going to get it good and plenty.'

I hit him at least twenty times, still not hurting him at all, when suddenly he began to stagger, to fool the crowd, then flopped. The referee rushed over, counted him out, and there over him I stood, the mighty victor, and you could really have toppled me with a feather!

Somehow I managed to get to my dressing-room, then flopped myself, so ill and weak I couldn't leave the place for an hour and a half. But my 'manager', Eppinger, came in and showed me a wad of bills. We counted them, $460 in all; the board bill was safe, and the sight of those greenbacks acted as a swift cure.

Following this fight, the Salt Lake papers spoke several times of my 'cleverness' and 'form', which certainly had been flashy that night; and about a week later Duncan MacDonald, the man who had refereed the contest, showed me a letter from Evanston, Wyoming, written, if I remember rightly, by a sporting man named Frank Hayes. There was a miner in that town, the letter went on to say, who 'couldn't fight a lick on earth', but had a backer to the extent of $1,000, 'if he took on some ordinary fellow'.

The cottage threatened to need more money, so MacDonald persuaded me to pack my bag, and took me up North to meet this miner.

We had not been in Evanston more than two hours when a rumour spread through the town that I was Jack Dempsey, the famous 'Nonpareil', then middleweight champion of the world. For some unknown reason I was supposed to be Dempsey, who, under the name of Dillon, had dropped off, trying to pick up that loose thousand. So this wise sporting man, Hayes, told MacDonald to return to Salt Lake with me, then to come back in a few weeks, billing me as Jack Dempsey, for an exhibition which would pack the Opera House and draw far more than the sum put up for the bout with the miner.

This advice we followed, bringing along with us, on the return trip, a third fellow whom we christened 'Danny Costigan', to help along the rumour, for that was the actual name of Dempsey's sparring partner.

At the station a good-sized crowd was assembled to meet 'the middleweight champion', and this looked promising for a good house; but at the hotel I ran into danger, when I was surrounded by a number of people from Brooklyn, Dempsey's home town, all very eager to talk about the Bridge and the beauties of Flatbush Avenue; and the nearest I had been to this lovely city was Salt Lake! There were so many of them that I was forced to arrange a signal with MacDonald, just a scratch of my head, when the questions about the home town came too thick and fast. MacDonald then would come breezing into the group and say: 'Excuse him a minute, boys, I've got something important to tell him', and he would lead me to safety. I believe I scratched my head all that day.

This Brooklyn slant of the affair finally got so on my nerves that I was afraid to go to the theatre until just before the bout. MacDonald and I did take a peek and found it packed to the peanut gallery with miners and cowboys all eager to see the fighter with the wonderful record on those bill-posters outside. All of them seemed to have guns on their hips and I began to wonder what would happen to me if they found out I didn't belong to that record.

Hurriedly we slipped away and we wandered around, until Mac, being a good Scotchman, decided we ought to have a drink. We entered one of those old-fashioned saloons with gambling layouts and men at the bar, each with a gun strapped on his belt – there seemed about a thousand to me – those fellows, you know, who shoot the lights out.

But we didn't want to duck and swung open the door. Just as we were crossing the threshold we spied a big fellow waving a gun in the air. Bang! he crashed it down on the bar and with an oath declared angrily: 'I tell you, that fellow is *not Jack Dempsey*!'

Suddenly I was not thirsty any more and I became an ardent Prohibitionist, a sprinter as well! We turned and must have run three blocks in nothing flat, fully expecting each second to be shot dead!

The town was small, but we managed to find a few dark streets, through which we wandered until the last minute, then slipped in the Opera House, and dressed in a private box so that our friends from Brooklyn could not trouble us.

I will never forget as long as I live the voice of the man announcing me as 'Jack Dempsey, Middleweight Champion of the World'. I expected a thousand voices to shout back: 'You lie!' and all that evening each time someone in the audience coughed, I thought it was the bark of one of those guns on their hips.

But I kept on, and I really did have something to interest people who loved boxing, and was in far better condition than on the night of the bout with the timid Frank Smith. And under these conditions, aided by the sight of those small black barrels, I outdid myself and would have amazed Walter Watson, my old boxing instructor. Before it was over, those in the audience who had doubted I was the real Jack would now have shot anybody that said I wasn't. But I couldn't drive from my imagination the scowl on the face of the man in the saloon and the sound of his gun crashing on the bar. To make sure I wouldn't meet up with its owner again, Mac and I took the midnight train for Salt Lake.

Not so long after this event, I met the original Jack, and asked the Nonpareil if he had ever visited Wyoming.

'Not that I remember,' he replied. 'I've passed through, but never stopped off.'

'Why,' I exclaimed, 'didn't you show in Evanston?'

'No,' he insisted, 'I never was there in my life.'

'Jack,' I said, shaking my head, 'I don't think you are telling the truth.'

He looked at me puzzled. 'What do you mean, Jim?' he asked.

'Why you were in Evanston and boxed with Danny Costigan just five months ago.'

'No, I never was there, Jim,' he repeated.

'Well, I tell you you *were*!' Then I let up and told him the story. We had quite a laugh over the affair, and so did Charley Mitchell, over the skating-rink battle, when he heard about that, as he did a few years later.

Perhaps someone will question the ethics of all this, and doubtless it wasn't all according to Hoyle. But I have never laid down in a fight in my life or fixed one. These tricks were the worst I ever pulled. It was rather harmless showmanship, and the spectators got their money's worth.

One day, not long after my return to Salt Lake, a bell-boy came to my room and announced: 'A gentleman downstairs to see you; name's Corbett.'

'Corbett?' I exclaimed. 'Well, show him up, he must be a relative.'

It was a pretty close one, too, for when the door opened I saw my father! He put his arms around me and said, rather pathetically: 'Jim, don't you think you'd better come home?'

He spent a couple of days with me and after a good visit together I yielded to him. 'Dad,' I promised him, 'I give you my word I'll be home in a little while, but I don't want to go with you now. I would look too much like a bad boy being yanked home by the collar.' So I saw him off on the train and told him he'd see me within a couple of weeks.

In the meantime I had spent everything I had and was flat broke, but I didn't want my father to know this.

Duncan MacDonald, who had refereed the fight with Smith and accompanied me to Wyoming, had become a bosom pal of mine, and he knew I was worrying about getting my tickets home and keeping my promise to Dad. He asked me how much I needed. I told him I had enough to travel second class, but he didn't like that idea.

'Jim,' he said, 'you don't want to take the girls home that way. They ought to travel first class. Here's the balance.'

Of course, I returned the loan not long after reaching home; but I did not realize his sacrifice until later, when Hayes told me Mac had pawned his watch, chain, and stick-pin to make up the sum. Mac himself never breathed a word. No, you can never make me believe there is anything 'close' about a Scotsman.

Although I had left the bank, the owners seemed still interested in me, and were good enough to get me a position in one of the concerns with which they were connected – the Anglo-Nevada Insurance Company. Here I worked after my return from Salt Lake, for about a year.

It was during this time that my old rival Joe Choinyski turned professional, and became very successful.

I happened to meet him one day and remarked: 'Joe, you're getting on pretty well for a pro.'

'Yes, I've been working a great scheme,' he explained. 'When I clinch with some of these fellows, the first couple o' times I always say: "Now come on and break away nice and gentlemanly", and the fellow breaks away clean and drops his hands. I do this three or four times, but the fourth time or so, I set myself and as he breaks away clean I shoot over a right. I nearly knocked that nigger Wilson out the other night that way.'

For some reason I stowed this away in my memory.

Now the only blots on Choinyski's record were several defeats by one Jim Corbett, given when Joe was an amateur. And all the credit he got for his hard work seemed to be: 'Yes, yes, you whipped So-and-so, and So-and-so, but you can't whip Corbett!'

That stuck in his craw!

In San Francisco there was another club almost as well known as the Olympic – the California Athletic Club; and in it were held some of the most prominent finish fights ever fought, for instance, the lightweight championship go between Jack McAuliffe and Jimmy Carroll, and the battle between 'Ike' Weir, 'the Belfast Spider', and his conqueror Jimmy Murphy, the Australian lightweight.

It was in this club that George LaBlanche knocked out the original Jack Dempsey with the famous 'pivot blow' after

Dempsey practically had LaBlanche defeated. There, too, Fitz-simmons made his first appearance in America in defeating Billy McCarty, and Charley Turner, one of the greatest middleweights California ever turned out, was knocked out after a terrific fight by Denny Kelliher of Boston, who, in my opinion, was the hardest hitter who ever stepped in a ring – and I do not except 'Lanky Bob' himself. Under the auspices of this club Peter Jackson defeated Joe McAuliffe, Patsy Cardiff, and George Godfrey; and a little later Jackson fought sixty-one rounds with me.

The directors of this organization realized that, on account of all the discussion going round, a bout between Choinyski and myself would prove a fine drawing card. So the sporting writers in San Francisco, all of whom frequented the C.A.C., thought they would try and work up Choinyski and Corbett into a fighting mood. One day this paper would come out with a story that 'Choinyski said so-and-so about Corbett', itemizing what he would do to him; the next day another would tell what Corbett had said and threatened, all made up out of wholecloth, of course. Then there would follow arguments in the town among the sports followers, as to the merits of the two men. Some preferring Choinyski on the ground that he was a professional and had more ring experience, declared that he would get revenge. Others maintained that I had too much natural skill, although I was an amateur; for I was still considered that, the two bouts in Wyoming and Salt Lake, having been fought under assumed names and peculiar circumstances, not being counted.

For a long time they couldn't stir me, as I had fully made up my mind I was not going to be a professional. However, they picked and jabbed away in their sporting columns, and in conversation wherever the sports met, until finally there appeared in the papers an article saying that Choinyski was going 'to take a punch at Corbett the first time he saw him on the street'!

It seems strange, these days, to think of putting so many personalities into print, but it must be remembered that this was a peculiarly local affair and that our meetings had been frequent over a period of years. Then, too, the California A.C., Choinyski's club, was the resort of all the sporting writers of the town because it was here that the famous professional fights occurred, while my club, the Olympic, was an amateur organization and did not hold professional bouts. I was the pet heavyweight of the Olympic, Choinyski the idol of the other organization, and they figured it would be a humdinger of a fight if they could only get the two to meet. So everything was deliberately done and every trick possible tried.

The day the article last mentioned came out, I went to my father and said: 'Dad, did you read in the papers what Choinyski said about me?'

'Yes,' he replied, looking up at me inquiringly.

'You'd better let me fight him then,' I told him.

He shook his head.

'No, Jim, you don't want to fight.'

'Now stop and think it over, Dad,' I pleaded.

Then, since I was convinced that Choinyski had said all that had been reported, though later I found out that this was not so, I continued: 'Look here, Dad, I'm not going to wait for Choinyski to hit me on the street, because the first punch is half the battle and he can hit very hard; so if I see him I'm going to get in that first punch. You don't want me to have a street fight, do you?'

'No,' he asserted, undecidedly.

'Then, why don't you let me fight him? The California people tell me money's no object.'

He thought awhile, and then replied: 'Jim, don't go in the club and fight for money. Go out in the hills and fight him for nothing. My boy, I don't want you to be a prize-fighter. That settles it.'

I was disappointed, of course, but I had to yield. 'All right,' I agreed finally, 'I'll make arrangements to fight him for nothing.'

5

THE sports writers had their wish, and finally Choinyski and I met at a newspaper office, in the room of the sporting editor.

As supporters and backers, I had with me Porter Ashe, who had married into the famous Crocker family, and Judge Lawlor, now Supreme Court Judge of the state, and the one who sentenced Abe Reuf to prison. With Choinyski were several faces familiar then and since in the sporting world, among them Ed Grainey, boxing referee and politician; Mose Guntz, the cigar manufacturer, an enthusiastic ring follower; and 'Tom' Williams, the horseman.

Porter Ashe and Williams grew so excited during the wrangling over the arrangements for the bout that they backed myself and Choinyski respectively for $1,000. It is perhaps unnecessary to explain that this was a big bet in those days. In fact, the relative value of money then and now must always be kept in mind in this story. Championship purses of those times would be scorned by 'pork-and-beaners' today, but there was more colour to the game then, I am sure, and a great deal more of love for it and professional pride.

There certainly was enough of each in this fight. I do not believe there ever was one that caused such excitement. It was a local affair, and at the time no one knew of it outside the state, but it has been told and retold since, hundreds of times, in sporting histories and reminiscences.

To give an idea of the intensity of the interest, I will list the various factions that fought in the fight. There were to be more than just the two fighters in the ring. The antagonists really were

Choinyski versus Corbett.
California Club versus Olympic.
Professional Sport versus Amateur.
Jew versus Gentile.
Labour versus Capital.
Golden Gate Ave. (his neighbourhood) versus Hayes Street (mine).

So you see there was quite a line-up of little feuds and grudges on each side. I had perhaps better explain the Labour and Capital slant by telling you that Choinyski at the time was a candy-puller and all the factory people were rooting for him, while my bosses at the bank and the wealthy business men who belonged to the Olympic were pulling for me to win.

Now the preliminary fights billed with an important bout usually take place between eight o'clock and ten or ten-thirty the same night in the same ring, but there were scores of preliminary bouts that were fought, in the weeks preceding our battle, in the street and bar-rooms, and started simply by arguments over the chances of the two principals.

No place had yet been arranged for, and as such an affair was outside of the law, finish fights being permitted only in licensed clubs, Judge Lawlor and Eddie Grainey were selected as a committee to locate a place reasonably safe from interference by the police. The next day Choinyski set out for a town about ten miles from San Francisco, where he was to train, I, in the opposite direction, establishing my quarters at Sausalito.

The police, it seems, were determined to stop the fight, thinking they would gain some glory if they succeeded. Several in uniform or plain clothes came to both quarters from time to time, hoping to pick up some loose information about the place selected, but we didn't know it ourselves. As I was 'turning in' on the night preceding the bout, one of my trainers slipped in the room and informed me that two detectives were across the street sleeping in an open lot, with one eye open, probably planning to follow us when we set out in the morning. How to escape them was the problem.

But a young fellow with us solved it. He was Hall MacAllister, Jr, whose mother had a summer home near by; and he appropriated her rig, which was fortunately a closed carriage, drove it over the lots back of the house that served as training quarters, and we slipped out of the rear door, entered the carriage quickly, and drove off, unsuspected. The two sleuths never dreamed that that fine rig, spanking pair of trotters, frothing at the bit, finely appointed carriage and all, was carrying a pugilist and his seconds. The boy MacAllister got into some trouble over his generosity, for his mother, a society leader, heard of it afterwards and was quite horrified, particularly when she read of it in the

43

papers, for it was written up as a very interesting incident connected with the fight. As a matter of fact, I do not believe that ever before had a fighter and his handlers been conveyed to the ring in such a fashion.

Leaving Sausalito, we drove for about an hour and a half until we reached an old barn somewhere out in the country – I never realized just where – and to my surprise saw about a hundred people waiting us. We were hustled into the farmhouse near by and into a room without any of the usual training equipment – nothing but an old bed, and that without mattress or blankets. They told me Choinyski had arrived and was in another room of the house.

In those days a great many men in San Francisco still carried guns, and usually we were not worried about it, so I was surprised when Judge Lawlor said to me: 'Jim, there is a lot of feeling over this fight and I am afraid there will be trouble and someone may pull a gun. Don't you think we had better search them before they are allowed in the barn?'

Someone went to Choinyski's room, and he agreed, and a few minutes later Judge Lawlor returned, his arms piled high with more guns than I had ever seen in one place in my life, and all loaded. I was told the same thing happened in Choinyski's room; so there was no one in the barn armed.

Another surprise came to me then when the Judge said: 'Jim, they are certainly out to win this fight. Mose Guntz has just hired Jack Dempsey (the original Nonpareil) for $1,000 to second Choinyski.'

As I knew Dempsey quite well and he wasn't very well acquainted with Choinyski, I realized that Joe's backers were leaving no stone unturned to win the fight and the money they had placed on it.

At last they told me time was up, to come over to the barn. We were to fight in the loft where a ring had been pitched. As I left the house I ran into Jack Dempsey headed the same way. We shook hands and he said to me: 'Jim, I'm going to second this fellow, but I'm only doing it because I am getting $1,000. I don't know him at all, and it's not because I want him to win.'

'That's all right, Jack. You can't *make* him whip me,' I replied confidently.

Then we went up the stairs and found the ring pitched in the centre of the loft and possibly a hundred men – of all sorts, from high-class gamblers to prominent bankers – all leaders in their line. Choinyski came up a few minutes later and we went into the ring.

Just before we were called up for instructions by Patsy Hogan, an ex-pugilist, who acted as referee, my friend Porter Ashe, who had bet the thousand with Williams, stuck $500 more in my hand saying: 'Now, Jim, when you go up there bet Choinyski this $500 that you will lick him. If you win, keep it.'

So I went up to the centre of the ring and met Choinyski, with this $500 in my hand, and we listened to the instructions of the referee. When that was all over I said: 'Joe, I'll bet you this $500 I'll lick you.'

Choinyski didn't seem any too anxious. He hung his head and shook it for 'No', so I turned to Dempsey: 'Jack, you're getting $1,000 out of this. I'll bet you half of it I'll lick him.'

He laughed and refused too.

'No,' he said, 'I don't want any of it.'

But time was being called, we advanced from our corners, and the fight was on.

When we came to the centre of the ring, each of us about twenty years old, in great condition, full of vitality and the picture of health, we went at each other in whirlwind fashion. During the first round we fought ourselves into a clinch and Choinyski said: 'Jim, let's break away nice and gentlemanly.'

Then, all in a flash, the conversation I had had with him, about a year before, came into my mind – when he told me of the time he had won his fight with Nigger Wilson and a lot of others, and how he would say the very same thing he had just said to me: 'Break away nice and gentlemanly'; that he would do this two or three times, then shoot his right over.

I didn't wait for him to do that two or three times; no sooner had he come out with this 'Break away nice and gentlemanly' idea than I shot over *my* right, hitting him on the chin and dropped him for a count of five. There was almost a riot, and it was a good thing that those guns were lying on the beds in the farmhouse!

We continued that furious style of fighting for three more rounds, and in the fourth, in hitting him on the head, I knocked my right thumb out of joint. So things kept up until the sixth

45

when the sheriff climbed up into the loft and stopped the fight. He seemed rather embarrassed about it.

'Boys,' he said, 'I thought the fight would be over by this time. I'm sorry to stop it, and if you will go over into the next county I'll "sit in"; but I have to stop it now that I'm here.'

So we tried to get a train at San Rafael and go to the next county, but when we reached the station, found it crowded. The people in all the little towns around had read the stories in the San Francisco papers telling about the fight and had also seen the many carriages and wagons driving up to this barn. So the news was spilled and it spread like wildfire. The crowds would have followed us if we had only gone over the county line, and the police would have been on our tracks again; therefore we decided to go back to our training quarters.

Before we left the ring the referee had ordered Choinyski and myself to take care of our gloves, to make sure the next time we met we'd have them with us, for boxing-gloves had to be made to order to fit a boxer's hand and could not be secured at a moment's notice.

For the next few days the committee was busy looking for another place for the continuation of the bout. It took them about a week to locate one, and by that time my thumb was in very bad condition and very sore. Finally Porter Ashe and Judge Lawlor phoned me, one evening, to come to San Francisco as they had the place all arranged. That night they put me on a train for a little country town called Benetia. From the station I was taken to the fine country home of Wilson Mizner, the author of *The Deep Purple* and other famous plays which later had long runs on Broadway. They told me we were to fight on a barge in the middle of the Bay, the following morning at eight o'clock, then put me to bed, telling me to go to sleep at once and get a good rest.

Can anyone in his wildest moments imagine a fellow going to sleep in a strange bed, with about twenty-five chaps outside walking around, some of them right outside my window, and all talking about the fight and thinking they were whispering, but getting so excited that I could hear every word they said? I did not close my eyes all night, but I didn't say anything to them about it for I knew they would worry more than I had.

They had a fine steak they wanted to give me, but the question was, how to cook it? The country house was deserted, all the family being away, and there were no servants and of course no fire in the place. But someone built a fire out in the field and they broiled this huge steak for me, which they thought would bring victory. You see that in training I had graduated now from egg and sherry to steak, although if there's anything I detest it is a rare steak, and all those trainers insist on giving it to you almost raw! By the way, it was cooked by a boy who was raised with me, called 'Forty' Kenneally. He was given this nickname because a horse that could go in 2:40 in those days was considered pretty fast, and Kenneally was a good sprinter and could travel in quick time himself.

No one in the world wanted me to win more than my friend Forty, for he had been given one of the worst beatings he ever had in his life by this same Joe Choinyski. They had fought several times in boxing tournaments, and terrific fights they were; but Choinyski had always come out on top. Naturally Kenneally had looked forward to this fight ever since it had been talked about, and he would have given up ten years of his life rather than not be on hand to see me defeat Choinyski! And no one but himself must cook the steak. He not only cooked it, but stood over me making me eat every mouthful, almost to the 'T' bone; and that operation over he never left my side for a second.

Breakfast over, we received notice to leave the place for the shore, then to row to the barge where we were to fight. Now, if I do say it myself, I have always, even in bad moments, had a sense of humour (possibly it's the Irish in me). As we were starting I looked around at all the boys who were very nervous by now, and said with a solemn face: 'Someone must stay here and watch this house until we get back – someone that I can trust.' I looked over the heads of the rest at Kenneally and nodded at him. 'Forty, you're the man. You stay here and watch this house until the fight is over.'

His eyes grew bigger and bigger and I shall never forget the look on his face! I have told you about how Blub Gallagher looked when he saw me sitting in the drug store eating ice-cream soda with a fellow I had come to lick. Well, his look of disgust was bad enough; but it wasn't a patch to what came over Forty's face then! He always stuttered when he got excited, and, to add to his eloquence, his mouth was at the moment filled with bread! He said: 'J-J-J-Jim, I-I-I'm a f-f-friend of yours, b-b-b-but I'd c-c-cut my r-r-right arm off b-b-b-before I'd m-m-miss this f-f-f-fight!'

I eased up on him then, told him he could go, and his face was all grin. The next thing we knew we were in a rowboat headed for the barge out in the Bay, and I can remember so well a part of the conversation in this boat. A dear loyal little friend of mine, by the name of Gene Vancourt, talking of the coming battle, said: 'Jim, do you think you can stand a licking? You only have one hand, you know, and you're certainly going to take a lacing, even if you win.'

'Gene,' I said, 'I don't know myself whether I can take a licking or not; I never got a really good licking and don't know how I'll act under fire, but I hope to find that out today.'

After rowing awhile, we reached this flat boat which was anchored in the middle of the Bay, and saw people on deck and the ring already pitched. We climbed up and everybody we knew seemed to be there – Choinyski and all of his friends, and possibly a hundred people besides – the same crowd that attended the previous struggle in the barn. (I found out afterwards that five of these very prominent gentlemen from San Francisco had fallen in the water while being transferred in a rowboat from the tug to the barge and had very nearly been drowned. But that didn't seem to dampen their spirits.)

Choinyski and I got our clothes off and stepped into the ring. Obedient to the referee's instructions, I had taken care of my gloves and had mine on my hands. But, though I didn't know it until afterwards, Jack Dempsey, having learned about my bad hand, had determined to turn the fight into a bare-knuckle contest, in which Joe would have the advantage, and had tied a rock to Choinyski's five-ounce gloves and had thrown them overboard.

So it was that Choinyski stepped into the ring without any gloves. 'Where are your gloves?' asked the referee.

'Lost them,' Choinyski mumbled, looking a little sheepish.

Then the referee came over to me and said: 'Choinyski has no gloves.'

'Well,' I replied, 'you told us to bring our gloves and I have mine. I am here, ready to fight.'

'Jim,' he said, 'you don't want this fight without fighting for it, do you?'

'That's right, I don't,' I told him. 'I'll keep these gloves on and let him fight with his bare knuckles.'

At this there was an uproar and someone suggested that Choinyski wear skin gloves; and a prominent business man who was present threw in his driving gloves and these they put on Choinyski's hands.

All of which sounds very brave on my part, but I had quickly figured to myself that my injured hand would be better off with a five-ounce glove than bare. He put on the skin gloves which, I noticed, had three heavy seams running down the centre, and the battle started.

As we stood there in the broiling sun (we didn't get started until noon) little did I figure that this was to be the very toughest battle that I had ever fought or was to fight, one in which I was to receive more punishment than I have ever had in all my other battles put together; more, in fact, than I have ever seen inflicted on any other prize-fighter – and I have seen all the famous battles of the past forty years!

We started off in the whirlwind fashion of the bout in the barn, two healthy young fellows hating each other through envy and jealousy inspired by our supporters and played up through all the years preceding. Choinyski, knowing that I had a bad right hand, started rushing me from the start, and I had to win with my left hand alone.

A sturdier, tougher fellow than Choinyski never stepped into a ring and I had my work cut out for me. As he came toward me I would bat him with my left, right in the face, and the more determinedly he came on, the more determined I was to meet him with a straight left hand right in the face. The two first rounds I had his face looking like a piece of liver.

In the third round I led for his face, he started to duck, and I landed on his forehead with my left and broke this, too! I knew it was hurt, but how badly, in the excitement, I couldn't tell; but as the rounds went by it got so sore that each time it landed it hurt me almost as much as it did Choinyski.

Now Choinyski would get in a terrific blow every little while. He was kind of sweet on hitting me in the left eye with his right hand, and he had my face 'busted up'.

c

49

So the fight went on at this terrific pace, round after round, and my left hand was throbbing and hurting so that the only time I would risk hitting him was when I had to protect myself from his leads.

About the tenth round I discovered that I had foolishly put on the wrong kind of shoes, the rubber-soled sort that amateurs wear in a gymnasium. They are all right there, but when you get out on a hard floor in the hot sun and they begin to blister your feet, I tell you you are going through something! Each of my soles was one great water blister. With these bothering me so, and Choinyski still so full of fight, I thought less of sparing my right hand; so I fixed it up with my trainer – Delaney – to call out every once in a while: 'Jim, it's time you used your right now.'

Before I would start my right I would, as they say in boxing, 'telegraph' the blow, purposely. I really didn't want to hit him, but wanted to make him afraid of that hand and I began swinging it very often and soon had Choinyski thinking it wasn't hurt quite as badly as they had said it was. This threat made Choinyski, to get away from the blow, go to my left, and that gave me a chance to use a little left-hand hook which they knew nothing about in those days; in fact, it had not been used before – nor had I myself used it before. It was just discovered through my great need. In using this left hook I found I could save the two knuckles that were hurt (those of the third and little finger) by hitting with the side of my hand and the first knuckle.

The wild swing at him with my right would force him to duck to my left; then he was in a position for me to hook him with my left, that is, with the first knuckle and the side of the hand; and of course the blow fell with double force, since he was practically ducking into it himself.

I hate to make my story of this fight agonizing for any women readers I may have, but I must tell it as it happened because it was an historic fight, and by this time Choinyski's face was badly cut up, especially at mouth and nose, and he was a free bleeder. There was not so much blood spilled from me except a little from the mouth, for I never bleed easily. However, my eye was nearly closed and there was a swelling around the cheekbone. The 'claret' from Choinyski flowed pretty freely on the deck and spattered the spectators; and finally we found ourselves slipping around the deck in our own blood.

Right here I should say, for the sake of those not initiated in prize-fighting, that the blows that cause blood are not really the most painful ones. In ordinary life the slightest tap on the mouth may make your mouth bleed. Many people visiting Denver, unused to the high altitude, bleed from the nose, and even a hot day will affect some susceptible ones the same way. The blows that really hurt are those alongside the jaw or the head – those that almost knock you out but don't – and the solid punches in the short ribs or in the stomach or any place around the body. (Of course I am not now considering the foul ones such as the rabbit punch on the back of the neck or those given below the belt.) When a really painful blow is delivered, spectators seldom realize it, but when they see blood most of them think a man is being murdered, and he may hardly feel it. For instance, Carpentier was badly hurt in the in-fighting by those short body blows which Dempsey landed on him in their historic fight, although most of the women spectators in their seats thought the two fighters were having a fine time going through pretty motions, since no one was badly cut up.

By this time the sun was very high in the sky and hot, and I could see that its rays, beating down pitilessly on Choinyski's raw face, troubled him a great deal. As for myself, Choinyski, you will remember, was using the riding gloves lent him by one of the spectators, and they had three heavy seams down the back, and each time a blow glanced by my face or body it left three angry red welts on my skin. I looked like a zebra – not striped with yellow, but with red, and the sun made these wounds pain horribly.

So the fight proceeded without ever a pause. We did not stall much or wrestle all over the ring, but blow succeeded blow fast and furiously. Probably a great deal of this fight could be characterized as slugging, since, though I did use my head, in the way I have described above, and was quick and fast, I was still an amateur and had not yet acquired the scientific skill one gains through experience; in fact I learned more about fighting in this contest than I ever knew before.

Things continued like this until the fourteenth round. Whenever I was forced to hit a straight left-hand punch the pain from the broken hand shot clean up through my arm, and in this round suddenly I grew weak and once, if such a thing is possible, fainted while still standing up, both arms dropping and everything growing hazy in front of me.

It was a critical moment, for there I stood with arms by my side, and there was an awful silence for a few seconds. Choinyski looked at me and thought I was pulling some trick. But a few seconds later his supporters realized that I was not faking, that I was in a position to be licked, and I heard a terrific shout from them, and with the shout I got a horrible punch on the right eye.

From that time on all through that round everything was black in front of me. All I could sense was the feel of the blows that Choinyski rained on me right and left. I was not 'out', I was just groggy and instinctively kept my head rocking with his blows and managed to keep my chin out of danger, though totally uncovered, my hands still at my side.

So they kept coming, regular and well timed, which was an advantage in a way, for I was able, with the little sense I had, just to 'ride them', as they say, getting hit alongside the head and the eye but not once on my chin. If just one had landed there I would have been down and out for the count.

The round ended at last and I can remember my seconds leading me to my corner – I didn't know where it was – and sitting me down in my chair.

I must now tell something that happened at this stage of the fight and which I learned afterwards. My two older brothers, Frank and Harry, were just spectators there and it looked as if I were going to be licked. Frank, wanting to find Harry so that they could sympathize with each other, found him at the stern of the boat, his head over the gunwale and looking into the water, crying. 'What the hell are you doing over here?' said Frank.

'I can't see Jim licked,' sobbed Harry.

'Well,' said Frank, 'this is a hell of a place for you to be if he is getting licked!' and he 'belted' him in the nose and they had another skirmish outside the ring because Frank thought Harry had left me in the lurch!

Now I remember that just before the next, the fifteenth, round started, Delaney said: 'Are you all right?'

I replied: 'Yes, I'll pull through.'

So I went up for the next round and of course Choinyski was at me like a fire horse going to a four-alarm fire, trying his best to put me out. As I was weak and my head was still quite foggy, I clinched and held on for a while, and in a very few seconds my brain cleared and when I broke out of the clinch I wanted to make Choinyski think that I was all right, although I was still a trifle off. So I feinted at him and tried to do a nice little side-step (as I had been doing before for the effect) but I pulled an awful 'bone', for when I started this side-step I nearly fell on my face and showed Choinyski that my legs were wobbly! Picture a drunken man reaching for a post and you have me then!

That was great for Choinyski's supporters! They thought they had me licked! And no question about it, I was well on the way to defeat! So I clinched at every opportunity, while he was trying his darndest to end the fight right then and there.

Now the tricks in clinching are only a few, in spite of some people's ideas to the contrary. All one can do to weather a rocky round is first grab for your opponent's arms, catch him wherever you can (at wrist or shoulder or elbow), putting your head on the other fellow's left shoulder, and then stay as close to him as possible.

The real skill consists in knowing just when to grab him and when to let go. If one doesn't time these manœuvres carefully he is in more trouble than before. I have seen hundreds of fellows defeated just because they didn't understand these points and didn't know what to do when they were in trouble. For instance, as I write these words, a fight I saw night before last occurs to me: that between Berlenbach and Delaney at Madison Square Garden. Berlenbach didn't know what to do when he was groggy; all he knew was aggressiveness. He had no defence. One of Berlenbach's friends has just phoned me, asking me to teach this young fighter some of these points I applied thirty-five years ago, and he is coming down to my house tomorrow night to learn something from my past experience – about clinching, particularly.

I have, too, often read accounts of how a man was worn out by his opponent's leaning all his weight on him in a clinch. That is a false idea. Jeffries, weighing 230 pounds, leaned on my 180 at Coney Island for twenty-three rounds and it never

53

affected me in the least, for when a man is leaning on you, that is the time for you to relax, and if his weight *does* get too much for you, all you need to do is to go down on one knee and let the referee see that your opponent is wrestling with you. All such points are important parts of the boxing game and a knowledge and use of them are what constitute generalship in the ring. So I clinched with Choinyski and weathered this storm by knowing just what to do.

I started up for the sixteenth round with the old pep, but the sun was beating on my face very disagreeably. Still, I figured to myself, it must be hurting Choinyski's face even more because he is more badly cut than I. Now this flat boat had just two pillars, about two feet in thickness, rising from the sides with a little platform or deck upon them and a little pilot or lookout house in the centre above. By accident I found the spot where this gave just enough shadow to cover one man from the sun, and I backed over into that little oasis and did as much fighting as I possibly could, standing there.

When the seventeenth round came, instead of coming to the centre of the ring, Choinyski walked right over to the sheltered place and stood there waiting for me to come to him! From then on the battling was as much to see who could hold this advantage as for the victory at the finish. In fact most of our fighting was done by those pillars.

Each round after the fourteenth, when it looked as if I were headed for defeat, that is, when I would clinch with Choinyski in a certain part of the ring, I could hear someone repeating the Lord's Prayer. The voice went on muttering, round after round. Finally it came to me that the owner of the voice must be praying for me because my opponent was of another religion, and one that does not use that prayer. So in one of these rounds (I do not remember just which, but towards the end of the fight) when I came to this same place, it happened that Choinyski's back was against the ropes and I could look right over his shoulder at a little old fellow whose lips were moving in prayer. I recognized him as a little Irishman by the name of Tom Riley, a friend of our folks, and no one ever knew how in the world he got there. But there he was, leaning on the ropes with his eyes shut, little spatters of blood on his face, praying! I don't really think he once opened his eyes after that fourteenth but he could tell by the noise and the excitement that the fight was still on, and he did all he could to help by praying until the fight was over!

We battled at this terrific pace to the end, which came in the twenty-eighth round. Choinyski was rapidly tiring, not only from exertion but also from the great loss of blood from his nose and mouth, and I myself had been suffering the tortures of the damned from the hot sun, my blistered feet, the raw welts all over my body and the pain from my left hand, as well as the terrible handicap of not being able to use my right.

We were sorry-looking sights, they tell me, when we came up for the twenty-eighth round. I saw the condition Choinyski was in and felt that one good left-hand hook would finish him.

People who have not engaged in ring battles, and many of those who follow them pretty closely, do not realize the mental attitude of the fighter or the processes of thought he goes through. A fighter, at least a scientific and experienced one, has no time to think much about fear or defeat, victory or the purse. Of course, between rounds, if his principal second is not holding him in conversation, which is usually the case, or in flashes such as at that time I have described when, relaxed in the clinch, I looked over Choinyski's shoulder at the little old praying Irishman, he can dwell on such things. But for the most part all a fighter can think of is the action – that is, of what the other fellow is going to do next and what he himself must do next. Occasionally his opponent may do something absolutely unexpected, something he never did in a fight before in his life and one has to change one's whole tactics entirely. Decisive plans of action frequently come from a wise handler, but if the fighter is skilful, from his own brain, as he rests between rounds, or in sudden inspirations as he fights in the ring.

There is one policy that I have always carried out in my fights, if I thought a man was beginning to tire a little, I would always turn and watch my opponent's gait when at the end of a round we were both walking to our corners. A man who is bothered in the head or in the legs is more or less like a man who has had a little too much to drink – he shows it plainly in his walk, or dragging his legs. That was Choinyski now, the old snap all gone.

Well, we came up for the twenty-eighth round. And a more

fatigued pair of men than us two I don't ever remember seeing. Yet both were still full of determination to win. I know I realized, and I'm sure Choinyski did also, that the end was not far off; human endurance could not last much longer.

There was one invaluable thought which occurred to me early in this fight. As I said, this was the most punishing one I was ever in, and somehow I learned then a principle that stood me in good stead in all my later fights – that is, to reserve a little strength for a crucial moment; never to go quite to the limit at any one time until that moment comes. I felt then, and also felt in my later conflicts, that I had some reserve strength for one final spurt. To save this I relaxed at every possible moment through the fight, not only between rounds, but as we clinched, when I would let him frantically try in his eagerness to push me away, while I leisurely held on and watched him waste his efforts and energy. Then I would break away just as deliberately and slowly as the referee would allow. By this tactic, which is also a part of ring generalship, I was slightly fresher than Choinyski in spite of the injuries with which I began the fight.

I now felt that if I could get my left-hand hook in on Choinyski I could end it all, and that was what I started out to do. As my trainer and I had arranged when the twenty-eighth round started, Delaney kept shouting: 'Now, Jim, cut loose with that right hand. You can finish him with one good punch. Come on now, let that right go!'

As if following his advice, time after time, I deliberately pulled my right back and swung 'haymakers' at Choinyski, intending to miss him; and I got him going, as I have described before in this story, towards my left, only he was not going quite so fast. Again and again I swung the right, deliberately, missing by a little, and watched him duck in an arc towards his right and towards the threat of my left. Slower and slower came his motions and, it seemed to me, as I watched him, like those of the swinging pendulum of a clock beginning to die down.

With this slackening I could see the end to all the gruelling pain I had been through and victory within my grasp, and the thought gave me strength. I called on that last reserve, swung my right hand and, as he came over more slowly than ever to the left, put everything that I had in the world into my left – whole fist now, not caring whether I would smash every bone in that hand, because I meant it to be the final blow – and timed it so perfectly that, as he reached the end of the arc, it landed squarely on the vital point of the jaw and down he fell. As the referee stood over him counting ten, I also counted to myself, to be certain I got the right count. I was so tired that I was sure if he should get up again I would drop dead!

So ended this battle, which Billy Delaney, the most famous of all seconds, said was the fiercest he ever saw, either before or since.

And it is a remarkable feature of this fight that I fought this whole battle with my left hand. I never landed with my right once – in fact, couldn't even close it tight!

As soon as the fight was over we were carried on to the deck of a tug that lay alongside, then as soon as I could get on my feet I went to Choinyski's cabin and shook his hand, turning the old feud into a friendship which has lasted ever since. He is now instructor in the Pittsburg Athletic Club, and every time I go to that city he and his wife have dinner with me.

We were then each taken to a Turkish bath, and for seven hours I sat on a steamer chair, my blistered feet in two pails of hot water, and my hands in two other pails of the same hot liquid, hot towels in addition on my zebra-striped face.

I suppose I should say something dramatic about how the two factions acted after the fight was over, but to tell the truth, I was so tired I do not remember a single thing about it aside from the one big cheer.

I had no fights during the following year, and when I came to exercise again I found the knuckles of my left hand so flattened that I couldn't even hit the punching bag with a straight left, but would have to left hook it with the first knuckle. This injury, however, turned out an advantage, for it perfected the left-hand hook, of which I think it is everywhere agreed in sporting circles I was the originator.

6

THE following year I was employed in the auditor's office in the
City Hall of San Francisco and engaged in no ring battles, simply
taking exercise at the club pretty regularly to keep myself fit.
Still, this period was not without its suspense and excitement.

Not a little of the latter was caused by a new weekly paper,
the *California Illustrated World*. In the very first issue they
printed on the front page a picture of 'James J. Corbett',
labelling him 'The Coming Champion of the World', with these
words underneath: 'Pin this in your hat!' Complimentary
copies of this number were mailed all over America and practically every known sporting man received one. This was just
about a year and a half after the great battle between John L.
Sullivan and Jake Kilrain, in Mississippi, which was the last
heavyweight championship contest fought with bare knuckles
and under the old rules. In this scrap, after a terrific struggle,
Sullivan managed to best Kilrain.

For the benefit of those who are not familiar with the old
London prize-ring rules I should explain that these regulations
not only provided for bare knuckles, but allowed wrestling with
and throwing your antagonist. When one contestant was either
thrown or knocked down the round was ended and not before.
It was only after such a turn in events that an intermission or
rest of one minute was granted. A good ring general could
actually fight a thousand rounds under these London prize-ring
rules and make the fight less gruelling than a modern twenty-
round contest. All he would have to do would be to clinch,
fake a fall, and pretend the other fellow threw him, and he could
gain a minute's rest and end another round. So rounds would
frequently be of only five seconds' duration, with a sixty-second
rest following each.

Conditions, of course, are much more practical under Queensberry rules, which prevail to-day. These forbid wrestling,

demand five-ounce gloves, and three minutes of boxing before the minute's rest. If a man is knocked down or falls, he must get up without any assistance, within ten seconds, and continue the fighting, or he loses. Thus the present system is much more severe than the old and results in more action.

After the Sullivan-Kilrain fight William Muldoon, the famous trainer and present Boxing Commissioner of the State of New York, took a show on the road, composed of wrestlers and boxers, and headed by Jake Kilrain as his star. About a month before Mardi Gras week, they hit New Orleans and one day were gathered at the gambling-house of 'Bud' Renaud, one of the most famous sporting men of the South in the old days.

Muldoon and Kilrain and some of the 'sports' around the place were talking about getting someone to box Kilrain during the carnival, and they couldn't for the moment think of any new face that would arouse interest. Someone suggested Dominick McCaffrey, who at that time was considered one of the cleverest boxers in America, but Kilrain turned down the suggestion, saying: 'I want something easier than that.'

It happened that a complimentary copy of the *California Illustrated World* lay on the table, displaying James J. Corbett's picture on the front page and flaunting in their faces the threat: 'Coming Champion of the World!' I ought to explain, I think, that this prophecy had been bravely put in the paper under the instruction of its owner, who had seen me box from boyhood up and even before the last Choinyski fight had prophesied great things for me. After that he had grown absolutely convinced there was a rosy future for me.

One of the sports picked this paper up and asked: 'Who's this?'

They all looked at the picture and had a big laugh!

Then Renaud spoke up: 'What's the matter with sending a telegram to this paper? Maybe we can get that kid.'

So it came about that the manager of the San Francisco paper sent for me one afternoon. I went down to his office and he handed me a telegram addressed to me in care of the paper. I opened it and read:

Will offer a purse of twenty-five hundred dollars, two thousand to the winner and five hundred to the loser. Your railroad fare to New Orleans and return if you will box Jake Kilrain six rounds Mardi Gras week.

I was dumbfounded, but also very proud that I was recognized as a boxer of enough merit to cope with a man like the famous Kilrain, and I was also tickled to think that my name was known outside of California! So, boylike, without consulting my father or anyone I immediately telegraphed my acceptance.

Of course the newspapers got hold of the news and a lot of the sporting editors grew very solicitous and expressed their sympathy and all that. To think that a kid like me was foolish enough to go down there and fight a man like Kilrain! A lot of my friends tried to talk me out of it. The old saying that 'familiarity breeds contempt' held in this case. My closest friends did think I would be a great fighter *some* day, but they never dreamed for one instant that I was then ripe enough to tackle a man like Kilrain, at the early age of twenty-one and with only one professional fight behind me – that with Choinyski – which, by the way, really first established my status as a professional.

The money for expenses was duly forwarded to me and the day before I left for New Orleans I went over to visit Jack Dempsey, the Nonpareil, who was training for a fight at Alameda, across the Bay from San Francisco.

When Dempsey heard what I was taking on he laughed. 'Corbett,' he declared, 'Kilrain will never lay a glove on you. You'll make a "sucker" out of him.' And he said it as if he meant it! Whether he did or not, I fully agreed with him, I was that confident!

Then he added: 'If you'll wait awhile I'll give you letters of introduction to some big men from New York down there for the winter.' After a time he returned and handed me half a dozen letters to some of the most famous sportsmen of the day, including the old plunger, Phil Dwyer; Ned Kearney, who owned the big Van Tassel & Kearney horse exchange down on Eleventh Street, New York City, also rather prominent in politics then; Pat Duffy, of New Orleans, and Dave Gideon, the racehorse man. I put these letters in my trunk.

So I set out on my journey, about two weeks before the fight, with only fourteen days for training, four of which were to be spent on board a train. On the way down, whenever the train stopped for meals at one of the old Fred Harvey stands, I would sprint and run during the wait.

One day the West-bound Limited pulled into the station just after our own train, and the West-bound passengers were getting off as I was sprinting up and down alongside the track. Much to my surprise I ran into Mr John W. Mackay, the father of our present Clarence H. Mackay, one of the big figures in California when it was a young state, and also one of the owners of the bank in which I had worked. He stopped and looked at me. I looked at him, without speaking for a moment. Then I greeted him.

'Is this Jimmie Corbett?' he asked.

'Yes, sir,' I confessed.

He looked puzzled, then asked: 'What in the world are you doing here?'

'I have left the bank and am a pugilist now,' I informed him a little proudly.

'A pugilist—huh!' he retorted. 'And where are you going now?'

'Down to New Orleans to fight Jake Kilrain.'

'Well,' he said, 'I hope you get a damn good licking!'

'I won't get whipped,' I told him, 'and I'll be back soon to open an account in the bank!'

It seemed an awfully long trip, but finally, one beautiful morning, I arrived in New Orleans. Since I knew not a soul in the town and Bud Renaud was the one who had guaranteed the purse, I had wired him asking him to meet me at the train. As I got off I looked up and down the platform, but didn't see anyone there who seemed to be looking for me. There was one very dignified appearing gentleman waiting, but I didn't imagine it was for me, but after almost all the passengers had gone from the station I caught him studying me. I looked at him in turn, and finally he took a chance and asked me my name.

'Jim Corbett,' I replied.

Well! I never saw such a look of disappointment, pity, and sympathy mixed and stirred up all together, come over a man's face! Though tall and weighing about 165 pounds, I was very skinny and undeveloped, with a long and none too strong neck.

'My name's Bud Renaud,' he finally said.

Then he escorted me to his carriage, treating me with great courtesy, and drove me to his home, which was in his apartments over the gambling resort, a beautiful place, by the way, on Canal Street, the main thoroughfare of New Orleans. During the drive he inquired: 'Boy, have you ever seen Kilrain?'

'No,' I replied.

He looked me over again. 'You're not very big, are you? Why, you're just a kid! What makes you think you can whip him?'

'I don't know,' I answered, 'I just think I can.'

After luncheon in his apartments we set out to look the town over, and in the evening he took me into one of the famous old restaurants of the South and introduced me to William Muldoon and the man I was to fight, the redoubtable Jake Kilrain.

Judging from the way they talked to me I must have appeared something of a 'boob' to them, but I let them kid me as much as they wanted, and did not betray that I was wise to them, always replying very meekly and politely!

The next day, Renaud took me out to a German garden where a lot of other fighters had trained and where a fellow named Smith was then preparing for a preliminary fight billed for the same night on which I was to meet Kilrain. I started boxing with Smith and going on the road with him, trying to get in the best condition possible in the few days remaining.

Now after all the well-known sports of the town had seen me at Renaud's gambling-house, there was of course some speculation as to my chances with Kilrain. Most were a little disgusted, I found out after the fight, feeling that Jake had too soft a mark. In this company was the famous 'Mike' Donovan, who died up North recently and who for years was the instructor of boxing at the New York Athletic Club. Phil Dwyer, Pat Duffy, and the others I mentioned in connection with the letters of introduction (which I had not yet presented) were also in this party, and they appointed Mike Donovan a committee of one to go out to the training quarters the next evening to size me up and have a talk with me.

Accordingly he came, introduced himself to me, and started to quiz me as we stood in the bar attached to the place in which I was training.

'Have you ever seen Kilrain, young fellow?' he said.

'No,' I replied.

'Have you any idea how he boxes?'

I told him I hadn't, and as all the time I could tell that he was trying to draw me out, and also from the way he talked that he knew a whole lot about boxing, I said to myself: 'I'll give him an "earful" to take back to the Kilrain quarters.'

For at least an hour we stood there in that bar, he asking all sorts of questions about boxing and fighting, most of his inquiries involving the finer points. Finally I asked: 'How heavy is Kilrain?'

'He'll weigh about two-ten to two-fifteen,' he replied.

'Well,' I said, 'Sullivan licked him!'

'Yes,' he said. 'But it was a pretty tough fight.'

Finally he took hold of me and said: 'Now this fellow Kilrain has a great left-hand body punch, also a trick like this, sometimes when he hits straight with the left for the head his head is over here and sometimes it's there.' And he illustrated it with his own head. 'Now what would you do if his head was over here?'

I looked him in the eye and replied: 'Mr Donovan, I'll go fishing for his head until I find it, no matter where it is!'

He grasped me by the hand. 'Young fellow,' he exclaimed, strangely enough, with almost Dempsey's exact words, 'you're going to make an awful "sucker" out of Kilrain. He won't lay a glove on you. Why, you know all about boxing!'

So he went back to the gambling-house and told the group: 'This fellow Corbett is going to make a monkey out of Kilrain.'

They all laughed at him, but nevertheless it made them more interested in the stranger's chances, for Donovan was the only one who had visited my training quarters.

But the following afternoon Phil Dwyer, Pat Duffy, and the whole crowd came out to look me over. Of course at that time I knew nothing of Donovan's report to them. They introduced themselves to me and we sat on the veranda of the little hotel and they started to cross-examine me too. One of their questions came in almost Donovan's very words: 'What makes you think you can beat Kilrain? You've never seen him fight. He's one of the greatest pugilists in the world.'

'Well,' I said, 'I not only think so myself, but Jack Dempsey thinks I can beat him too.'

Right away came a voice: 'Do you know Jack Dempsey?'

'I box with him and know him that well,' I replied.

Their surprise over this information made them feel a little foolish, I suppose, after having talked to me as if I were a novice, and from then on I dropped that role and they treated me with some respect.

'Now that you are out here, gentlemen,' I remarked, 'I have

letters in my trunk addressed to several I see here. They're from Jack Dempsey.'

At this, they seemed more surprised than ever and when I produced the letters we found that four of them happened to be written to men in the crowd. Immediately they became my friends and warmed up to me and we had a nice chat, which continued until they left.

On the day of the fight I left off training, and went down to visit the city. Seeing a big café which seemed to be very popular, and being curious to hear the talk of the fight, I entered and found a crowd of men at the bar. Someone recognized me and I was introduced. While I was being presented, one of the men, a great, strong six-footer, looked me up and down as if he were quite amused. 'You're the fellow who's going to fight Kilrain tonight!' he exclaimed, then laughed as if his heart would break.

'Yes, sir,' I said, in a very low voice.

He slapped me on the back and indulged in another horse laugh. 'If you stay four rounds with Kilrain, kid, I'll make you a present of a hundred dollars!'

Well! There was nothing he could have said that could have hurt my feelings more, and as I had about fifty odd dollars in my pocket, I came back with: 'You won't *give* me any hundred dollars; but I'll bet you fifty that I'll be there at the end of the sixth.'

'No, no,' he insisted, 'I'll *give* you a hundred dollars.'

'You couldn't give me anything,' I replied. And we had quite a heated argument which almost ended in a fight. However, after a while, I left without any serious row occurring.

I will never forget what a splendid character Bud Renaud was! He was a personal friend of Kilrain's, but he had a very kindly feeling towards me and showed it in a nice though not exactly encouraging way. His wife, knowing I was all alone in the city and thinking I was going to be killed by Kilrain, whom they idolized and thought unbeatable, felt sorry for me too. So they came out to my training quarters and had dinner with me before the fight and I could tell from the tone of their conversation and from the way in which Mrs Renaud would look at me from time to time, that they really thought I was going to be very badly hurt, and that they would not give much for my chances. Nevertheless, they tried their best to cheer me up, not realizing that I didn't really feel the need of such support.

64

Just before they left I asked Mr Renaud if he would send a telegram to my father in San Francisco for me?

'Why, certainly,' he said; so I wrote out the message, and as near as I can now remember it, this is what I wrote:

Never felt better in my life. Will whip Kilrain sure. Love to Mother and all.   Jim.

I handed it to him, saying: 'Will you be sure this goes right off, please? I want my father to get it before the fight.' Then I added: 'You can read it, if you like, Mr Renaud.'

He did, and I only wish I was capable of picturing to you the look on his face! After getting over his amazement, he said, in the way people talk when they try to break bad news gently: 'Jim, do you think it's advisable to send this telegram? You know you have never seen Kilrain fight.'

I slapped him on the back and replied: 'Mr Renaud, I appreciate your sympathy and your kindness to me and I'll never forget it; but I feel in my bones I'm going to beat Kilrain!'

This was almost too much and they went off to send the wire, and I went to the Southern Athletic Club, where the fight was to be held. The preliminary bouts were already on when I arrived, and walking down the aisle I sat in the audience and looked at the fighters, no one paying the least attention to me – not that I wanted it, but the indifference showed what a stranger I was and how little known.

Here I waited until Smith came on, for I was quite anxious to see what sort of a showing this young fellow I had been training with would make. I saw him all right – knocked stiff – and helped carry him into a dressing-room, which, by the way, was the one I was to use. A nice beginning, but I brought him to, not only through sympathy, but because I needed him as a second. Then I started getting into my things.

I had everything on but one shoe when Muldoon came into the room and said in a domineering manner which I did not like: 'Hurry up, young fellow, and get in the ring! The referee and Kilrain are waiting for you!'

'Just a minute,' I retorted, 'I've got something to say about that!'

'Well, what is it, what is it?' he replied, impatiently.

'Hold your horses and I'll tell you,' I said. 'You say the referee is in there?'

'Yes, yes, and you'd better not keep them waiting.'

'That so?' I came back. 'As it happens I haven't been consulted about any referee. I want to look him over,' and then we had a few stiff words.

However, it ended in his going out and telling Bud Renaud and the directors of the club that the young fellow had weakened and it looked as if he weren't going to fight.

I should perhaps explain that this ignoring of me on the part of the directors was natural; Kilrain was the big card, and none expected me to have a chance with him, so they didn't consult me about a number of things. It was not that they were deliberately unfair, they just thought it would be wasting time. But considering all things together, they were certainly taking me lightly.

Within a minute the directors and Bud Renaud, and all of the audience who could get in, had rushed in the room. One of them spoke up. 'I'm the President of the club,' said he. 'What's the reason for your trying to back out?'

'I'm not,' I replied politely, 'and there's no trouble at all, only I came a long ways to box Jake Kilrain, and this contest tonight means an awful lot to me, though it seems to be a joke with you people. I want to know who the referee is and I want to meet him and talk with him. I think that much courtesy at least is coming to one of the principals.'

'Why, that's all right,' he said, seeming to feel a little easier now, and out they sent for the referee, who walked in a few seconds later to be introduced. Lo and behold! Who was he but the fellow who had wanted to give me the hundred dollars if I stayed four rounds with Kilrain!

I knew my chances were slim with him as the third man in the ring, and looking him straight in his eye, remarked: 'You've been appointed referee?'

'Yes,' he answered.

'I've no doubt but you stand pretty well here and are a gentleman.'

'I certainly am a gentleman, sir!' he came back at me.

'That's fine,' I took him up quickly, 'and since you're a gentleman, if one of the principals in this contest objected to your being referee, you, being such a gentleman, would naturally resign.'

66

'I certainly would,' he replied.

'I'm glad of that, sir, and also that you are a gentleman,' I declared, 'because I happen to object to your being referee!'

He walked out in a huff and then there was a round or two of talk! Finally, without any intermission, I said: 'Wait a minute, gentlemen' – I was addressing the whole room, Muldoon included – 'don't think you're not going to see a fight. You're going to see one, all right. But I came from San Francisco all alone and you all think I'm going to be murdered. Now I don't think so; I think I'm going to win tonight. Now, what do you think of that?' Here I paused to let this sink in, then I went on: 'And if I win by one point I don't want to be robbed by a referee this fellow Muldoon here picks to save Kilrain's reputation for him. If I win by an inch, I want it; and if I lose it there will be no kick coming. Now I'll take anyone in this crowd for referee – and I don't know any of you.'

Up stepped one of the finest looking men I ever gazed upon, handsomely dressed, a regular fashion plate, in fact. He was the amateur boxing champion of the club, a cotton broker, and a member of one of the best families in New Orleans, I was told later. Rather excitedly, Ned Violett – that was his name, though I won't swear as to the spelling – declared: 'I'll referee this fight!' And if ever sincerity and fairness show in a man's tones, it certainly did in his!

I liked him at once and I said: 'He'll do me, gentlemen. Now go on out and I'll be ready in the shake of a lamb's tail.' So I put on the other shoe and went out into the ring, where Kilrain was waiting for me. The announcer came over and asked me my weight. I said 'About 165', and he announced the weights: 'Corbett, 165, Kilrain, 190!'

I jumped up from my chair and said, laughingly, in a voice that everyone near the ring could hear: 'Just a minute. If Kilrain weighs 190, I weigh 130. Change those weights.'

At this there was considerable laughter among those at the ringside, who seemed to catch the sarcasm quick enough; and the first round started. As we met in the centre I feinted at Kilrain a couple of times. Then, too swiftly for the audience to count them, I hit him six punches right on the nose, and the spectators began throwing their hats in the air.

In the second round I hit him at will and a bad cut appeared above his right eye. He was a good boxer of the old school but was being considerably out-pointed, for I was confusing him with a brand-new style of fighting, although I was not quite aware of it myself. Jack Dempsey (the original – always remember that) had recognized this and looking back I can see that in his conversations at training quarters Mike Donovan had betrayed his enthusiasm and belief that I had something altogether new. Perhaps it was just as well that I had just my boyish confidence then, without a full realization of my actual ability! I might have grown too cocky and worked less industriously.

The six rounds went along like this, I hitting him practically whenever I chose, the audience frantic with surprise and excitement. At the call of 'Time!' at the end of the bout, almost before the referee had time to give the decision, which he did – and to me – the audience had swarmed down the aisles and the leaders had lifted me on their shoulders, carrying me around the building and hailing me as the next champion of the world! They took me into my dressing-room, where I changed clothes as quickly as possible, and then was ushered into a carriage and taken to the smartest club in New Orleans, the Pickwick Club, if I remember rightly. Here they opened several cases of champagne and wined and dined me. It was a glorious night for a boy of twenty-one.

On the next day I had no sooner entered Bud Renaud's place than Kilrain came in, sore as a boil because this unknown kid had put it over on him. 'Corbett,' said he, 'I want to fight you again.'

'No,' I replied. 'I've got your name on my list. Now I'll go and get some other names on my list.'

'What for?' he said. 'You didn't lick me last night.'

'Anybody looking at your face would think I did,' I replied, and he turned quite nasty and for a minute it looked as if there was going to be a second battle right then and there, but Bud Renaud came in and escorted Kilrain out of the place, apologizing to me for the latter's actions.

After the fight I had sent my father a wire as follows:

Won with hands down. Love to all.

Now my father was a quaint old Irishman, and he knew just as well as anybody in the world what I meant when I said 'Won with hands down', but he loved to hear people explain the meaning to him. They tell me he was all over San Francisco that night, with the telegram in his pocket. When congratulated on 'Jim's success', he would reply: 'Yes, but he sent me a telegram and I don't understand it', and so he'd produce the telegram! The fellow would read it and repeat the words: 'Won with hands down.'

'Yes,' father would say doubtfully, 'but what does he mean by that?'

And it was music to his ears to hear them reply: 'Why, Kilrain was easy; Jim was just playing with him; he just walked away with him.'

'Is that what he means?' he would inquire doubtfully, trying hard to appear indifferent; and he must have gone through this act with everybody in San Francisco!

So you see, now that I was successful my father got over his disappointment at my leaving the bank, and forgave me. He seemed no longer to have any objections to my being in the professional ring, and had all the typical Irishman's pride in a son that was a good fighter.

7

I become Boxing Instructor at the Olympic – Peter Jackson is offended – My First Glimpse of Sullivan – What happened in the Five Bar-rooms – I attain my Weight and am matched with Jackson – Dad wants to disown me.

WHILE my friends were now convinced that I had at least a chance of becoming a champion some day, I was sure that I ought to be a little bit heavier before taking on any more important fights. Luckily the directors of the Olympic Club, where I had spent the happiest days of my youth, took it into their heads just then to ask me to become instructor. This solved my problem, for if I signed up I would be compelled to be on hand every day, developing myself for the time when I should take up pugilism as a career. The bargain was struck and I taught boxing at this club every day for about a year.

I had not been in this position long when the papers announced that the great negro fighter, Peter Jackson, was coming from Australia to San Francisco. He was at that time considered without an equal as a boxer anywhere in the world. Shortly after his arrival someone brought him around to the club and I was introduced to him.

A very trivial incident, harmless in itself, aroused this great fighter's animosity toward me. It seems that right after being introduced to me he asked where 'young Mitchell's place' was. I told him and he inquired: 'Are you going up that way?'

I said 'No', for, as it happened, I really intended going in another direction.

Only a short time after he had left, the man whom I had wanted to see at a place at a considerable distance from 'young' Mitchell's dropped in the club and our business was transacted there. Forgetting all about having told Jackson that I was not going up that way, I then started toward 'young' Mitchell's, and as luck would have it ran into Jackson coming back. I was about to go up and speak to him, when he gave me a funny look and a very stiff bow. Something was the matter! I didn't realize for several hours afterwards what in the world it was. Then it finally dawned on me that possibly he thought I had declined to walk with him because he was coloured.

Bad feeling grew out of this little incident, and since he had been brought over here by the California Athletic Club, the professional club, rival of the Olympic Club, naturally the members of the former didn't try to heal this injury to his pride. Then too they had never gotten over the last Choinyski fight.

Not long after his arrival Jackson made his first appearance in San Francisco, boxing with a local heavyweight, Jack Sullivan. I attended the bout with a chap, Billy Dick by name, who I had always thought was a friend of mine. As we both sat watching Jackson, Dick asked: 'What do you think of him?'

'Well,' I replied, 'he's a very clever man, but no cleverer than I am!'

Following this bout, I ran into Jackson on several different occasions and he never paid the least attention to me.

One day I stopped at the C.A.C. and there were six or eight fellows in a group, Jackson among them. I shook hands with everybody, but Jackson didn't offer his hand, nor did I offer mine. Some fellow spoke up and said: 'Why, you know Peter, Jim?'

I said: 'Yes, but there's something the matter with him, and I don't know what it is.'

One of the other fellows turned to Jackson. 'Peter,' he said, 'what's the trouble between you and Jim?'

'He's been talking about me,' Jackson declared.

'Anything I've said behind your back I'm not afraid to say to your face,' I told Jackson. 'What's been repeated to you?'

'You said,' he replied, 'that I was over-rated.'

I tried to recollect any such speech and at first couldn't, but suddenly it dawned on me that the only time I had ever said anything at all like that was the night I first saw him box; so Billy Dick must have repeated my remark: 'He's no cleverer than I', and stretched it.

So I said: 'Yes, in a way, I made that remark; but it was never meant to be repeated to you as I thought I was expressing my private opinion to a friend. What I really said, though, was that I didn't think you were any cleverer than I.'

Well! Somehow he got hot under the collar over this harmless statement and said: 'Why don't you fight me then?'

'Maybe I will, some day,' I replied.

'What do you mean, "some day"?'

'I'm not quite big enough for you yet, but if ever I can put on a few pounds, I'll be after you.'

'It can't be too soon for me,' he replied. 'I'd just like to give you a good licking!'

'You'll have that chance, all right!' I answered, and in a few minutes left the club, more determined than ever to acquire the needed weight!

Jackson spent the months following meeting all the heavyweights they could rake up out in California. In rapid succession he defeated George Godfrey, the coloured heavyweight from Boston, Patsy Cardiff, and Joe McAuliffe, then toured through the country towards the east licking some more, and even went over to England, cleaning up everything in sight in the British Isles. Flushed with his triumphs, he returned to America and wanted to fight John L. Sullivan. But the champion drew the colour line.

All through this period, I was up in the club, working away, developing myself and trying for extra poundage and not neglecting to see Jackson each time he fought in the vicinity.

While he was training for his fight with the famous Joe McAuliffe, the latter's backers asked me to box with Joe at the training quarters because he was in need of a fast man to work with. So I went out one day to box with him and he would not allow anyone in the room. We were there all alone – and I knocked him all over the place. A few weeks later (this was in 1891) Jackson fought McAuliffe and defeated him. During the fight I watched every move of the big negro's and figured out a system of fighting him by which I might have a 'look in'.

At last, one happy night, I mounted the scales and found to my delight I weighed 172 pounds, stripped, and the thought flashed across my mind that now was the time to make a jump up that pugilistic ladder, right to the top. 'Sullivan will not fight Peter Jackson,' I argued to myself; 'Jackson has defeated practically every well-known heavyweight in America, Australia, and England. No one of prominence will take him on. Now is my chance!'

At the same time I recalled that a meeting of the directors of the California Athletic Club was booked for that evening, and, dressing quickly, I went to the phone and called up the secretary. 'Are the directors in at their meeting?' I asked, then told him it was Corbett inquiring.

He told me they were sitting in, and I explained my reason for the call. 'They have been wanting me to fight Peter Jackson for some time,' I declared, 'and I've just made up my mind I'll fight him.'

'Wait a minute,' he replied. 'I'd better speak to the President.'

The President, 'Lam' Fulder, came to the phone and I repeated what I had said to the secretary.

'Will you come down to the directors' meeting at once?' he asked.

'Yes,' I replied and hurried on down.

Into the room I went and told them I would fight Jackson at their club, but they'd have to put up the biggest purse that had ever been offered anywhere in the world – a $10,000 purse – and one and all nearly dropped dead!

'Why,' they shouted, when they'd gotten back sufficient breath, 'Corbett, you're crazy!'

'Not on your life,' I said. 'I'm all right at the top. Now listen here, and I'll show you folks something,' and I explained my plan, by which each man who wanted to see the fight must first join the club, paying the dues, $66.50. Those who were already members could be taxed a few dollars extra to see this special bout, and so the sum I had named would be raised.

We argued until three o'clock in the morning, and they finally gave in and agreed, and Jackson and I were matched before the meeting broke up, to fight to a finish, six months from that date, for $10,000, the biggest purse ever offered up to that time.

Then I took a trip down to New Orleans to see Jack Dempsey and Bob Fitzsimmons, and after that contest went to New York. On my way back to San Francisco to train for the Jackson fight I stopped off at Chicago, where John L. Sullivan was appearing in a melodrama called *Honest Hearts and Willing Hands*.

I had seen him first when I was about fifteen years old and he was travelling through the country, offering a thousand dollars to anyone he couldn't knock out in four rounds. He was very successful at this sort of game, and when he came to San Francisco, I told the door-keeper of the theatre where the champion was to appear, how crazy I was to see the performance. Some folks never have been boys, but the door-keeper had, and he sneaked me into the theatre at four o'clock in the afternoon, and there I sat, in the first balcony, until 10.30 at night, when they entered the ring! And there for the first time I saw the great John L. and conceived a boyish admiration for his fine physique and courage.

From what I have read and heard, I imagine most people picture Sullivan as stout, sluggish of motion, heavy of foot, always standing in one place, and equipped only with a right-hand swing. This was perhaps more nearly though never quite true of him in the latter part of his ring career, but as I remember this famous man at twenty-six years of age he was about 5 feet $10\frac{1}{2}$ inches, weighing two hundred pounds or so stripped, and perfectly built. He had light legs, a wonderful neck and shoulders – not too thick or badly proportioned – and was a terrific hitter with both hands. In addition, he was pretty quick with his feet and hands and as fast a heavyweight as Jack Dempsey is today.

That was John L. Sullivan when he was twenty-six. Mind you, I do not from the above description mean to give an idea that he was a highly skilled boxer; he really was in the slugger class and I have often thought what a great slugging match a fight between John L. Sullivan and the present Jack Dempsey would have been, if they only could have been matched while each was at his prime!

Time went along while I, still an amateur, kept on improving until, a few years later – I must have been about eighteen then – John L. Sullivan was matched to fight the ex-champion of the world, the famous Paddy Ryan, in San Francisco. I shall never forget having dinner one evening with my dear old father and mother and the rest of the family, and hearing Dad grow enthusiastic over his visit that afternoon to Sullivan's training quarters where they had seen him go through his stunts. Dad really grew quite excited as he talked, and finally even mother broke in. 'Yes, and he shook hands with us!' she said proudly, then told us all he was 'a very fine man'. But little did they dream that their son, sitting right at the table, was one day going to take the crown away from the man they admired.

A few weeks later I saw the fight with Paddy Ryan. Of course I was older and knew more about boxing than I had that day I sneaked into the theatre; and I spent more time getting points than in hero-worship. Whatever put the thought into my youthful head I don't know, but in my heart I felt that with agility and science, and a certain system that could be worked out, I could beat him some day!

With this one idea in mind I think I took better care of my health than any boy that ever lived. I was conscientious about my exercise, going to bed early and getting my proper rest, and following a careful diet. Sometimes I would spend the whole afternoon walking out by the ocean and getting whole lungsful of fresh air and exercise. I was very abstemious, too, in smoking, limiting myself to a couple of cigars a day (I never smoked cigarettes).

It was about this time that I cut down on drinking. Up to then I had thought it was smart to go out with a lot of fast young men and stand up to the bar and drink, although I never really liked it.

And now at last here in Chicago had come my chance to meet

the great John L. Sullivan! So I sent a messenger boy over to the theatre with money and a note asking for a private box, but Jimmie Wakeley, a New York sporting man, one of Sullivan's backers, sent the ticket for a box, and also the money back to me with word that Mr Sullivan would be pleased to have me as his guest.

I went over and sat all alone in this private box watching the performance. After the first act Sullivan sent for me and I was taken back to his dressing-room. He had a bottle of whisky on the table and Ed Williamson, the famous baseball player, then with the Chicago Ball Club, was sitting in the room with him. When I entered Sullivan took me by the hand and it seemed as if he was trying to break it – a great 'stunt' with him. Then he offered me a drink. I thanked him, but said I didn't drink, and he growled out something that sounded pretty scornful, then remarked: 'You're matched to fight that nigger?'

I nodded.

'Well, you shouldn't fight a nigger!'

'No one seems to want to take him on,' I explained, 'and it's a great chance for me to take a step up the pugilistic ladder.'

Although Sullivan was nice to me, I knew he was trying to impress me with the fact that he would be a rough customer if I ever met him; but all the time I was laughing up my sleeve at all that 'stuff'!

When the show was over I determined to leave, and held out my hand. 'Goodbye, Mr Sullivan, I'm glad to have met you.'

'Now wait,' he replied, with a gesture like some lord. 'I have a hack outside and I'll drive you downtown.'

He was beginning to show the signs of all the liquor he had drunk and I felt I would really much rather get away and go to my room. Nevertheless, when he insisted, I said 'All right', and he pushed me into this hack.

We must have stopped at ten saloons on the way downtown. Everybody knew him; crowds followed him everywhere. There was no doubt about his possessing a wonderful personality, and I think he was the most popular pugilist that ever lived. Certainly his whole-hearted way took people, although he was very rough and blustering in his manner.

When we reached the first saloon and walked into the place, as usual all gathered around Sullivan. He introduced me: 'This young fellow's Jim Corbett. He's going to fight that nigger Jackson.' Then, after presenting me to the crowd in this way, he ordered drinks for the house and hit the bar with his fist, growling: 'I can lick any —— in the world!'

Of course that made rather a fool out of me, as I was being talked about in the papers at the time as the coming champion; but I laughed it off and we went along another few blocks and stopped at another saloon. Again he walked up to the bar, introduced me, ordered a drink for the house, pounded his fist on the bar and swore: 'I can lick any —— in the world!'

He did this in four or five places on the way downtown and I was beginning to feel very much humiliated, since it looked as if he was trying to belittle me. At least I felt that way.

Finally he said: 'Now I'll take you down to Mat Hogan's place.'

Mat Hogan's was one of the most popular cafés in Chicago and all of the high-class sports hung out there – such men as Bill Pinkerton, the great detective, Mike McDonald, the big politician, Max Blumenthal, and Abe Levy; in fact all of the prominent sporting and racehorse men that figured in the papers thirty-odd years ago.

I tried my best to get away from Sullivan, as I didn't want to go in Hogan's place and have him hit the counter with his fist before all those people and tell them he could lick any blankety-blank in the world – meaning me in particular. But I couldn't make my escape, and he evidently thought he was making an impression on me because I was so meek and taking it with a smile. But the smile was not on the level!

Undoubtedly he figured to himself: 'Here's a young fellow coming on pretty fast. I may have to meet him in the ring some day and I might as well throw the fear of John L. into him now!'

So I now made up my mind, if he pulled that speech in Hogan's place I was going to 'call' him, and of course not knowing him very well, it was a very serious thing for me! But I determined that whatever happened I could not afford to have him make a fool out of me before all those well-known men of the sporting world.

So we walked into Hogan's, and after introducing me to a lot of these people, once more he banged his fist on the counter and made the old boast: 'I can lick any blankety-blank in the world', this time looking at me with a particularly ferocious and contemptuous glance.

I was pretty well worked up by this time. This doesn't mean that I lost my temper, for as a rule I sometimes get excited over trivial things, but am very cool in crises, no matter how resentful I may feel.

I looked him right in the eye and said: 'Mr Sullivan, you have made that remark several times in my presence this evening. You are the champion of the world and everybody is supposed to think that you can whip any —— in the world. But I am in the same profession as yourself and it's hardly courteous, and I don't want you to make that remark in my presence again!'

There we stood, each man in the room holding his breath, we holding each other's eyes! He looked at me, and I could see a wicked flash in his, but he couldn't outstare me and he saw I wouldn't cow. Coolly I watched the look of anger change to one of bewilderment. To think that this young kid had the nerve to 'call' him before his friends in the most fashionable sporting place in Chicago! He was stunned.

Then, all of a sudden, to my surprise he put his arm around me and said very affably: 'Aw, come on and have a drink!' Then he looked over his shoulder at his friends and blustered out, making a joke out of what he had really meant: 'What do you think of this kid?'

I let the thing drop there. But I found out a very important thing about John L. Sullivan that night: we were there for several hours and he never repeated that remark, and he now treated me with a lot of respect and friendly familiarity, and in my heart I knew that when he met a man who looked him in the eye and was not afraid of him he would be surprised and bewildered, because previously everyone had trembled at his very name! So I made up my mind that he would 'listen to reason'. I put a peg in that.

The next day I left Chicago and went on to San Francisco to begin training for my fight with Peter Jackson.

It was a great blow to my father when he heard the news. He did not like the idea of my fighting a coloured man! You see, when he had first come to America he had landed at New Orleans where mixed bouts are disliked more than in any other place in the country, and he had inherited this prejudice to the full. So he wouldn't speak to me for months!

I took up my training in the old quarters at Sausalito where

Choinyski had prepared for his fight with me. My father never came near the place, but sometimes my mother and brothers and sisters would come out to see me.

Finally the excitement over the fight reached such a pitch that my father's Irish blood was roused; naturally he did want to see his son win. So my mother persuaded him to come over and call on me, telling him I was worried about his refusal even to speak to me, and it would hurt my chances and perhaps cause my defeat.

I will never forget the talk I had with my father the first time he came round. 'Dad,' I told him, 'the only reason that you don't want me to fight this coloured man is that you think I am going to get licked; but if you thought I was going to win you wouldn't mind so much. You have it in your head that when I went into pugilism I jumped on the Vestibule Limited for Hell. Nothing like that at all, Dad. You've a son who can whip John L. Sullivan and you don't know it and can't believe it. Now I'm going to fight Jackson, Dad. If you stop me from fighting him here, I'll go over to Australia, or England; but when I sign to fight a fellow I'm going to fight him.'

So finally I got the old gentleman feeling pretty happy and he used to come over quite often to see me.

My brother Harry at this time had a milk route, and a few years before, while he was ill I had gone out to live at his home, getting up at four o'clock in the morning and starting out his wagons for him, and I realized how hard his life was. One Sunday, about four months before the fight, I took a day off and went over to see him. He was out in the stable at his work, dipping a sponge in the soapy water of a bucket by his side and swabbing a set of harness. He didn't see me at first, and I watched him for a while, feeling sorry for him, then hailed him. 'Harry, I've a very bright idea.'

'Yes?' he said, without turning, sort of weary-like.

'Why don't you sell out this milk route? You told me there was a fellow who wanted to buy it. Then with the money you can open a big café in the city and put the name "Corbett's" up on it. Some day soon I'll be champion and you'll make a lot of money with that name up there.'

He took one look at me, a glare of disgust, then went on dipping the sponge in the water and swabbing the harness, laughing at me all the while.

'All right,' I said; 'you think it's a joke, but I'll tell you what I'll do, Harry. In this fight with Jackson the winner gets $8,500 and the loser $1,500. Carroll, the wholesale liquor man, is one of the directors of the Club. You sell out this place to the fellow who wants to buy it and I'll sign over my loser's end to Carroll and put that and what you'll get together and we'll open the place before I fight Jackson. You'll make a lot of money.'

'Would you do that?' he asked, dropping his old sponge at last.

'Yes, I'll do it,' I replied; and a few days later he did sell the place, I signed over my loser's end of the purse and my brother opened a café in San Francisco. It was one of the landmarks there for many years afterwards.

8

Nervousness in the Ring – The Fighter who never budged an Inch – Jackson's Famous 'One-Two' – Sixty-one Long Rounds – The Ghost in the Steam-room – 'Parson' Davis.

FOR the Jackson contest I trained for four months and secured Billy Delaney (who had prepared me for my fight with Joe Choinyski for nothing) as trainer – on a salary at last. At that, he assured me that if I lost this fight he would not ask anything for his services.

Peter Jackson's manager was the picturesque 'Parson' Davis, who had also managed Charlie Mitchell, Jack Burke, 'the Irish lad', Frank Glover, and a host of other celebrities. Oh, what a credit to pugilism Davis was, and how different from some of our fight managers of today!

Parson Davis looked his nickname. He was a fine-looking man with grey hair, and his clothes were always made by the best tailors, and always black. Whenever he was to introduce a pugilist to an audience in the afternoon he would put on a black cutaway; when he presented the principals in the evening he always donned evening clothes.

I was very fond of Parson, and although he was managing Jackson when I was matched to fight him, that didn't interfere with our friendship. He believed Jackson had a walk-over and felt sorry for me; and I used to kid him considerably about this confidence which to me was decidedly misplaced.

During one of these chats, he showed his friendship by asking me if I wouldn't agree to have the loser take $3,000, and the winner $7,000, of this $10,000 purse, thus increasing the defeated man's end. I knew he was doing it just through his liking for me, because, as I said before, he thought it was a 'cinch' for Jackson to win. But I refused.

One day, less than a month before the fight, Jackson hurt his ankle in stepping out of a buggy, and in those days, as in this, the newspapers made a lot of a slight injury; from the space given it one would have thought his ankle had been *broken* and that he wouldn't be able to fight, but it was only a little sprain and in a week he was out on the road again, running and training, and in as good condition as he ever had been in his life. I knew this, for Delaney had a personal friend watching him every day.

The betting was 100 to 20 on Jackson, and the only bets that were made were on rounds. My supporters didn't expect me to win – they were simply betting I would stay so many rounds, the wager-limits varying from four rounds to twenty-five. They didn't think I had had enough experience and were afraid I was too light to defeat this great fighter.

About two weeks before the fight I began to speak disparagingly of Jackson whenever his name was mentioned in interviews with reporters the papers sent to me. My object was to 'get Jackson's goat', for I knew he would read what was printed, also to let him know I wasn't a bit afraid of him. This, I believe, is one of the most important things to get over in a fight: the short ender should always try and convince his opponent that he himself hasn't lost heart and feels sure he will be the victor. I have followed this practice throughout my career.

Jackson took to heart some of the things I said – just as I had hoped. So much did it affect him that he sent Bill Naughton, the famous sporting editor of the *San Francisco Chronicle*, over to my training quarters to tell me that the verbal agreement Parson

CORBETT *v.* PETER JACKSON

Davis had made about $3,000 to the loser 'didn't go now'; that the money would be divided according to the articles of agreement – $1,500 to the loser and $8,500 to the winner!

I told Naughton to go back and tell Jackson that this division suited me perfectly and that if he (Jackson) preferred, I would fight him, the winner to take *all*! Bear in mind that if he even accepted this proposal, I would have been in considerable of a fix, for I had already signed over my loser's end on the purchase of my brother's café. It was a bluff, pure and simple – a little part of what might be called the diplomacy of the ring. Luckily my offer was not taken up.

Meanwhile I got in perfect condition and Jackson was never in better shape in his life, contrary to the reports of some of the sporting editors who said he still had a bad ankle.

On the afternoon before the fight, 21 May 1891, I went over to San Francisco. Although I had a big contract on my hands in facing one of the greatest fighters of all times, I had the boyish confidence that only youth can have. I often wonder now how I ever passed it!

About five o'clock (we were to fight about ten) I had a bite to eat, and, to the surprise of everybody (it was the only time I ever did such a thing in my life before a fight) I fell sound asleep at seven o'clock, and they wakened me at nine!

I have often read reports of fighters who were so calm that they took naps before a battle, but it is my experience that this is usually 'bunk', as the boys say. I know that this was the only time I was ever so fortunate myself, and I never saw one of the many fighters with whom I have been in the hours preceding the entrance into the ring that had this good luck. They usually have their minds pretty well concentrated on the fight; in fact some of them think too much about it, and it's very hard on those fellows who keep the tenseness to themselves and don't 'unbutton' to some friend.

Whenever I felt that way before a bout I would take some close pal and say: 'Come on, let's take a walk and have a chat; I'm thinking too much of the fight.' And off we'd go and talk about something else.

Jim Jeffries, when he was training for the fight with Jack Johnson, couldn't think of anything else but Johnson. He'd even go out fishing – not to fish, but so that he could sit down on the bank and worry about the fight undisturbed, while apparently just waiting for a bite. On the day of the big event in Reno he came out of the house at noon, looking as if he hadn't slept in three months.

I was acting as his adviser, and to distract him suggested a game of cards and five of us started a round of 'Hearts'. Jeffries in that game actually played spades for diamonds and clubs for hearts, time after time. The other boys thought he was just kidding, but I knew he couldn't tell the colour of the cards. So I upset the table and broke up the game as though in a joke – because I was afraid the people standing by would 'get on to him'.

The greatest case of nervousness I ever recall was that of a young fellow from Syracuse named Joe Dumphy. I had boxed with him on several occasions when I visited his city, had seen him fight, and knew him to be a pretty good man as far as natural ability went. And he did come along pretty strong, well enough to be matched with Dan Creedon of Australia, the big event of his life as Creedon was looked upon as one of the greatest middleweights in the world.

His big night came around all right; he and Creedon got in the ring; but when 'Time' was called, Dumphy stood in the centre of the ring with his hands up, just like a statue; he couldn't move hand, foot or head! Creedon feinted at him, went up near him, walked around him, and this fellow just stood there – didn't budge the fraction of an inch! Everyone began to laugh and thought he had a trick up his sleeve and were waiting for him to spring it, but I knew Dumphy so well that I was sure he was just paralysed from nervousness.

At last, after walking round and round this statue for a while, Creedon got over being puzzled and walked up and gave him a smash right in the face. And still Dumphy never moved arm, foot or head – just stood there, immovable, like one of those living pictures you see sometimes in vaudeville. Well, do you know, Creedon walked up and hit him four or five punches in the jaw and knocked him down and they carried this joke fighter off, he never having moved one step or hit one blow in the whole fight!

On the night of the Jackson fight thousands of people gathered in front of the old Florence House where I was stopping, and cheered me and wished me good luck as I drove away in the carriage. At my mother's house my parents had arranged to get the news of the fight, round by round, over the telephone, and all the neighbours who had known me since I was a boy, were on hand too. There was Julius the barber, the first one who ever shaved me; Devecchio the butcher, Cohen the grocer, Lippman the dry-goods store man; and our neighbours, old Mrs Blanchfield, the Quinns, the McAnerneys, the Fogartys, the Carneys, the Boyds, and Mrs Raven, a sweet white-haired old lady who was my mother's chum. All evening they ran in and out, laughing and crying and praying, or comforting one another. I guess they had as many thrills over that telephone as anyone at the ringside.

Meantime I arrived at the club and went to my dressing-room, and they told me Jackson was already on hand. The referee, Hiram Cook, came into my room as I was putting on my fighting togs and said he would like to have Jackson and me settle on the details then; in short, he wanted to give us his instructions before we entered the ring; so I said: 'I'll go in Jackson's room with you and you can give us our instructions there.'

Now I knew that Jackson was under the impression that I was afraid of him because of his great reputation and long experience. This would have been natural, for I was only twenty-one, and this was the biggest fight for which I had ever been matched. So I wanted to convince him that I wasn't afraid of him at all.

Of course, this idea of 'getting the other fellow's goat' is nothing new. It has probably been attempted in every ring fight since the first; but the methods vary. As one comedian has one way of working up to his situations and his laughs, so every fighter has his particular system of getting the other man's 'goat'. Most fighters simply take the obvious way of insulting the other man by some nasty remark or slur, but I usually adopted a carefully thought-out plan.

I went into Jackson's room, to confront one of the most magnificent specimens of physical manhood I ever saw! There stood this negro, stripped to the waist, 6 feet $1\frac{1}{2}$ inches in height, weighing 204 pounds. Even at that weight he was so splendidly proportioned that he looked lean. I might add that Jackson, from my own knowledge of him, was one of the most intelligent pugilists that ever stepped in a ring; and that statement goes for either black or white!

What I am about to tell may sound a trifle 'fresh' on my part; but please remember that I had an important object in view. I was much lighter and had to mentally upset – if such a thing were possible – this formidable antagonist who thought I was simply a child in his hands. And the betting odds fully justified his confidence. There wasn't a 'wise one' who gave me a look-in.

'Now, gentlemen, we want to decide on just how you want to fight,' the referee began. 'I will read off these articles of agreement for you; there are a few little points we want to decide upon before you enter the ring.'

Then he read off the customary rules until he came down to the article, 'Hitting in the Clinches'. 'Now,' he said, 'do you want to hit in the clinches, or not? Decide on what you want now.'

In spite of the irritating things I had previously said about him, all of course for a purpose, Jackson said very magnanimously: 'Any way Mr Corbett wants.'

And I went right back at him: 'Any way *you* want it!' Fresh, sure! But I had to do it.

He repeated, with great politeness: 'Any way you want, Mr Corbett.'

'Never mind that stuff,' I replied, 'Any way *you* want it!'

He looked at me in amazement and I could read in his eyes the question: 'What in the world makes this kid think he can whip me?' And this was just the impression I wanted to make!

As a matter of fact, I would have preferred looking out for ourselves in the clinches, since Jackson was a fighter of the Jem Mace school and I had built up for myself an assorted, or miscellaneous style which included the best of everything now in vogue today, but a surprise at that time. However, it meant more to me to impress him, so I insisted: 'Anything *you* want, Mr Jackson!'

This went on back and forth for a few seconds until finally I said: 'You can look out for yourself in the clinches and I'll look out for myself.'

This bewildered Jackson even more, because it seemed a foolhardy thing for an 168-pound man to agree to look out for himself in the clinches with one weighing 204! However, that was the arrangement and other minor details were settled in the same manner.

When we were through the referee said: 'Now we'll toss up for corners.'

Again I spoke up: 'It's not necessary. Let him take any corner he likes.'

Jackson, still very polite, replied: 'Then I'll take the "lucky" corner I've always had.'

So that was settled.

Just before the referee left the room Jackson made one request. 'Mr Corbett,' he said, 'I have always gone in the ring last and my opponents have always allowed me to do that. It's a little superstition I have. Would you mind going in first?'

'You're a little superstitious about it?' I inquired.

'Yes,' he said. 'I have never gone in the ring first in any of my fights.'

Suddenly I remembered how much superstition meant to one of his race, and I snapped back at him: 'Well, tonight's one time you'll go in first all right!'

Do you know, we were in that dressing-room for forty-five minutes and he wouldn't budge an inch! He simply would not go in that ring ahead of me!

Finally the directors came up to the room and tried to persuade me to grant his request, but I said: 'No. He's a hundred to twenty – a five to one shot. He goes in that ring first if we stay here all night!'

As a compromise it was agreed that we would enter the ring at the same time.

Now the corner of the ring he had chosen was nearest the stairs that we descended; my corner was the farthest from the stairs and I had to circle the ring to reach it. We came down the stairs side by side; he reached his corner and stood there, his hand on the rope, waiting for me to reach the opposite corner. When I got there, he kept his eye on me, and I paused purposely. There we stood on our toes, like a couple of sprinters waiting for the bark of the pistol. Chuckling to myself I gave him a nod, as much as to say 'Are you ready?' lifted up the rope, and put my head under, as if to enter. He went through and I ducked back! You never saw a more irritated man in your life!

So we entered the ring and they put the five-ounce gloves on us – without bandages, as they were not used in those days. We went through the usual preliminaries and the battle started.

At once he sprang at me like a panther or some mountain-lion, trying to whip me as quickly as he could, since all the bets were on rounds.

Now I had decided not to swap punches with him, for he was too big; I intended to rely purely on my speed and footwork, and at once followed this plan of campaign. And I needed all my quickness, particularly to offset his best weapon, which I had noticed he used in other fights, his 'one-two' punch, one of the most effective I have ever seen. Sometimes I hear this parti-cular punch spoken of, these days, as if it were something new. But it's the oldest punch in the game (a right, quickly following a left lead) and Jackson was an expert at it; but he had a better one than the boys fighting today. They 'one-two' for the head only. He would not only do this, but would vary this practice by leading his left to the head, following up with a terrific right to the body. In all my career I never had a man make me travel so fast or make me think so quickly! No matter in what direction I would dash, this big black thing was on top of me, trying to 'one-two' me to death!

I was ducking round and round, clinching and doing every conceivable thing I could to stay on my feet – somehow never losing the least particle of my youthful confidence!

He was crowding me hard and I had tried so many different things that would be effective. None worked, until finally I struck something that did. It was simply dashing my left shoulder right into his breast when he rushed me. He didn't mind this manœuvre for a couple of rounds; at last it seemed to disconcert him. For each time he crowded me too much I would dive in and hit him with the point of my shoulder in the breast. Now it was not a 'foul', because he was coming to meet me – therefore practically running into my shoulder!

So we went on until, in the eighth round, he began to complain to the referee about this shoulder work, and I said: 'If you don't like it, keep out of the way of my shoulder!' I knew positively that I was within the rules!

In the sixteenth round his left came for my face, quickly followed with a right-hand body punch, the worst I had ever received up to that time in any fight! When I went to my corner after the end of that round, it hurt me so I couldn't help putting my hand up to my side – a childish thing to do – and Delaney grabbed hold of my arm and pulled it away and quietly gave me the devil for showing how much I had been hurt. But it was instinctive.

Following that punch, I felt a chill all over my body and mentioned this fact to Delaney. He asked an attendant to close the windows in the club, thinking possibly that there was too much cold air for me, but that was not the trouble; it was that terrible blow.

That started me figuring. If I got very many of those I knew he'd lick me, sure. So I fooled around for a few rounds trying to find some way of blocking this 'one-two' punch for the head and body.

I found that he usually tried this trick after a stiff left that he thought had hurt me. Finding I was hurt, as soon as he could he would let a left go for my head; but this purposely had no force in it – it simply balked me and drew my hands up, and then in came that terrific right for the body while my hands were up.

Through necessity I at last figured out a way to block this stunt. Knowing now that the left would have little force behind it and was to be followed up immediately with the dangerous right, I did not now attempt to get away from the left except by making a slight turn of the head, and then quickly shot out my left for the pit of his stomach.

Sure enough, bing! bing! his right would shoot out, following his left, but my left had already been sunk in his stomach and his right glanced off my arm! So that method blocked the famous 'one-two' for the rest of the fight except in one or two unlucky instances.

Of course all the time my head was at work his was too, and he was trying to think up something to offset my new defence. He did, and a little later, when I decided he was set for the old 'one-two', and I let my countering left go for the body, he shot a terrific uppercut under my left arm and just grazed my chin! That was a big surprise to me, something new at that time – and very dangerous!

I wanted to discourage him from trying that again, and I knew it wouldn't do to let him think it bothered me. So I went right in then for the next couple of rounds with my left-right for his body as if that uppercut didn't bother me at all, but each time moved my head a little farther to the right which made him miss me farther with that uppercut by just so much more margin. He tried it five or six times and suddenly, instead of letting the left go for the body I hit him a left-hand hook alongside the jaw, and he became discouraged and never tried the uppercut again. As it was the blow in the fight that bothered me more than anything else, what a load was off my mind when he stopped using it! But all through that night the fear that he might try it again remained with me and it was lucky for me he didn't realize this, or he might have changed the course of the fight.

We went on battling furiously and the audience, from the first round on, kept up a continual cheering and yelling. As a matter of fact not one in that room sat down for the first hour. It certainly was a furious pace that we kept up and every single blow known to boxing, and every fair trick, was tried by one or the other of us.

Up to the twenty-eighth round I did not slug with him – I was hitting single punches. In the twenty-eighth he got me in a corner and hit me a terrific right-hand punch on the side of the head and dazed me. I felt that he had me going and called on all the reserve I had, for it looked for a moment as if I were going to be licked. Suddenly I let both hands go with all the power I had in me, and slugged him from that corner clean across the ring into his own.

A second or two of this and he was helpless, with his arms by his side just like Dempsey, when he was pushed back into the ring after Firpo had knocked him out of it. I lost *my* opportunity just as Firpo did that night. Instead of steadying myself and hitting him one good punch and winning the fight, I wanted to hit him a thousand punches in a second, and the consequence was I simply had him dazed, not out, when one accurate blow might have turned the trick; and the gong sounded, as it did for Dempsey. Jackson was saved and I went to my corner, fully as tired as he, from my exertions!

When we came up for the next round he was as full of fight as ever and we fought up to about the thirty-fifth, as near as I can recall, when I felt I was getting pretty tired in the arms.

And I noticed that he didn't seem any too fresh, also that he was not crowding me so ferociously as he had in the first half of the battle; and Delaney kept repeating, while I sat in my corner after each round: 'Remember, no matter how tired you are, Jim, the other fellow is no better off!'

So we went along and fought in spurts. We would gain a little strength and now Peter, now I, would try for a minute to catch the other napping so that we might land a couple of good punches and perhaps win the fight. It was a finish fight and when we reached the fiftieth round I was more tired than ever. I can recall now a wonderful thing about Peter Jackson that showed how intelligent and resourceful a fighter he was.

When one is very tired in a contest the eyes become tired as well as the body; one does not see any too keenly and the other fellow always looks rather fresh to you. At the end of each round – I can see it all clear in my memory – each of us would bluff it out when the gong sounded for the end of the round. I'd look over at him, trying to appear as fresh as a daisy, and as if I were going to eat him up the next round; he'd catch me with the same dashing look. But looks can't kill you nor put a man down for the count of ten!

In the fiftieth round I loosed a left-hand hook as Jackson was letting the right go for my head. Our arms became tangled and I wrenched my left a trifle. That is the only incident of the ten periods, from the fiftieth to the sixtieth, that I now recall as important.

Just before the sixtieth, Jimmie Wakeley, John L. Sullivan's backer, the one who had sent me the tickets to see Sullivan in the show in Chicago, came over to my corner and said: 'You've got that fellow licked now if you'll go right in and finish him.'

'How do you actually feel, Jim,' Delaney inquired. 'That fellow is pretty tired over there. I know you're tired too, but how much have you left?'

'I feel I've just one good rally in me,' I told him, 'and I think after that I won't be much good.'

Remember by this time my hands were numb through keeping them clenched so long. I would go up and hit Jackson with my hands open and actually didn't know they were open, so dead were they. Towards the latter end of the fight the perspiration brought out all the hair in the gloves, forming a ball, which I used to work around into the palm of my hand; holding this was the only way I could tell my hand was clenched.

After my remark just quoted, Delaney decided the best thing to do was to keep going up to the scratch every count and giving all I had, since we couldn't last much longer. I had already told him that my legs felt all right, for I was not tired below in spite of all the footwork I had done; but my arms were as heavy as lead.

'Just keep up that little spurt and keep going up to the scratch; you'll last longer than he will,' advised Delaney, and that we decided to do.

Most of the gamblers had bet that Jackson would whip me in anywhere from four up to twenty-five rounds and had lost all their bets. As the fight continued so long they had plenty of time to connive and figure out how they could save their money; so during the sixtieth round the referee left the ring for half a minute – a strange and illegal proceeding – and I found out afterwards that he consulted with some acquaintances who had put up a lot of money on Jackson.

What did he do in the sixty-first round, without any reason or warning, but stop the fight and call: 'No contest. All bets off!'

In a jiffy Jackson's seconds started pulling off his gloves. If I hadn't noticed their actions, I would have been perfectly satisfied, I was so tired; but that showed me that he was not anxious to continue, while my seconds were in no hurry to pull off my gloves. So I protested right away. Lam Fulder, the President of the Club, and Hiram Cook, the referee, had both known me since I was a boy, and it didn't seem to me possible that they could do such a rotten thing to a man! When I protested I didn't realize the referee had said 'No contest' – I thought he had called 'A draw'.

Fulder grabbed me by the shoulder and exclaimed: 'What the hell are you kicking about? You have fought the greatest man in the world a draw and you will get $5,000. What's the matter with you? Don't you know when you're well off?'

Too fatigued to argue any further, and really half glad that the gruelling fight was over, I let my seconds lead me towards my dressing-room, when what did I see but Jackson, who was just ahead of me, fall right on his face, exhausted. They had to pick him up and carry him to his room. Then I knew I had been robbed.

I want my readers to know that I am telling this as gospel truth. I do not believe in alibis and am willing to admit defeat. During the course of this story I will tell things that are to my discredit as well as to my credit; but that was one time when I was 'jobbed'! I have never forgiven that referee and Lam Fulder, the President of that club! To take away a victory when it was just about to be won, after four hours of fighting, and from a boy they had known almost since he was born, to save a foreigner, and for what? Just to protect a few hard-boiled gamblers! How a man can do that is beyond me!

Well, anyway, it was considered just the same as a victory for me out at my mother's house, where they had received the news of the fight round by round over the phone. This had been too far away for my father, however, he was so excited, and he came down to the club, where the street was blocked with people.

'I'm Jim Corbett's father; let me get in!' he kept shouting, until they made room for him. Finally, to my surprise, he walked into my dressing-room, put his arms around me and kissed me! I noticed his watch chain hanging loose and asked him: 'What's the matter here?' He put his hand in his pocket and found that someone had 'touched' him for his watch, probably as he was worming his way in! I had presented him with the watch and reproached him: 'It's too bad you lost it, Dad.'

The loss didn't seem to worry him at all; he grabbed hold of me and hugged me again and said: 'To hell with the watch. You whipped the "nigger"!'

After Dad left they took me over to a Turkish bath and put me in the steam-room for about an hour. If you have ever been in such a place you will realize that one can recognize a person outside the glass door, but cannot make out the outline of his features clearly, once he is in the room and enveloped in the clouds of steam.

I was sitting there all alone when I saw a big form shadowed on the glass door and recognized Peter Jackson. He entered and sat right next to me. I said nothing, knowing he did not recognize me, but I watched him. He was all doubled up, with his hands on his stomach, moaning. Evidently his body was sore from the left-handed punches I kept putting in for four hours. Suddenly I spoke: 'You don't feel very good, do you?'

'Is that you, Mr Corbett?' He was startled.

'Yes.'

'You were a great man tonight,' he said. 'The quickest man I ever saw in my life; it was just like boxing a ghost!'

'Well, Jackson,' I said. 'I'm glad it's all over now and I hope I'll never have to fight a man as good as you are again. All those things that I said about you which were put in the papers and my conduct during the whole affair, I apologize for, and I want to let you know I was just trying to annoy you as much as I could. I figured you were taking me lightly and I thought I'd worry you a little and make you think a young fellow who had all this confidence must be pretty mysterious and maybe might have an ace in the hole.'

'How do you feel, Mr Corbett?' he asked.

'My arms are so tired I can hardly lift them, but my legs seem to be perfectly all right.'

'My legs are awfully tired,' he replied; 'I can hardly stand.'

I was anxious to get away from the place as soon as possible because I had promised my brother I would go out to the house and see my mother and father and sisters who, I knew, would wait up for me to come, and it was then about four o'clock in the morning. So I bade Jackson goodbye and went out.

When I reached home you would have thought it was eight o'clock in the evening! The house was packed with neighbours; we had something to eat; there was singing and dancing, and we stayed up the rest of the night. I even indulged in the dancing myself, tired as I was, and waltzed with my mother!

That night I thought Peter Jackson was a great fighter. Six months later, still being tired from that fight, I thought him a great one. And today, after thirty-three years, as I sit on the fifteenth floor of a New York skyscraper writing this, I still maintain that he was the greatest fighter I have ever seen.

By this time my brother Harry's café had justified my prophecies. To my satisfaction and his surprise the name over the door, 'CORBETT'S', did draw a lot of business. On lots of nights you couldn't even get in the place, and he agreed at last that it was better than swabbing off harness and getting up at four o'clock in the morning to start out milk wagons. And he didn't treat me as a joke of a fighter any longer.

9

Sullivan insists on Dress Suits — He throws Overboard my Cigars — I take on all Comers — Mike McGuinness of the Gas-house and his Little Bag.

THE day after the fight with Jackson, I went to the club to get my half of the $10,000 purse, and all they gave me was $2,500. I wouldn't accept this and went to a lawyer, but he advised me to take it, which was good counsel, because the club broke up soon afterwards on account of this very bout. So my supporters around town, after hearing that I was robbed of both fight and purse, planned a testimonial to be held at the Grand Opera House in San Francisco to make up the loss.

John L. Sullivan, then on his way to tour Australia with his company, was billed with his play, *Honest Hearts and Willing Hands*, for San Francisco, the week of this benefit, and some of my friends thought it would be a good idea for me to ask Sullivan to box with me at this benefit. I promised them I would.

At his opening I had a private box. It happened that I was late in arriving and Sullivan was already on the stage. When I walked into the box and sat down, the whole audience stood up and cheered me to the echo! This was the first time in my life that I was so greeted at a public performance and it surprised me; in fact, annoyed me, because I had not realized I would be noticed and saw I was interrupting the performance and did not want Sullivan to think it was a grand-stand play on my part.

After the first act I went back to his dressing-room and told him about the testimonial they were planning for me and asked if he would box with me? To make sure of his coming I offered to split the receipts with him. He very kindly accepted these liberal terms and everything was arranged.

The day before the benefit Sullivan sent word informing me that we would box in dress suits. The fellows handling the benefit said this would make a joke of the affair and displease the audience. They asked me to persuade him to box in his tights. I saw Sullivan at the Baldwin Hotel and told him I thought the people would be disappointed to see us appear in dress suits — it would look like a burlesque show – and they would think they weren't getting their money's worth. But he insisted it was the only way he would box – in evening dress! – and as he was champion, of course I had to consent. We appeared that night on the Grand Opera House stage in this soup-and-fish rig, much to the disgust of everybody. When the event was announced we removed our coats and started the first round. I had seen Sullivan fight a couple of times and had also seen him box, so I thought I would not do any footwork with him at all, but would stand still and swap punches with him. In a real fight this would have been very dangerous; but by adopting this course in this exhibition affair, which was not at all for blood, I might possibly get a line on his most dangerous attacks and not give away much of my own defence, particularly my footwork.

We boxed and swapped punches all through the first round, which was very short – about a minute – as Sullivan was fat and out of condition. I was pretty fit, though still very tired from that long fight with Jackson about four weeks before.

In the second round we went at it in the same way and were slugging pretty fast, toe to toe, when suddenly Sullivan dropped his hands by his side and stuck out his jaw towards me, trying to make it appear that he was *allowing* me to hit him. He thought I would keep on boxing, and ran no danger himself as it was a tame exhibition fight and I could not afford to try and put him out. He also expected me to continue my punches and it would look to the audience as if he were just playing with me and letting me hit him whenever he wanted.

So I also dropped my hands and held *my* face out to *him*! At once I saw a wicked look in his eyes.

After the round was over I went to my corner and said to Billy Delaney: 'Billy, I can whip this fellow!'

'Honest?' says Billy. 'Well, don't say anything about it now. Keep it to yourself.'

So Sullivan and I went through the third and fourth, which ran along like the others – just a bloodless exhibition. The audience was more or less disgusted that we didn't put on fighting togs and hammer each other's heads off. However, there was a packed house and the affair more than made up for the sum of which the California Athletic Club had robbed me.

George Thatcher's Minstrels, then showing in San Francisco,

made me a flattering offer to go with them on the road to box in or between the acts, and I accepted.

While up North with this troupe, I wrote a friend, Frank Phillips, asking him to visit the boat the day Sullivan was to sail and present a box of cigars to him with my compliments. A few days later I read that Sullivan had sailed and, shortly after, received a letter from Phillips telling me that he had taken the cigars to the boat, and had presented them to Mr Sullivan 'with Jim Corbett's compliments'. To Phillips's great surprise the champion had grabbed the box from him and thrown it overboard!

To save my life I couldn't understand this action! I thought and thought, but couldn't remember what in the world I had ever done to Sullivan to incur his enmity. I had boxed with him at my own benefit, and even given him half the receipts.

Finally it dawned on me. Like all fighters, he too, although the champion of the world, could be disturbed mentally, and I decided he was jealous of my growing reputation. Even back in those bar-rooms in Chicago he must have had a 'hunch' that here was a youngster coming along whom he would have to meet some day; and now since the Jackson fight, and the exhibition bout, everyone was hailing me as the coming champion. That must have galled him!

So I sat down and wrote a letter to the Olympic Club in New Orleans, which at that time was offering big purses for Sullivan to fight Frank Slavin of Australia or Charley Mitchell of England. I told them that when Sullivan returned from Australia they could offer a purse for a fight between Sullivan and myself and they could count on me being already signed! I asked them to 'keep it private, as Sullivan is so popular I would rather have the offer come from the Club; I don't want to come out publicly and challenge him. It would look like a grand-stand play on my part'.

Thatcher's Minstrels closed in Omaha. It was the end of their season and the company was to disband. I was still a little tired from the Jackson fight, and one day while walking up the street with an actor named Gene O'Rourke, I told him I would like to sign up with some show to box between the acts, or do something like that. A season of this would give me a chance to rest up before I fought again. Immediately O'Rourke left me and telegraphed to William A. Brady, now a famous theatrical manager, but at that time not so very well known. Brady wired me from New York, offering $500 a week to appear in his show *After Dark*, an old English melodrama.

I went on to New York, met Brady for the first time in several years (we had been acquainted as kids out in California) and I went on the road. Much to my surprise, for I had never travelled around through New England before, I found I was quite a drawing card. Soon I began to get over the stale feeling that followed the Jackson fight and grew restless, feeling I ought to get in action.

One day I dug up 'Bill' Brady in a little hall on Sixth Avenue. He was rehearsing a new show and I called him out on the stairs and said: 'Bill, I've just got on to myself.'

He looked at me in a funny way and said: 'Why, what do you mean?'

'I'm a drawing card,' I replied.

'Well, what of it?' he demanded, not admitting anything in particular.

'I don't want to work for someone else; I want to work for myself.'

'Got any plans?' he asked.

'I want to fight,' I told him. Then I took hold of him by the collar and said: 'I can whip John L. Sullivan!'

He looked at me as if I had paresis!

'Now you take me around to some of these burlesque shows and let me fight – meet all comers – and I'll show you I can fight all right.'

My confidence may have helped. Anyway, the idea struck him as a good one, although he didn't for one minute think I could whip Sullivan! In short order he arranged with the Central Theatre in Philadelphia to have a variety show, and billed 'James J. Corbett, the California Wonder', as a headliner, and had me offer $100 to any man who would stand before me for four rounds.

The first week was so successful that I was booked for three more weeks in Philadelphia, meeting a different man every night.

As long as I live I shall never forget the first night I opened at the Central.

On Monday afternoon I walked up past the theatre to look

at the big sign out in front: 'James J. Corbett, the California Wonder, Offers One Hundred Dollars To Any Man Who Will Stand Before Him Four Rounds!'

It looked lovely, but at the hotel where I stopped, several people had told me there were a lot of very tough men around — fellows who could really fight, though they were not so well known outside of Philadelphia.

'Who do you consider the toughest man I will have to meet?' I asked.

'Mike McGuinness from the gas house,' was the answer.

This had me guessing a little and picturing what an awful 'flop' I'd be if I failed to make good, for most of my work had been in long finish fights where I could take my time and study out my opponent's methods and watch for openings. That had not trained me for quick and early finishing. Of course I had no fear of being defeated, but was a little afraid I would not be able to stop all comers in four rounds; and failure to do so would be poor publicity!

Still worrying a little about these things, I went into a small saloon near the Central Theatre — not because I was at all thirsty, but simply to see if I could get some information about my 'prospects', particularly this 'Mike McGuinness from the gas-house.'

Behind the bar stood one of those little 'hick' bar-tenders with a stubby moustache like those you see in Tad's cartoons.

'Give me a glass of ginger ale,' I said, 'and have a drink yourself.' So I got into conversation with him.

'What is this going on over at the Central Theatre this week?' I inquired.

He kept on polishing up a glass as he replied: 'There's a "guy" from California opens there tonight. Name's Corbett, but they call him "The California Wonder", and he offers a hundred dollars to anybody he can't stop in four rounds. It's dollars to doughnuts he gets his "block" knocked off before the week's over!'

'Is that so?' I inquired, with a show of mild interest.

'Sure!' said the bar-tender, and I gunned for more information.

'Who do you consider will be the toughest man this fellow Corbett will have to meet?'

'There are a lot of tough "birds" around this neighbourhood,' he answered; 'but he'd better look out for Mike McGuinness of the gas-house!'

'Why? Who is he?'

'"Who is *he*!" Mike Connelly, the Ithaca giant, came on here a few months ago and asked the same question. He met all comers, includin' Mike, and Mike walked on the stage and hit him on the jaw and very nearly knocked him out. Connelly was lucky to go through the four rounds himself. This here bird they call "The California Wonder" just don't know what he's up against!'

'The California Wonder' walked around the streets that afternoon very much worried!

That night I passed through the alley leading to the stage door and found quite a crowd gathered there. I thought they were waiting for the gallery door to open and as it was early I felt pretty proud. 'House sold out sure,' I said to myself.

When I got inside I asked one of the stage hands when the gallery door opened? 'Why, it is open,' he replied.

'No,' I said. 'The gallery birds are all out in the alley trying to get in.'

'The gallery door doesn't open on the alley,' he answered. 'It's on the other side of the house.'

'Well, then, what's that crowd doing out there?' I inquired, a little puzzled.

'Oh, those fellows! They're fighters — want to get a crack at that hundred dollars.'

At once I sent for Brady, my manager, and posted him about Mr McGuinness. 'I understand he is a tough fellow,' I said, 'and from what they tell me in this burg I may not be able to put him out in four rounds. We don't want to pick him if we can avoid it.'

As soon as I appeared on the stage for my act those fellows poured on after me like an army, and like a drill-major I started calling the roll, going around and asking each his name. There was one big fellow who stood apart from the crowd, with a little grip in his hand. He was about 6 feet 1½ or 2 inches, raw-boned, and looked as if he was in good condition. After getting the names of several I went up to him and asked him his.

'Mike McGuinness!'

I acted as if this meant nothing to me and paid no further attention to him, continuing to question others standing around. At last, calling Brady aside, I whispered: 'That big fellow over there with the little grip in his hand is McGuinness. Tell him we've engaged someone for tonight – he can come around tomorrow night if he wants to.'

This Brady did and McGuinness went out.

I looked the crowd over to see if I couldn't pick out something 'soft' for myself and chose a fellow by the name of Joe Donovan. Although he was fairly big, I thought I could throw a scare into him, for he had a weak face. So I arranged with my sparring partner, Jim Daly, to take this fellow down and make him dress in the same room with us. While we were dressing Daly exclaimed: 'Jim, will you ever forget the night you hit that fellow over in Buffalo?'

'Yes,' I said, mournful like, 'I was very much scared that night; I didn't think he'd ever come to!'

Of course Donovan was taking all this in. So after a while I began again: 'But, Daly, that fellow in Jersey City had me more frightened than any of them.'

'Aw,' he said, 'that wasn't anything! You split one of his ribs, but a fellow can live with a busted rib! It's dead ones I worry about.'

I glanced at Donovan out of the corner of my eye and could see that his hands were shaking as he laced his shoe; so, as a parting shot, I added: 'Daly, you know when they get fresh with me I just slam it across; that's all!'

Well, we returned to the stage and when 'Time' was called this fellow was so frightened that he started running with the first punch I aimed at him, and ran off stage back of the scenes and I chased him!

The stage was empty and the audience hooted out front, and Brady came running back.

'I'll give you a hundred dollars whether you stay or not; go on there – we have to have a show,' he said to Donovan.

'I wouldn't go on there if you gave me *five* hundred!' replied Donovan.

This made us do some quick thinking, and as a substitute for the frightened man I seized a fellow with a nice little 'corporation', but very big and weighing about 220 pounds. He

99

afterwards became my sparring partner and was quite a famous character, 'Con' McVey. While he was dressing, to calm the audience, which was raising the devil, I went on and gave an exhibition with my sparring partner, so I didn't have a chance to work on this second fellow's nerves.

When the bout with Daly was ended, McVey was ready. I seemed to be myself again, not worrying at all about the act being a flop. So McVey and I shook hands and went at it. He was a big, aggressive fellow, but didn't know anything about boxing, and his stock in trade was nothing but wild-swinging 'haymakers'. I just played around with him for a couple of rounds and, as I had expected, being in no condition, he began to get tired. In the third round I put him out.

As the first night seemed to be a success, I felt rather happy and the next evening went over to the theatre at an early hour again. Who was standing at the stage door, with the little grip in his hand, but my friend 'Mike McGuinness of the gas-house'! I walked right up to him and said: 'I'm very sorry, but you'll have to come tomorrow night – we have someone for tonight.'

'All right,' he answered, and went away.

I went on that second night, and everything was nice and rosy for me.

The third night came and with it my friend McGuinness, with his little grip in his hand, to the stage door. Again I told him: 'We have someone for tonight. Come around tomorrow.'

'All right,' he replied, not 'phazed' a bit, and off he went.

So I stalled McGuinness off each night that week. Now I was doing such a wonderful business that they transferred my act to another theatre, called the Lyceum, quite a distance from the first one. 'This,' I said to myself in relief, 'is where I lose McGuinness!'

But the first night I opened at the Lyceum there was my friend McGuinness standing at the door waiting for me! I will never forget it! I got so I imagined I could see McGuinness when I went to bed at night and when I got up in the morning; in fact 'The California Wonder' was about as much mentally disturbed as his opponents of former fights had been!

The third week I went to a place on the outskirts of Philadelphia called Kensington – and, sure enough, me bold McGuinness was on hand! By this time the newspapers had gotten on to it and Brady came to me one morning while I was still in bed and exclaimed: 'Look at this!'

In the article he pointed out was an awful roasting handed me by one of the sporting editors. He said I had sent McGuinness away from the stage door every night and declared I was afraid to take a chance with this local fighter.

Of course, as soon as I read that my mind was made up: I would have to take on Mr McGuinness. There was no other way out. But we thought we would discourage him as much as we could and put him to all the trouble possible.

So that night we had him come to the dressing-room, to put his togs on, and Brady went out and told the audience some pathetic things – about how unkind that sporting editor was to say Mr Corbett was afraid to meet Mike McGuinness, and all that. Further, to show our sincerity, he explained to them, we had just been saving Mr McGuinness for the end of the week, to wind up nicely and give them a little treat. Then he bellowed out: 'I take great pleasure in introducing to you Mike McGuinness of the gas-house, whom Mr Corbett will meet tomorrow night.'

And McGuinness came out on the stage and received an ovation.

The next night he was on deck all right, waiting for me, the little grip in his hand. He was as welcome as the income tax today!

Jim Daly, my sparring partner, and I took him down to our dressing-room to put him through the 'third degree' as we had all the other fellows, trying hard to throw a scare into him. When McGuinness started lacing his shoe, that was Daly's cue to start talking.

'Will you ever forget, Jim, the night you hit that fellow in Buffalo and he was out for three hours?'

'Yes, Daly,' I replied, 'I thought that fellow was dead and would never come to. But that lad over in Jersey City was worse!'

'Aw,' said Daly, 'a couple of broken ribs aren't anything! A fellow don't die from that!'

I glanced at McGuinness as he laced his shoe and thought I heard him mumbling something to himself. My spirits rising, I winked at Daly and we watched for the medicine to take effect.

So we listened, but McGuinness was humming a little Irish ditty, 'In sweet Dublin city, where the girls are so pretty', and wasn't paying any attention at all to what we were talking about!

I made up my mind at last that there was one fellow who wasn't going to be afraid of me. No matter how much trouble we put him to, in sending him away night after night and 'razzing' him and all, he had been patiently waiting for his chance. All he wanted was to get on that stage with 'The California Wonder'!

I had my own manager referee the bout this night and also control the time-keeper; so before we went on the stage I said to Brady: 'I must stop McGuinness in four rounds, if the four rounds take four hours!'

'What do you mean?' he asked.

'Let the first round go five minutes,' I answered. 'The audience never kicks at a fight's being too long. And let me know about ten or fifteen seconds before you call "Time".'

You see, I was figuring that I would have to get some of the steam out of this fellow before I took any chances of getting near him, if he was such a dangerous man as they all said.

So 'Time' was called and McGuinness came to me like a wild man. He had me ducking and slipping and running away, and in his wildness he hit a bit of scenery that projected out from the wing and knocked it down.

With my great experience I could have hit him at will, but, as I said, I was a little leery about my ability to finish him in the scheduled four rounds, for he probably had a pretty tough jaw, and much as I out-pointed or beat him up, if he wasn't out, I would lose the hundred and a lot of prestige. The easiest way was to let him keep going and get him winded. All the time I was 'sprinting', I was quite relaxed, and he was spending all his strength.

He went along at this pace for a full two minutes, swinging those ferocious haymakers all the time, but at last he paused to get his breath; or tried to, rather, for I didn't permit that for a second.

'I never saw a Protestant I couldn't lick!' I shot at him as soon as he let up.

Well, being a true son of the McGuinnesses, he started calling me all sorts of names and came at me like a maniac! That was just what I wanted! And every time he stopped to take his breath I would make a feint at him as if I were going to hit him, and would say something else to hurt his true Irish soul.

He began to run down like a clock, going slower and slower from this terrific pace. Finally I was tipped off by Brady that I had ten or fifteen seconds to go; so suddenly, instead of running away, I stopped short and put everything I had in a left-hand hook and caught him alongside the jaw, knocking him groggy. He almost went down with the punch.

'Time' was called, and as he went to his corner I turned and looked at him walk and could tell he was a bit drunk from the punch; so I sat down in my corner and took ten or fifteen long, deep breaths.

McGuinness was no sooner in his chair than I gave the wink to Brady. 'Time' was called, and he was up again! I didn't want him to get over the effects of that punch! I went at him again and hit him a right-hand punch alongside the jaw and he fell into me, with both arms around me, almost out. The referee was trying to break us, but McGuinness wouldn't let go. Finally he said: 'Don't you think we'd better stop before we kill the two of us?'

I laughed and stepped back and had them lead McGuinness off. I didn't want to give him the finishing touch.

Now I am going to make a confession: This name, 'Mike McGuinness', is fictitious – for a reason. This happens to be one of the very few stories in this book that I have told in vaudeville, most of them being new ones I dig up out of my memory as I write. When I used to tell this story from the stage, it was my custom to put in the man's real name, but during one vaudeville engagement in Philadelphia I was much surprised to receive a letter from a lawyer who represented the widow of 'McGuinness' – he had died just a little while before that time – asking me not to use the name, as the widow felt it was giving her and her daughters too much of the wrong sort of notoriety. Now, in my heart of hearts, I had always felt regretful about poor 'McGuinness' and wished I could have done him a good turn later; so the least I could do was to submit to the wishes of the widow of this gallant Irishman!

IO

THE next day came a thunderbolt in the sporting world – the
challenge shown below. The comparison is no exaggeration,
for it created more stir than any similar defiance would today,
so popular was Sullivan, and so invincible was he considered.

SULLIVAN'S CHALLENGE

St Paul, Minn., March 5, 1892. – The following was given to the
Associated Press this afternoon:

To the Public in General and Frank P. Slavin, Charles P. Mitchell,
and James Corbett in Particular: On the 25th day of August 1890, I
formed a partnership with Duncan B. Harrison and entered the theatrical profession. Mr Harrison and myself made contracts covering two
continuous seasons, including a trip to Australia. These facts were
well known to everybody, they having been published in almost every
paper throughout the civilized world. I also keep my contracts, a fact
well established by reference to my entire career.

Ever since the existence of this contract between Mr Harrison and
myself becoming known, this country has been overrun with a lot of
foreign fighters and also American aspirants for fistic fame and
championship honours, who have endeavoured to seek notoriety and
American dollars by challenging me to a fight, knowing full well that
my hands were tied by contract and honour. I have been compelled to
listen to their bluffs without making reply on account of my obliga-
tions. But now my turn has come. Our season ends about June 4, and
we do not resume again until September 12. This gives me over three
months' time to prepare.

I hereby challenge any and all of the bluffers who have been trying
to make capital at my expense to fight me either the last week in
August this year or the first week in September this year at the
Olympic Club, New Orleans, La., for a purse of $25,000 and an
outside bet of $10,000, the winner of the fight to take the entire purse.
I insist upon the bet of $10,000 to show that they mean business,
$2,500 to be put up inside of thirty days, another $2,500 to be put up

by May 1, and the entire $10,000 and as much more as they will bet to be placed by June 15, the *Advertiser*, of New York City, Colonel John Cockerill, editor, to be the stakeholder. We are ready to put up the entire $10,000 now. First come first served.

I give precedence in this challenge to Frank P. Slavin, of Australia, as he and his backers have done the greatest amount of blowing. My second preference is the bombastic sprinter, Charles Mitchell, of England, whom I would rather whip than any man in the world. My third preference is James Corbett, of California, who has achieved his share of bombast. But, in this challenge, I include all fighters – first come, first served – who are white. I will not fight a negro. I never have, and never shall.

I prefer this challenge should be accepted by some of the foreigners who have been sprinting so hard after the American dollars of late, as I would rather whip them than any of my own countrymen.

The Marquis of Queensberry rules must govern this contest, as I want fighting, not foot racing, and I intend to keep the championship of the world where it belongs in the land of the free and the home of the brave.

JOHN L. SULLIVAN,
Champion of the World.

Of course all of us in the Brady troupe were very excited. We could hardly believe that the champion had actually challenged me.

I didn't take much time to speculate about it, however, and as soon as I had read the last word I threw down the paper.

'Bill,' said I to Brady, 'put up the thousand to bind the bargain.'

'But,' he protested, 'where in hell can we dig up the other nine?'

'You can search me,' I replied, 'but we've got to get it. Someone in the Olympic Club has tipped off Sullivan – about my letter, I mean, and he's put that ten thousand dollar condition in purposely. He thinks that's the best way to knock me out.'

Now I really hadn't the faintest idea where to get that money and couldn't think of a soul I could get to back me.

The following week I went to New York. On the train I went over in my mind the names of all the men interested in sports who were at all prominent. There were a lot of them whom I had met or knew by reputation, but it seemed silly to approach them, for everybody thought Sullivan unbeatable.

Thirty-odd years ago there was a music-hall on Twenty-third Street near Sixth Avenue, run by Koster & Bial. It was here that Carmencita, the most famous of all Spanish dancers, made her first appearance in America. It was a great resort on Sunday nights, for all the high-class sportsmen, politicians, and 'round-town celebrities of New York, among them the Dwyer brothers, Frank and Phil, the great racehorse men; Colonel Jacob Ruppert, a youngster then; Jesse Lewisohn Johnson, another racehorse owner; Dave Gideon; Matty Corbett; Ned Kearney; 'Al' Smith; 'Honest John' Kelly; and Richard Canfield, the gambler; Stanford White, and picturesque characters like 'Diamond Jim' Brady.

So I bought a box and went down there unaccompanied, one Sunday night, hoping that I might have luck enough to run across someone who might be interested in backing me – a long chance, but I thought I would take it.

Seated in a box opposite to mine, with a party of friends, was a young lady I knew. Seeing that I was alone she beckoned to me to come over. I went, was introduced to her friends, and was invited to join them for the evening. One of the gentlemen in the party was a Colonel McLewee (I think that is right, but though my memory of people's faces and names is pretty fair my faculty for spelling the latter is the worst in the world). Later, he owned the great racehorse Gold Heels. That will help to recall him.

Colonel McLewee asked me what I was doing down there all alone.

'I am out on a mission,' I told him gravely.

'What do you mean?'

'You know I am matched to fight John L. Sullivan?'

'Gosh A'Mighty! What! Fight Sullivan!' he exclaimed. 'Do you want to get murdered?'

I answered 'Yes' to the first part, 'No' to the second.

He looked at me quizzically: 'And you think you can whip John L. Sullivan?'

I pulled up my chair close to his, looked him right in the eye, and started to tell him, as earnestly and convincingly as I could, all the reasons why I thought I could defeat the champion.

I must have been a good salesman of myself for once, for he said: 'My boy, I don't think you can whip Sullivan; but you certainly have a lot of nerve and you can just put me down for $5,000.'

Well! I was speechless! I couldn't believe it! I was really dazed and must have looked around at the girl doubtfully, for she said: 'If Colonel McLewee says he will do it, it will be done.'

Then he gave me his card and told me to let him know when I had to put up the first $2,500.

After a while I entered another group and met 'Matty' Corbett (no relation – just an old friend of mine), who owned a racing-stable in partnership with Jack McDonald, and I told my story to him and the people in that box. In fact, I think I went in every box of the theatre that night, and before I left I found I could have had $50,000 if I had wanted it!

Can you imagine a man walking into a theatre today and digging up from people he had never even met before a sum of money which would be equal now to $100,000, just to back him to meet Jack Dempsey, and all figuring that the nervy stranger didn't have a ghost of a chance? These people did it for me just for the sportsmanship of the thing.

But it would be utterly impossible these times, when boxing is simply a commercial proposition and there is no longer any sportsmanship attached to it. For there isn't – no, not in any shape, manner, or form. Why, a man won't enter the ring today, even though he is a second-rater, unless the loser's end is guaranteed to be more than a champion got for winning a fight thirty years ago. They won't take any chances at all.

I do not remember the exact date, but shortly after this memorable evening at Koster & Bial's I notified Colonel Mc-Lewee that I was going to clinch the match and had to put up $2,500 for the first instalment. For this sum he sent me his cheque.

Neither of the principals appeared at the negotiations, the managers attending to all arrangements. Charley Johnson acted for Sullivan and Brady represented me. They met at the *New York World* office and arranged the match, which was to be the first heavyweight championship battle ever held under the Marquis of Queensberry rules, to be fought with five-ounce gloves; all the other details too being exactly like those govern-ing fights today. The managers agreed on Phil Dwyer, the famous racehorse man, for stakeholder.

In the meantime the Olympic Club had offered a $25,000 purse; so the contest was fought for a $25,000 purse and a $10,000 side-bet, the winner to take all – Sullivan insisting on this last condition.

Now I have seen almost all of the fight managers of the last forty years, but I never met a smarter one than William A. Brady. He was the originator of all the business strategy they follow these days, only the prizes now are bigger. He was shrewd enough to capitalize all the interest and sympathy arising from the fact that I, comparatively a youngster, was matched to fight the champion, also from the hard condition that Sullivan had forced the winner to take *all* – something that had rarely been demanded by any champion.

So Brady booked a tour through the country and we hired theatres and halls where I met all comers, as Sullivan was doing from time to time, offering $100 to anyone who could stand up against me for four rounds. Before the match had been arranged I had appeared in Philadelphia in burlesque shows as an added attraction of the evening, the story of which experience was told in the preceding chapter; but now our 'stunt' was the sole entertainment of the evening.

Whenever the words 'James J. Corbett, now matched to fight the great John L. Sullivan' appeared on the bill-boards they acted like magic and we drew great houses everywhere we went. This had the additional advantage, also, of increasing the interest in the coming match, for I endeavoured to show in these bouts that I really was capable of standing up to the great John L.

At the end of the tour Brady arranged for a big night in Madison Square Garden. Here I met, in the one evening, three men of pugilistic standing, each weighing over 200 pounds, and stopped all three within the specified four rounds; and that without taking a rest between the sessions. My opponents were good men, too: George Spillings of Rochester, Bob Caffey of Philadelphia and Joe Lannon, Sullivan's sparring partner at that time.

I don't think a fighter ever lived, or ever will live, who was as popular with the masses, and especially with the Irish, as John L. Sullivan. Many of our Irish citizens hated me just because I had the insolence to fight him. One night, not long before the Sullivan match, I was boxing with a man at Miner's old Eighth

Avenue Theatre, and in the middle of one of the rounds some-one in the gallery called out: 'So you're the guy who thinks he can lick John L. Sullivan!' following the jeer with a bottle which came clear across the orchestra, just grazing my head, and breaking into a thousand pieces on the floor of the stage.

My unpopularity with the Irish struck me as rather peculiar, for everybody that ever belonged to me, as far back as we could trace, was Irish through and through, and Sullivan, like myself, was born in this country, of Irish parents. Of course this attitude was due to Sullivan's disposition, which was just the right mixture of good nature, aggressiveness, and temper for a fighter, so people thought; while I was always more controlled and a little too businesslike, perhaps, to vie with him in popularity. Then, though I entered saloons occasionally, I did not care to waste a lot of time standing up against the bars of any city I happened to be in. To me it was the most boring thing in the world to be mauled around by a lot of drunks; and, as my friends of the footlights say, there old John L. 'was on his native heath', at least at that stage of his career.

But Brady's pre-fight campaign did result in arousing among the better element a respect for my ability, and some support. At the same time his playing up of such things as my banking experience and my orderly way of living, together with my quieter manners and rather unostentatious style of dressing, brought to my bouts many people who had always thought it beneath them to attend a prize-fight!

Meantime, Billy Delaney had joined my camp and it was quite a surprise to many 'experts' who thought I should have engaged someone else. One night shortly after the articles were signed, the famous William Muldoon came to my table in the old Delmonico restaurant and offered to train me. He seemed quite earnest about it.

'Muldoon,' I answered him, 'if I should be lucky enough to defeat Sullivan and any trainer gets any credit for it, it will be a little fellow who isn't famous like you – you never even heard of him. He lives 'way out in Oakland, California, and his name is Billy Delaney.'

Delaney was, in fact, on his way east at the very moment, for I had written, asking him to sell out his business and come on to train me; which confidence showed that I thought our joint prospects were very bright.

About this time too I ran across another old friend I had not seen in a long time. I was strolling up Broadway when a chap came out of the shadows and hailed me: 'Hello, Jim, don't you know me?'

I took him under the arc-light and looked at him in wonder. He had no coat on and the night was very cold.

'It can't be Denny Gillen?' I said at last.

'Yes,' he answered.

'My God! Denny!' I exclaimed.

Now Denny Gillen had lived around the corner from me in San Francisco in the old Hayes Valley days and I used to box with him in the cellar. I had heard about his drinking himself out of all the positions he had held in San Francisco and that his case seemed hopeless. So, after asking him a few questions, I said: 'Denny, I know you can't stop drinking altogether; but if you could just taper down on your booze enough to run errands for me and the gang, I'll take you down to my training quarters. It will be a nice berth for you.'

He promised. So I fitted him up with an overcoat, gave him some money, and did the things for him that anyone would for an old friend. He hung around until I went into training, meanwhile trying to keep as sober as possible. Denny did very well, considering, although he had a 'still' on most of the time, but this was never bad enough for any but those who knew him well to detect. Then he came down to our camp and used to be great company as we sat around evenings talking about the old days when we were kids together.

There was quite a big dent in Denny's nose. It looked as if it had been broken once, in a fight, as I supposed, and one night I asked him about it.

'No,' he said, shaking his head sadly, 'it wasn't broke in any scrap.'

'How did you get it dented, then?' I asked.

But he seemed rather shy about explaining the cause of his misfortune. 'Oh, you fellows would laugh at me if I told you,' he said.

However, finally we coaxed him to tell us all about it.

'I was in bed one night,' he began, 'and had the delirium

tremens. All of a sudden I heard a lot of guns going off. Then a bugle called and I sat up in bed. Bands were playing, and I saw about ten thousand soldiers marching around the room. Some fellow yelled out: "We are at war! Fall in!" In all the excitement I jumped out of bed and joined in the parade with all these fellows marching around the room, and we marched and marched and marched. Finally they started marching through the keyhole. I tried to follow them, and in trying to get through the keyhole I broke my nose!'

Denny's history came to an end. Some time after this I left Denny with money for clothes and a ticket to San Francisco, but when I returned to New York I ran across him panhandling on Broadway. Poor Denny didn't last much longer, and a few weeks later I received word that he had died in a little rooming-house, all alone. There was not a soul to bury him, and I felt the responsibility was mine. So I arranged for the funeral and, wanting to give Denny a good one, invited George and Johnny Considine, who then ran the famous Hotel Metropole at the corner of Broadway and Forty-second Street, and later the new one of the same name in front of which Rosenthal was shot; also Eddie Burke, the racehorse man; Teddy Foley, Tim 'Dry Dollar' Sullivan, and others. They promised, but when the day of the funeral arrived they all seemed to have forgotten the 'date', and I showed up at the place of appointment to find no one there. It was ten o'clock in the morning – probably most of them were not even up.

As I rolled down Broadway in the carriage to the undertaker's, I spied a little Jewish boy I knew, Ed Meyerson. He seemed to be in an awful hurry and was almost racing over the sidewalk, but when I hailed him he came over to the carriage. 'Jump in here,' I ordered him gruffly.

'Oh, I can't!' he pleaded. 'I've a lot of business to attend to.'

'This won't take you a minute,' I replied. 'Jump in, I want to tell you something.'

He got in the carriage and I immediately told the driver to travel!

Little Meyerson tried his best to jump out of that carriage, but I grabbed his arms and explained the circumstance to him, and finally he promised to stick. So at the grave of poor Denny the only ones to pay the last respects were two little old ladies (one of whom ran the rooming-house where he had died), this little Jewish boy, who had never even met the principal of this last act, and myself! I was sorry, for I had tried to give poor Denny the send-off he and his old parents would have liked.

Sullivan started training at Good Ground, Long Island, and I pitched my camp at Asbury Park, N.J.

Never before had a pugilist trained in Asbury Park – which at that time was almost as strict in its regulations and as religious in its atmosphere as Ocean Grove. I will never forget the first few days of my training there. The neighbours did peek out of the windows at us, but very cautiously; none of the children in the neighbourhood were allowed to come near the training quarters; and I was supposed to be first cousin to the Devil himself.

Some of my trainers of course were of a rather rough type, and there were two or three of them who unfortunately didn't have very good manners. So when I saw the attitude of my neighbours I gathered the boys together, and told them that anything in the way of misconduct on their part reflected on me. I further explained to them the ideas of the people we were to live with and threatened to discharge any who did not act like gentlemen. They all, I am glad to say, followed out my instructions to the letter.

We had been there about three weeks, minding our own business and going about our work in a nice, quiet way, when one day two boys of about twelve or so, children of people in the neighbourhood, came around. I saw them and stopped punching the bag. 'Now, boys,' I said, as kindly as I could, 'I want you to go back home. Your folks don't want you to come here and I don't want you to try it again.'

One of the little fellows spoke up: 'My mamma said I could come over here,' he said, looking very disappointed.

'Your mother said you could come here?' I repeated, flabbergasted.

'Yes, sir!'

'All right, then,' I told them, 'I'd like to have you. Make yourselves at home.'

Gradually from that time on the children began to come around; finally the fathers dropped in and actually seemed to enjoy themselves.

MITCHELL AND CORBETT

One of my inseparable companions those days was a dog who had attached himself to me in a very strange way, while I was playing New Bedford, Mass., under Brady's management. I was getting into a carriage to go to the theatre when this pup jumped in and wouldn't be persuaded to leave. Brady wanted to throw him out. 'Jim,' he said, 'you don't want a dog like that; he's a mut!' And he was! I could see in him traces of bulldog, collie, spaniel, greyhound, black-and-tan, and a few other breeds; but oh! how that dog did seem to love me! So I let him stick, christened him Ned, and he toured the country with me.

At Asbury Park Ned was always unhappy if I was not along. Sometimes he would insist on accompanying me on the Boardwalk and everybody was amazed to see this awful-looking animal following me. Often I'd lock him up when I went out. One night when I started for the New Brunswick Hotel, then the fashionable one in the place, I had to cross a bridge leading over the lake. Ned broke loose and succeeded in beating me to the hotel, for when I reached there I found the women gathering up their skirts and hustling out of his way, for he was wringing wet and covered with mud from his swim across the lake!

At this time Brady's daughter Alice, now the famous moving-picture star and legitimate actress, was a baby in arms, and as much as that dog loved to go out with me, he somehow got it into his old noddle that it was his duty to care for that baby in the carriage, and when the nurse took her out he would cast longing looks after me as I walked off, but never once left his charge.

I had some original ideas about training at this time; that is, they were considered erratic then, although some of them have since been adopted. For instance, it was considered very dangerous to allow a man to drink water when heated from exercise. I noticed that I did not enjoy, in fact could hardly swallow, my evening meal after a hard day's training. I had no appetite, only a fierce, burning thirst, for the stiff exercise had made me feel feverish inside. I figured this out and adopted a new course, much against the advice of all my trainers.

When the day's work was over I would go to a spring, take a dipper of water, rinse my mouth out half a dozen times and gargle my throat. Then gradually I would let a little trickle down. When I felt cooler I would repeat the process. Thus it took about half an hour for me to empty that dipper; but I found that after that I did not lack for appetite and enjoyed my evening meal enormously. You see I simply adopted the principle of treating my machinery as one does an automobile – you do not pour a lot of cold water into a heated engine, but let it dribble in gradually.

Then I formed the habit of going down to the most popular ice-cream parlour about ten o'clock at night, and eating a couple of plates of ice-cream, to the accompaniment, which I could hear, of sarcastic remarks from observers in the place.

'There's the fellow who is going to fight Sullivan,' one would say.

'What! That chap eating the ice-cream?' a companion would inquire in surprise; then everybody laughed at the ridiculousness of it. 'Sullivan will fairly murder him!' came the anvil chorus.

I told some of my ideas to a Dr Pancoast, a well-known authority from Philadelphia, who had a summer home in Elberon, and he also thought I used very bad judgment. In those days you must remember a typhoid fever patient was never given cold water or ice-cream, but now it is allowed; so my routine was justified by latter authorities.

It happened that horse-racing was at its height then at Monmouth Park, N.J.; and occasionally I took a day off and went over there, thinking the rest would do me good and probably prevent me from going stale.

Now these little details are not as trifling as they seem. They are very important, for they were innovations in the nineties, and I feel I owe what success I have had to my thinking for myself and not following rules blindly, not only in the ring but in my preparations for it.

And to show how important such things seemed in the eyes of the papers and public, I need only tell of an incident that occurred just before the day when Colonel McLewee's second instalment, $2,500, was to arrive and be turned over to the stakeholder.

At the races I met an old friend of mine, George Morgan of California, who invited me to dinner at a very popular resort at Pleasure Bay. During the course of the dinner he ordered a pint of champagne. I felt that a little would do me good, so took a glass of it. That was all that was necessary! The next day the Associated Press sent out the report that 'Jim Corbett was off on a "bat" at Pleasure Bay!'

I was shocked when I read it, but more so when I received a letter from Colonel McLewee telling me that he had seen this story in the papers and of course must decline to put up the next $2,500! I was left flat and I didn't sleep a wink that night through worrying about it.

Phil Dwyer, the stakeholder for the coming fight, and who, by the way, was a great friend of Sullivan's, was at Long Branch with his stable, so I rushed madly over to him, the day following the receipt of the Colonel's letter, and showed it to him. He saw that I was pretty much upset and tried to cheer me. 'My boy,' said he, 'you have nothing to worry about.'

'Why!' I exclaimed, 'he refuses to put up my deposit!'

'I'm stakeholder,' he replied. 'And if none of your backers come through with their money, your ten thousand is up anyway. I'm stakeholder!'

He meant, of course, that he would make good the $7,500 shortage if my backers failed; and he did this, mind you, although he was Sullivan's friend, through sheer sportsmanship, wanting to see me get a square deal! There were great boys in the old days!

Dwyer then asked me how much I weighed, and being so frightened at McLewee's falling down, I was afraid to tell him my exact weight, thinking he might get the idea in his head that I was too light to fight Sullivan and he might therefore weaken, so I told him I weighed 192 pounds, when I really weighed 178 – a white lie, for which I hope I may be pardoned, under the circumstances.

'I'll be over in a couple of days to see you train,' Dwyer added as I was leaving, and a few days later he came to my training quarters accompanied by 'Dick' Croker, then chief of Tammany Hall, and they watched me work out for a while.

'Do you really weigh 192 pounds?' Dwyer asked me, as I stopped.

'Yes, sir,' I assured him.

'Where do you weigh yourself?' he then inquired.

'Downtown, in a butcher shop.'

'Well, you come over tonight to the hotel after your dinner.

There's a butcher shop next door to our hotel, where they have some wonderful scales. We'll see what you really weigh.'

I got cold all over, but concealed my fear. 'All right, sir,' I agreed, 'I'll be over,' and made the date for eight o'clock.

As soon as they were gone, I called Brady, Delaney, and all my handlers, and we were in a terrible 'stew', all of us thinking that if any of the backers once learned I weighed only 178 pounds, they would leave me flat. So we decided to take the iron weights out of the pulleys, each weighing four pounds apiece, and stick three or four of them in my trousers; which I did. Then Delaney and I drove over to Long Branch in a hack.

Dwyer was standing in front of the hotel waiting for me. He took me into the butcher shop and said: 'Get on the scales.'

I started removing my coat, when he stopped me, saying: 'Never mind your coat. Leave it on.'

'All right,' I agreed, a little relieved, jumped on the scales and –I'll never forget it – I weighed 197 pounds!

Dwyer looked at me in amazement! 'You're certainly a deceiving man!' he said.

But even as I was talking to him I could feel that the weights were slipping. We were standing on the asphalt pavement, and, taking his arm, I tried to hurry Dwyer toward Delaney, who was sitting in the hack, for the game would have been up if those weights had once fallen on the pavement!

As we were side by side, he didn't notice my peculiar gait, and just as we reached the end of the walk and while I was still talking to Dwyer, I felt one of the weights at my knee, so I put my foot over the curb and the iron dropped into the dirt without any noise and he never saw it at all. Bidding him goodbye, we went home, the day saved! I told this little incident to Dwyer after the fight and he had a great laugh over it.

As you have discovered, my relations were very friendly with Brady, and we got on very well together, so well in fact that when one day he said: 'Jim, you and I have no contract or understanding about what I am to get if you win this fight; don't you think we ought to sign papers of some kind?' I told him not to worry about any contract. 'Just let me give you whatever I feel like, you'll profit better than if we make it a business proposition.'

He agreed, shook me by the hand and said: 'Jim, that's good enough for me!'

Time drifted by pretty swiftly, and at last came the hour for our departure. I knew I had managed to overcome the prejudice of the people of Asbury Park against prize-fighters; but how much I did not realize until I was closing up quarters. As I took the hack for the train, dozens of children of the neighbourhood flocked around and showered me with little presents that touched me very much – cheap scarf-pins, flowers, handkerchiefs, cologne bottles. Then, to my great surprise, Mr Bradley who controlled Asbury Park and who had objected very strenuously to my training there sent the Beach Band to escort me to the station!

My last day's training up North was done in Madison Square Garden, a publicity stunt of Brady's that gives another evidence of his shrewdness. I ran around the track, punched the bag, and even ate my meals before a large audience which had paid admission to watch me. This netted us both a lot of newspaper space and a handsome sum.

At last we boarded our private car and started for New Orleans, breaking the trip two or three times, on the way down, for exercise.

We reached the city about four days before the fight, Sullivan being already on hand. He had been taken up by the Young Men's Club, the biggest of all in the state, while the smaller Southern Athletic Club, where I had boxed Jake Kilrain, opened its doors to me. The betting was three to one on Sullivan when we arrived in town.

There was one princely hearted man in New Orleans whose kindness I shall never forget. His name was Wormseley and he was one of the leading cotton brokers in the city. I had met him when I fought Kilrain, and he now actually sent his family away and turned his house over to me for a home during my stay in the city!

I I

I STARTED in to do some light training in the Southern Athletic Club and all the time thousands of people were in and out watching me. There were also large audiences at the other club watching Sullivan, and after seeing both of us, the bettors decided that instead of three to one on Sullivan the odds should go up to four to one. This increase was due, I think, to our difference in weights. (It was two-hundred and twelve; and one eighty at the ring-side.)

If I had ever relied much on others' opinions I wouldn't have had much confidence or strength left for the fight. Even my old friend from California, Tom Williams, who had backed me heavily in the Choinyski fight, and had also seen me fight my sixty-one rounds with Peter Jackson, blew into New Orleans and bet, so someone was kind enough to tell me, $5,000 on Sullivan. Not because I was hurt at all, but simply because I liked Williams, I wrote him a letter the day before the fight. In it I said: 'Tom, I understand you are betting on Sullivan. I'm not mad, but I wish you would switch your bet and put it on me. I'm in splendid condition. You saw me fight Choinyski and Jackson. You know I can go the distance; and no man who has lived the life that Sullivan has lived can beat me in a finish fight.'

A few years later when I was going abroad, I happened to run into Tom Williams on the steamer. We were talking over old times and got down to this fight. 'Do you remember the letter you wrote me,' he said, 'before your fight with Sullivan, telling me to bet on you?'

'Yes,' I replied, and somehow managed not to grin.

'Well,' continued Williams, 'after I received your letter I went out and bet $10,000 more on Sullivan!'

I had also written to my father and figured he would receive the letter a day or two before the fight – which he did. I told him in what good condition I was, and prophesied that by taking my time and being careful I would win the fight between the twentieth and the twenty-fifth round; and my dear old Dad wore that letter out after the fight, just as he did the telegram after the Kilrain battle.

The excitement in New Orleans was intense from the start, as this was the first heavyweight championship fight ever arranged to be fought under the protection of the police. All other fights up to this time had been under London prize-ring rules and with bare knuckles, and, being against the law, had been pulled off in private.

Just before we left New York for New Orleans, I had told Brady to see how much money he could dig up to bet on me. He took all the money his wife had and what he could skirmish up himself, and it amounted to $3,000. All I had in the world on the day of the fight was $900 – we had used up so much for training expenses; but that morning I gave it to Brady and said: 'You take this $900 and the $3,000 you have, and go down and put it on me.'

'Jim,' he said, 'I'll bet my $3,000, but you had better keep your money. If we should lose the fight, that's all we'd have, and we'll have to ride the brakes out of town.'

So, after thinking it over, I took his advice and kept my $900, Brady going downtown to bet the $3,000 – four to one.

In a couple of hours he came back, all excitement, and exclaimed: 'My God, Jim! They're betting 5 to 1 on Sullivan!'

'That's great!' I replied. 'Did you put the money up?'

'No,' he answered, looking a little sheepish. Then he added: 'Don't you think, Jim, we'd better keep it in case you get licked?'

I got angry at this.

'You fool!' I blurted out. 'You were willing to take four to one, but now when it's five to one you get cold feet! Sullivan and I are just the same as when it was three to one: *we* haven't changed any.'

Then, pushing him out of the door, I gave him this parting message: 'Don't you come back here unless that three thousand is on!'

No sooner had Brady gone than in came the sporting editor of the *Cincinnati Enquirer*, Harry Weldon, one of the greatest supporters I ever had. He had prophesied that I would be the next champion of the world, before he had ever laid eyes on anything of me but my picture, and his confidence naturally touched me and later brought us together very closely. He was a big, fat, red-faced man, and he too rushed in, all excitement. I could tell by his manner that his confidence had been shaken by this jump in the odds to five to one. It seemed as if everyone was going back on me. But I held tight on to myself and as we sat on the trunk I remarked, coolly:

'Well, Harry, they've got you going, too.'

'No! No! No!' he insisted, but his manner gave the lie to his words.

'Yes they have,' I shot back at him, trying to put some iron in him, 'they've got you wriggling a little. Now I'll tell you something, Harry. I've seen Sullivan fight. I've boxed with him, and the only thing that will ever make me think that John L. Sullivan can whip me is when they bring me to and tell me I was knocked out!'

This boosted his confidence wonderfully and he went off very happy!

I had also noticed that the strain was beginning to tell on my trainers, and even Delaney. With all his coolness, he was trying to hum little songs to himself to make me feel he was happy and wasn't thinking about the fight at all. And others were whistling too loud and too often. All their actions, I could see, were so unnatural and unlike them. They were all doing it for the effect on me, and, if I do say it myself, I think I was the only one in the whole crowd that really felt normal.

To lead up to a climax, the club had arranged bouts between famous fighters to be fought on successive nights before the heavyweight battle – Monday night, George Dixon fought Jack Skelly for the featherweight championship of the world; on Tuesday, the wonderful lightweight, Jack McAuliffe, defended his lightweight title against Billy Meyers of Streator, Ill.; on Wednesday night, John L. Sullivan was to defend his.

McAuliffe gave Meyers an awful beating on Tuesday night, and it suddenly occurred to me that it would be a grand idea to have the last meal before I fought Sullivan with poor Billy Meyers. This did not strike me as ominous, for I was never superstitious – in fact, often defied and flew in the face of superstition purposely. This annoyed my companions considerably sometimes, and only a few days before, in Charlotte, N.C., where we laid off on our way to New Orleans, I had almost given Delaney heart failure. I hadn't noticed the number on my room when the bell-boy took me up, and while I was sound asleep that night Brady came up and hammered on the door. When I asked 'What in hell is the matter?' he shouted back: 'My God! don't you know? You're in Room 13!'

'Get out of here and let me sleep!' I called back. 'I don't care what number it is. I'm going to stay here!'

So now when I suggested that I go out with the loser, Billy Meyers, there was a terrible uproar. 'Why, he's a "Jonah"!' they said.

They begged and pleaded with me, but I insisted on going and dragged them all out there with me!

Meyers came down into the dining-room and met us. I knew him very well and liked him very much. He had a big black eye and a cracked lip, and I started to 'kid' him about these marks of his battle. 'You may look worse than I do when Sullivan gets through with you tonight,' he retorted.

'No, Billy,' I replied. 'Sullivan won't have to hit me as many times as McAuliffe did you, to lick me. If it's done, it will be done with one punch!'

So we talked and joked with each other, and finally, about nine o'clock, we started for the Olympic Club.

Now the following incident comes back to me as I write these words, thirty-three years afterwards:

As I was starting to put on a light summer suit, with a straw hat and a little bamboo cane to match, Delaney exclaimed: 'My God! You're not going to the fight that way, are you?'

'Certainly, Mr Delaney,' I replied, examining myself in the mirror, as if I thought I looked grand.

It was too much for him. He wanted me to go to the arena like the usual short-haired, big-sweatered type of pug with a scowl that would scare people, and here I looked like a dude that a good man could break in two. For a moment he couldn't say anything; simply looked his disgust.

'What difference does it make how I'm dressed going up?' I continued, as I gave a little extra twist to my tie. 'I don't expect to fight in these clothes.'

But it did make a difference to Billy, and he started to protest.

I had begun the conversation in fun, but possibly I was getting a little nervous as the hour drew nearer; anyway we had a heated argument which lasted until I cut it short. 'This is the way I'm going and that settles it,' I said, and out I started, cane, straw hat and all.

The streets of the city were black with people, and as our carriage was working through, all I could hear from every side was the murmur: 'Sullivan', 'Sullivan', 'Sullivan'! Not once did I hear the name of 'Corbett'; it was all Sullivan in the air.

We reached the club and I stepped out. As I walked in at the door, right ahead of me hurried my old friend, 'Mose' Guntz, from San Francisco, the one who gave Jack Dempsey a thousand dollars to second Choinyski against me. After that incident we had become great friends, and have been such ever since.

He turned around at my hail and started to speak cheerfully, but when he saw my get-up, he looked kind of embarrassed and strange, and although he didn't *say* anything about my trimmings I knew what effect they had on him, also that it wouldn't be but a couple of minutes before someone would tell Sullivan that Corbett came to the club with a cane in his hand and a straw hat on, like a dude! I could picture the look on Sullivan's face when he heard this news.

When I reached my dressing-room, one of the club managers came in and announced: 'Sullivan wants to toss up for the corners.'

'Let him take any corner he likes,' I answered as I started to get ready. 'He's going in the ring first anyway.'

Word immediately came back that *I* was to go in the ring first. However, the question was settled by Brady's going down to Sullivan's dressing-room and tossing a coin.

Now the only reason for my insisting that Sullivan enter ahead of me was the wonderful ovation I knew Sullivan would receive. Just then I felt quite calm, and I didn't want anything to excite me in any way, and it was possible his great reception might. But Brady had won the toss and finally it was announced that Sullivan was in the ring.

My seconds and I started down the aisle. The seats were banked circus fashion and only a few of the audience could see us, but I could see the ring and Sullivan was not in it. The managers had lied to me. So I stopped.

Now Sullivan thought I was in the ring, because I had started and enough time had elapsed for me to get there. As I stopped and turned back I met Sullivan, for the first time since I had boxed with him in San Francisco at my benefit. I looked him in the eye and said: 'You're the champion and I'm the short end. You're going in that ring first, if we stand here all night!'

This enraged Sullivan, who was always aggressive in manner, anyway. He gave a roar like a wounded lion, strode down the aisle, and bounded into the ring. Never before or since have I heard an ovation equal to that given him as he came through the ropes.

I said a little prayer to myself: 'I hope to God I am as cool in the ring as I am now', and then, as the cheers subsided, skipped into the ring, receiving the usual reception that any fellow would get from an audience, which meant about as much as: 'Well, anyway, he showed up!'

About six months before this I had had a conversation with my dear old friend, Judge Lawlor, of the Choinyski fight days, in which he asked me how I thought I would fight Sullivan – what I thought my tactics would be. And I distinctly remember telling him the most important thing in my fight with Sullivan would be to convince him that there was one man he was going to meet who was not licked before the fight started.

'How are you going to do that?' inquired the Judge.

'I don't know myself; but I've got to do it, some way.'

When I entered the ring I noticed that the floor was of turf instead of boards, on which I had always trained and fought. My shoes were of the solid sort used nowadays and I wondered how my feet would hold on turf. As soon as I entered the ring I started dancing around, and found that my feet would hold pretty well – in fact, much better than I had expected – so I was considerably relieved.

There was a reason, you see, for these jumping-jack antics that night, but I wish someone would tell me why present-day fighters do the same thing. They have been training on boards, and are fighting on boards, and using the same shoes and everything, so there is no reason for the practice unless to cover up nervousness. But it has been followed generally by fighters ever since that night. It is funny how customs and habits go down from generation to generation.

Meanwhile, Sullivan sat in his corner trying to catch my eye, his clenched fists on his knees, elbows out, and his head thrust forward in an ugly fashion. He had a wicked eye.

Now, as I had always done before, I was trying to convince him that he was the last person or thing in the world I was thinking about. I was bowing to people I didn't even see, smiling at entire strangers, waving my hand and talking to my seconds, laughing all the time.

Finally the referee, whose name was John Duffy, called us up to the centre of the ring for our final instructions. We walked up, Sullivan with his arms still folded, looking right at my eyes – not in them, for I never met his stare – and rising and falling on his toes without a pause. I waited for the referee, my gaze on him, and you could have heard a pin drop in the place. You wouldn't think 10,000 people could be so quiet. At last the referee got down to 'hitting in clinches'.

'When I tell you to break,' he told us, 'I want you to drop your arms.'

Immediately I grasped the referee by the shoulder – mind you, all for the effect on Sullivan – and sneered: 'That's very well for you to say, "Drop your arms when I say Break!" But suppose this fellow' (even then I didn't look at Sullivan, just jerked my thumb at him) 'takes a punch at *me* when *I* drop my arms?'

'If he does that he'll lose the fight; and you'll lose, too, if you try it,' Duffy answered.

'Then what about clinching like this?' I asked, and took hold of the referee and put my elbow up under his chin, pushing his head back, and repeated: 'What if he does this?'

'That's a foul, of course,' he answered. 'The one that does it will be cautioned once. If he tries it a second time he loses the fight.'

'All right,' I said, as gruffly as I could, 'that's all I wanted to know.'

Then, for the first time since entering the ring, I looked Sullivan square in the eye and very aggressively too. He stopped his rising and falling on his toes and stood staring at me as if he were petrified, so surprised was he at this sudden change in my attitude, and I saw at once it had the effect I intended: I had him guessing!

In a very cocksure manner I jerked the towel from my

124

shoulders, turned my back on him and ripped out: 'Let her go!'

This piece of business had its effect not only on Sullivan but also on the audience, for they cheered me louder then than they had when I entered the ring. They must have come to the conclusion: 'Why, this fellow thinks he can whip Sullivan. We'll see a fight!'

'Time' was called, and the first round was on.

Now I knew that the most dangerous thing I could do was to let Sullivan work me into a corner when I was a little tired or dazed, so I made up my mind that I would let him do this while I was still fresh. Then I could find out what he intended doing when he got me there. In a fight, you know, when a man has you where he wants you, he is going to deliver the best goods he has.

From the beginning of the round Sullivan was aggressive – wanted to eat me up right away. He came straight for me and I backed and backed, finally into a corner. While I was there I observed him setting himself for a right-hand swing, first slapping himself on the thigh with his left hand – sort of a trick to balance himself for a terrific swing with his right. But before he let the blow go, just at the right instant, I side-stepped out of the corner and was back in the middle of the ring again, Sullivan hot after me.

I allowed him to back me into all four corners, and he thought he was engineering all this, that it was his own work that was cornering me. But I had learned what I wanted to know – just where to put my head to escape his blow if he should get me cornered and perhaps dazed. He had shown his hand to me.

In the second round he was still backing me around the ring. I hadn't even struck at him yet, and the audience on my right hissed me for running away and began to call me 'Sprinter'. Now I could see at a glance that Sullivan was not quite near enough to hit me, so suddenly I turned my side to him, waved both hands to the audience and called out: 'Wait awhile! You'll see a fight.'

That made an awful 'sucker' out of Sullivan, as the gallery birds say, and it was quite unexpected. And since he didn't know that I knew he couldn't reach me when I pulled this stunt, he was the more chagrined. So he dashed right at me, angry as a bull, but immediately I was away again. At the end of the round

125

I went to my corner and said to Brady and Delaney: 'Why, I can whip this fellow slugging!'

At this there was a panic in my corner, all of them starting to whine and pleading with me.

'You said you were going to take your time,' they said. 'What are you going to take any chances for?'

'All right,' I replied, to comfort them, 'but I'll take one good punch at him this round, anyway.'

So far Sullivan hadn't reached me with anything but glancing blows and it was my intention, when the third round started, to hit him my first punch, and I felt that it *must* be a good one! If my first punch didn't hurt him, he was going to lose all respect for my hitting ability.

So, with mind thoroughly made up, I allowed him to back me once more into a corner. But although this time I didn't intend to slip out, by my actions I indicated that I was going to, just as I had before. As we stood there, fiddling, he crowding almost on top of me, I glanced, as I had always done before, first to the left, then to the right, as if looking for some way to get out of this corner. He, following my eye and thinking I wanted to make a getaway, determined that he wouldn't let me out this time!

For once he failed to slap himself on the thigh with his left hand, but he had his right hand all ready for the swing as he was gradually crawling up on me. Then, just as he finally set himself to let go a vicious right I beat him to it and loosed a left-hand for his face with all the power I had behind it. His head went back and I followed it up with a couple of other punches and slugged him back over the ring and into his corner. When the round was over his nose was broken.

At once there was pandemonium in the audience! All over the house, men stood on their chairs, coats off, swinging them in the air. You could have heard the yells clear to the Mississippi River!

But the uproar only made Sullivan the more determined. He came out of his corner in the fourth like a roaring lion, with an uglier scowl than ever, and bleeding considerably at the nose. I felt sure now that I would beat him, so made up my mind that, though it would take a little longer, I would play safe.

From that time on I started doing things the audience were

126

seeing for the first time, judging from the way they talked about the fight afterwards. I would work a left hand on the nose, then a hook into the stomach, a hook up on the jaw again, a great variety of blows, in fact; using all the time such quick side-stepping and footwork that the audience seemed to be delighted and a little bewildered, as was also Mr Sullivan. That is, bewildered, for I don't think he was delighted.

In the twelfth round we clinched and, with the referee's order, 'Break away', I dropped my arms, when Sullivan let go a terrific right-hand swing from which I just barely got away; as it was it just grazed the top of my head. Some in the audience began to shout 'Foul!' but I smiled and shook my head, to tell them: 'I don't want it that way.'

So the next eight rounds continued much in the fashion of toreador and the bull, Sullivan making his mad rushes and flailing away with his arms; rarely landing on me, but as determined as ever. Meanwhile I was using all the tricks in my boxing repertoire, which was an entirely new one for that day and an assortment that impressed the audience. Then I noticed that he was beginning to puff and was slowing down a little.

When we came up for the twenty-first round it looked as if the fight would last ten or fifteen rounds longer. Right away I went up to him, feinted with my left and hit him with a left-hand hook alongside the jaw pretty hard, and I saw his eyes roll. Quicker than it takes to tell it, I saw that I had then the same chance that I had had in the fight with Peter Jackson, but had failed to take – the same chance that was Firpo's when Dempsey stood helpless before him, and which he also failed to take.

This time I did not let it slip. Summoning all the reserve force I had left I let my guns go, right and left, with all the dynamite Nature had given me, and Sullivan stood dazed and rocking. So I set myself for an instant, put just a little more in a right, and hit him alongside the jaw. And he fell helpless on the ground, on his stomach, and rolled over on his back! The referee, his seconds, and mine picked him up and put him in his corner; and the audience went wild.

As Sullivan struck the floor, the few people who were for me jumped up and yelled, but the mass of that vast audience were still as death; just clenched their hands, hoping their champion would rise. When the last count ended and it was over beyond doubt, then came an uproar like Niagara tumbling over the cliffs, followed by the greatest shower you ever saw, of hats, coats, canes, belts, flowers from buttonholes, everything, falling on me and my seconds and all over the floor of the ring. I have often thought what a business I could have started down in Baxter Street with such an assorted stock!

So the roar of the crowd went on. I should have felt proud and dazed, but the only thing I could think of, right after the knock-out, was Sullivan lying there on the floor. I was actually disgusted with the crowd, and it left a lasting impression on me. It struck me as sad to see all those thousands who had given him such a wonderful ovation when he entered the ring turning it to me now that he was down and out.

In justice to the man who had reigned so long as champion of the world, I think it is only fair to say that I was not fighting the Sullivan I had seen and admired in San Francisco at the Paddy Ryan bout, then twenty-six and in the pink of condition; but a man who had not been careful of his habits and who had enjoyed too much the good fellowship and popularity the championship brings. I got him when he was slipping; and that goes for all the champions down the line.

It is very hard to tell, as you gaze down the list at all the defeated champions of the past, which was supreme. As I got Sullivan when he was slipping, so Jeffries got Fitzsimmons; Johnson defeated Jeffries; and Dempsey, Willard. And so, too, when Dempsey starts to slip someone is sure to get him. Like the pitcher that goes too often to the well, the champ will go once too often to the ring, and be broken in the end. And all argument as to their respective merits is foolish and futile.

After the first uproar had subsided a little, it seemed as if everybody in the audience wanted to hug me. Captain Barrett, Chief of Police, was standing near and I said to him: 'Please don't let this crowd get hold of me. I want to go up in my room and be with the people I was with before the fight started.'

Somehow I still had the feeling of resentment and couldn't stomach that crowd. He and his men forced a lane for me by using their clubs, and at last I reached my dressing-room. Brady and the whole gang were there and wanted to take me out to see the town and all that. 'No,' I said. 'I promised the Southern

Athletic Club that whether I won or lost this fight, theirs would be the first place I would go to; and that's where I'm going.'

They had opened their doors to me, you see, when I had fought Kilrain, and I thought I owed it to them. So we took a hack and drove there. They had hung a banner across the gymnasium with my picture on it, and when I went in some of them actually cried with joy to think I had come there after winning the fight. I made a little speech to them and then went up to Mr Wormseley's house, where I had been staying, and they had champagne galore. There was one fellow there – I couldn't remember his name, but I knew he was on the 'water wagon' and had been a hard drinker at one time – who said: 'Jim, this is the first drink I've had in two years!'

I took it away from him and told him: 'You're not doing me a favour by drinking that tonight. Please don't!' And he didn't.

It isn't that I never took a drink, but as I wanted to keep fit I have only taken liquor on occasion and almost always in moderation. That night I saw a chance to give an example to the young fellows, and I ordered a glass of milk. They drank all the wine around there, but Jim Corbett, the champion of the world, took a glass of milk! This incident was wired all over the world and was published in many newspapers.

I have always figured that this moderation helped me to what success I have had. There was another aid, and that was ability to throw off or control any tendency to worry.

Now I maintain that anyone can keep from worrying, except of course when misfortunes are crashing all around. It is just a question of will-power, which can be developed by practice just as I developed my ability to say 'No' when the fellows wanted me to dissipate back in the old San Francisco days. But it was a gradual development.

It is hard to describe how I put myself in this mental attitude before the fight. By not worrying, some people will think I mean utter relaxation, but that is not quite true. Relaxation is all right for a vacation or for sickness, but this is not the proper way to keep from worrying when one has a hard job ahead. The mental attitude must be preceded by a determined effort of the *will*, which controls the nervous system. In other words, one has first to clench his mental muscles and set himself with determination;

then will follow the calm, deliberate poise – a sort of iceberg coolness, if you will – that is necessary for any achievement.

Now I had *willed* myself into this state which held during the long months preceding the fight. One thing was on my mind at all times: 'You can't win this fight if you lose your nerve; you can't win this fight if you lose your nerve. Worry will weaken you.'

I would make this resolve several times a day, then deliberately turn my attention to something else. I had so gained this control over my nervous system that even when the fight had ended and the championship of the world was in my hands, I did not give way – I was still the same iceberg, or the same cold, controlled machine, that I had been in the ring; in fact I could not unwind myself for two or three days afterwards, even to become the companionable friend that I liked to be with all I know.

This mental condition was the cause, together with my disgust at their fickleness, for my efforts to avoid the crowd. I realized that some day, too, they would turn from me when I should be in Sullivan's shoes lying there on the floor.

When I got to bed that night my mind was so full of many things that I couldn't sleep. The championship was a great achievement; my ambition was realized. But I got to thinking of that $6,000 mortgage on father's house and the livery stable, which had impressed me so as a kid, and the next day I wired my father asking him to let me know at once just how much he owed. He replied that $10,000 would cover everything; so the first thing I did with the money I won was to send $10,000 of it home.

The night following the fight, Brady and I sneaked away to a restaurant where we thought we would avoid the crowd. But as we sat there we noticed on the other side of the room a table all set for a banquet. One by one a number of men entered, and I recognized several of them, men from all parts of the country. They spotted us and came over, shook hands and congratulated me; said they had all bet on Sullivan, but were 'glad to see a good man win', and the like.

Finally the banquet was ready to start, but there was one empty chair. I saw a number of them look over at me, then whisper to one another. Finally two of the gentlemen rose, came over again and asked if Brady and I wouldn't join them? We accepted, another place was made for Brady, and I sat down in the vacant chair. Of course we talked the fight over and one thing and another, until finally the chairman got up and said: 'I think we had better be honest and tell Mr Corbett that we all came down here and bet on John L. Sullivan. We are all friends of his, and this banquet was to have been a surprise for him after his victory. Of course we wish it could have been Sullivan that won, yet we're all mighty glad that an American has taken his place, and not Slavin or Mitchell.' Then he wound up: 'Now since Sullivan will be in bed for a few days and cannot be with us tonight, we are glad to have you, Jim Corbett, as the guest of honour!'

Then we all stood up and drank the health of the defeated ex-champion. The next day we started North.

12

The Lady in the Box – Miner's Bowery Theatre – The Meetings with Slavin, Charley Mitchell, and the Sporting Squire – The Match with a Famous Englishman – Harry bets too heavily – A Short but Fierce Encounter.

ON the way up from New Orleans we stopped at Birmingham, Atlanta, and others of the larger cities *en route*, and gave exhibitions which brought us something. Then when we reached New York, Brady ordered a play written, named it *Gentleman Jack*, got together a company, and we toured the country. It was a very prosperous season and we netted jointly about $150,000.

In writing the story of a professional career one hesitates to draw in one's family, but as my wife has helped me so much during the twenty-nine years we have been together, I somehow cannot help telling of the little incident of our first meeting, which even after so long a time still sticks out strongly in my memory.

I was playing in Kansas City in this melodrama, *Gentleman Jack*, and one afternoon gave a box party to Miss Maxine Elliott, her sister Gertrude (later Mrs Forbes-Robertson) and James A. Herne, the famous old actor, then out with *Shore Acres*. Before the curtain went up and while the audience was naturally paying considerable attention to Miss Elliott, who was a reigning beauty of the day, another equally beautiful, but with light hair, entered the opposite box, and the interest was divided. There was much guessing as to the identity of the newcomer, who, the spectators supposed, was another actress and guest of honour. I knew nothing of the excitement until my manager came back and I asked if Miss Elliott and her party had arrived.

'Yes,' he replied, 'she's there, but you ought to see the beauty sitting all alone in the box opposite her.'

So I took a peek through the curtain. Now I have always admired Miss Elliott, but I am afraid I didn't cast many glances in the direction of her box that afternoon!

After the matinée I went down to the Midland Hotel for my dinner, and who should walk into the dining-room but the Lady of the Box! I happened to know the gentleman with her, and he came over and invited me to sit at their table. I didn't need any coaxing! Two years after that we were married, on 15th August 1894. I am now 57 years old, and still I feel like a young man of twenty-five. I have been successful and happy since leaving the ring, and I owe all my success and great happiness to her.

After our successful trip with *Gentleman Jack*, we returned to New York. Meanwhile the newspapers were working up interest in a fight between Charley Mitchell and myself. The former had been in America during the months preceding my fight with Sullivan, and was considered one of the most prominent contenders for the championship.

I was engaged to box at Miner's Bowery Theatre one week and didn't know that they had Mitchell and Slavin, who was also a leading figure in pugilistic circles, booked for the same dates. Finally the management decided that, since I was matched to fight the great John L., I would be the drawing card, and they put me on, cancelling the acts of my two rivals. They both resented this, naturally enough brooding over the slight, and one night, after a round at the old Hoffman House bar, they decided they would go down to Miner's and give Corbett a good licking.

I was standing in the lobby when they walked in and Mitchell came up to me and tried to pick a quarrel. Among other things, he said: 'Why, I'll fight you right here for a five-pound note!'

'You won't fight me in a bar-room,' I replied. 'Boxing is a business with me. But mark what I say: I'll fight you some day and I'll whip you, and I'll get a lot of money for doing it!'

This didn't satisfy him, and he insisted on 'mixing it' right then and there, but the manager, Mr Miner, came up and separated us. That was all there was to it, but of course the papers had to come out and say that Mitchell had given Corbett an awful 'calling down'; also that Corbett 'had turned yellow' and 'had refused to fight Mitchell'.

The insults I did not forget, but it was just as well to get a little cash with my revenge, I thought, and when Mitchell, who had returned to England, finally issued a challenge to fight me to a finish for a $10,000 side-bet and the largest purse offered, I accepted at once.

There figured in the papers frequently, in those days, an English sportsman by the name of 'Squire' Abingdon Baird. He seemed to have a ton of money and was constantly spending it on his racing-stable and theatrical productions, in which famous beauties, particularly Lily Langtry, were starred. He also seemed quite as infatuated with Charley Mitchell's prowess as a fighter as he was with the beauty of the 'Jersey Lily'; and Charley Mitchell really was a mighty man.

He was the first who ever knocked John L. Sullivan down, and that too when Sullivan was at his best. This great feat was accomplished in the old Madison Square Garden. Later they were matched for a second go in the Garden, but though Mitchell was on deck, quite fit, Sullivan showed up intoxicated and the bout was postponed. The meeting-place was transferred to France, where they fought a finish fight for the championship, with bare knuckles, under London prize-ring rules. This resulted in a draw.

When the challenge and acceptance appeared in the English papers, it was announced that Squire Abingdon was coming with

Mitchell to bet on the side as much money as all the sports in America could raise together.

Well, the two arrived, and the morning on which the articles were to be signed, Richard Canfield, who owned the famous gambling-house at Saratoga, also the one even better known, on Forty-fourth Street, New York City, went over to the Gilsey House to see a friend of us both, 'Al' Smith. There he handed him fifty bills of a thousand dollars each, to 'talk turkey' with the 'Squire', and Al immediately jumped on the 'L' and went down to the World Building in Park Row, where the match was to be made.

After the articles were signed, and my ten thousand put up, Al turned to the 'Squire'.

'I understand you have come over here to lay all the money in England on Mitchell. Well, you're on. I haven't all the money in the U.S. with me just now, but here's fifty thousand as a starter, and there's plenty more where that came from.' Which, I think, was quite a good illustration of the courage of the sportsmen of those days.

However, when it came down to the colour of his money, the 'Squire' showed only $10,000, and his bluff was called!

It happened that the Duval Athletic Club in Jacksonville, Florida, offered the best purse, $20,000, the winner to take all, so their offer was accepted; and Mitchell started training at one of the Florida beaches, I about ten miles farther up the coast, at Mayport.

Charley evidently lightened his labours with considerable humour, for I was told several stories about him, one of which will serve as an example of his pretty keen wit. He was eating dinner at his quarters one night when the sunset gun went off. Leaning back in his chair, he exclaimed: 'Hello! my friend Corbett punching the bag!'

And he too had his way of getting people's 'goats' and disturbing them mentally, only he was cleverer about it than any man I ever met.

A very important thing happened about four days before the fight. I was playing handball; had gone through a couple of games at a furious pace, when suddenly I noticed that I did not perspire. I stopped and my trainer asked: 'What's the matter?'

Now I didn't want anyone to know of my predicament – not

even those closest to me – so I didn't answer him, but started walking over to the shower. Naturally the trainers followed and here Brady and Delaney also inquired: 'What's the matter?'

'I don't want a rub-down,' I said, 'just a shower and a dry rub with a towel,' and all at once I grew very irritable – no one could talk to me – I wanted to bite their heads off. Still, I kept the secret of the trouble to myself.

I fooled around until dinner time, then went to the ice-box, took a quart of champagne and drank the whole quart. Brady and Delaney tried their level best to stop me and I abused them unmercifully; so much so that Brady cried, and I was an outcast in the training quarters all that evening.

About nine I strolled down the beach in the moonlight, and when I returned, there sat Brady, Delaney, and all my handlers in the parlour, heads cast down. I walked in, went out to the ice-box again, took a pint of champagne and drank that down, started laughing, singing, and 'kidding' them about how little they knew about training as I went up the stairs, then fell on the bed and soon was off to a sound sleep.

The next morning a knock came at my door and Delaney said: 'Get up, Jim; it's seven o'clock.'

'I'm not going to get up at all,' I replied. 'I'm not going to train today.'

'Now, Jim, please open the door and let me talk to you a minute.'

'Get out!' I called back. 'I'm not going to get up until noon!'

So I lay in bed not knowing what was going on downstairs, but pretty well able to imagine it.

At noon I got up. Brady came into my room, sat down on the bed and said in the most coaxing tone he could manage: 'We're pals outside of business and it's coming to me. Won't you please tell me, Jim, what this is all about?'

'I know exactly what I'm doing, Billy,' I answered. 'And I'm not going to tell you or any living soul what I'm doing; but I don't do any more training up to the fight!'

'And you won't tell me why?'

'I'll tell you just before the fight, but not till then.'

That ended it and I loafed until two days before the big event. Then, in the afternoon, I said to the trainers: 'You wait here. I'm going down the beach about a mile and a half, and will run back, and I want you all to be ready to give me a dry rub when I come in.'

And down the beach I started, all of them looking at me in amazement and wondering if I hadn't gone plumb crazy. I jogged down at a pretty fair clip, then doubled back at the same pace until about two hundred yards from the training quarters and then I sprinted in. When I arrived at the rubbing room, a most beautiful glow of perspiration came all over me, and I said to the boys: 'Come on now. I'll get under the shower. All you need to do is just rub me down with a towel.'

While I was dressing I looked at them and laughed. 'Now,' I said, 'I'll tell all you "fatheads" something you don't know and that none of you had the sense to notice. The day I stopped playing handball I did enough work to sweat an oceanful, yet I was as dry as a bone. Don't any of you know what that meant? Well, I'll tell you. It meant I was overtrained and hadn't any perspiration to come out. If I had continued training up to now, I'd have been tired after two rounds. Now I'm all right; but I don't do any more work until the day I fight Mitchell.'

It was not only because I wanted to teach these fellows a lesson that I kept quiet, but also to prevent the leaking out, through carelessness on the part of my trainers, of any news that might reach Mitchell and add to his confidence.

For the benefit of the young fellows coming along, in whom I always have the greatest interest, I would like to say here that I do not advocate going out and getting drunk every time one feels stale; but the facts in my case were these:

Although I never have drunk much, that is since those early San Francisco days, I knew that I was dry inside – dangerously so, almost burnt out. I had to get more liquid into me. My stomach at that time revolted at the taste of water and I could not take much, but I knew that with its 'kick' I could take more champagne than anything else. As a matter of fact, although I may have been foolish in the youthful days I have just spoken of, I am a strong advocate of moderation in all things. Lots of things that people look upon as harmful are all right and beneficial, providing one knows when to stop and does not carry on to excess. One can take too much medicine; eat too much, as well as drink too much and smoke too much. I do not even advise a man's giving up tobacco, if he can limit himself to a moderate number of 'smokes' a day. Temperance, or moderation, has been one of the secrets of such success as I have had; I have rarely overdone in my pleasures, and I am sorry to say many pugilists have shortened their careers in the ring by taking the opposite course.

During these weeks a great friend of mine frequently visited the training quarters – Porter Ashe, the one who put the $500 in my hand the day I fought Choinyski and told me to keep it if I won. One day he reported that he had been down in the village and had met one of Mitchell's trainers, Billy Woods. While they were talking, the latter was foolish enough to say that when Mitchell got Corbett in the ring he was going to call him a lot of names and get him mad, and then was going to whip him.

This didn't trouble me, in fact it amused me at the time, but another incident did cause me some worry.

A couple of weeks before the fight I had written to my brother Harry in San Francisco, who by that time had added a pool-room to 'Corbett's Café', where bets were laid on races and all sporting events. In my note I had told Harry to go out and 'bet his sox' on the result of the fight, but not to bet on rounds. What I really meant was just to bet some *reasonable* sum. But on the day before the fight, I received a telegram from Harry saying he had put every nickel he had in the world on the result, and not only that but had gone into debt to back me further. Never had I received any news before a big battle that troubled me as much as this did.

As I went to my dressing-room, all I was thinking was: 'My God! If I should lose this fight, Harry will be broke!' That didn't help much.

When we got orders to come to the ring, I went out first and Mitchell was to follow, I not caring about this particular point of precedence now. Of course I had a light bathrobe over my fighting costume, but the wind was chilly and Mitchell kept me waiting out in that ring one hour!

Talk about a fellow getting another one's 'goat'! I was like a raving maniac, with the telegram from my brother on my mind and this fellow keeping me there in the ring for that length of time. I couldn't even get a laugh out of a remark I heard from Steve Brodie, the famous bridge-jumper who, when some fellow hopped up and in a loud voice cried out that he would put a thousand head of cattle on Corbett, shouted back: 'Bring on your cattle!'

One thing I did notice, as I waited, was that the soldiers stationed around the arena by the Governor of Florida, who had made a grand-stand play about stopping the fight, were quietly entering, one by one, and taking their seats in the audience, their rifles on their arms.

Finally Mitchell did show up, and when he came in the ring I was not in a very good humour. I had disliked him ever since that affair in the Bowery Theatre and now he had kept me waiting until I was thoroughly chilled! To add insult to injury, he now looked over at me and winked and smiled – a very clever stunt – and it had the desired effect. All at once I turned so mad and was so wild to start that, as soon as we got the gloves on, I said to the referee, the famous 'Honest John' Kelly – he still walks Broadway – 'No shaking hands!'

Turning to 'Snapper' Garrison, the jockey, who acted as time-keeper, I yelled: 'Snapper, hit that gong!' And he hit it.

Before Mitchell had time to catch his breath the round had started, without any of the usual preliminaries, not even the shaking of hands. There was no method in this; he simply 'had my goat' and I was wild. I almost upset him too, but when with the gong's clang I sprang to the centre, he recovered from his surprise sufficiently to call out, very sarcastically: 'Hello! Started already?'

My answer to this was a left-hand swing, which he ducked. He went me one better by landing on my mouth and cutting my lip, and I don't think any bull in an arena, with the picadors after him, was ever madder than I was then!

But mad as I was, my rushing tactics were not quite as reckless as they may seem or as they would have been in fights with the heavier men of my previous fights, like Peter Jackson, who weighed 204 pounds, Sullivan, who weighed 212, or Jake Kilrain at 214. Mitchell had gotten down to about 168, while I, having gained four pounds during the four days' lay-off, scaled 182 and so could afford to slug with him; and as he had fought John L. Sullivan a draw I was anxious to settle all question of my supremacy once and for all time by licking him quickly. So it was not all temper that drove me to that mad rush.

However, Mitchell was skilful; and, taking advantage of my lack of caution, he shaded me this first round. I knew this, of course, but it did not affect my aggressiveness, for I was determined to make a quick finish of it.

In the second round I hit Mitchell a right-hand body blow which I think took all the fight out of him. His face seemed to turn purple, and with all his generalship he couldn't hide the fact that the punch hurt him. At the end of that round I knocked him down.

I do not consider out of order here an explanation contradicting a statement which was published in the papers after the fight, and which was believed by some of the excited people who had been in the audience. It was declared that I had struck a blow at Mitchell while he was still on the ground.

Mitchell, as a matter of fact, was on his knees, the referee still counting, and as I thought, too slowly, so I said to Kelly: 'Count faster!'

While I was talking to Kelly, I wasn't going to be caught napping, and from out the corner of my eye I could see Mitchell getting up off his knees and setting himself to take a punch at me the instant he got up and while I was still facing the referee. Just before he straightened up I turned and unloosed a punch myself, which he saw coming. To avoid it, he fell back again on his knees. This is the truth about the disputed blow.

With the gong's signal for the end of the round, I walked to my corner, and was just about to sit down when Mitchell quickly retraced his steps and, leaping at me ferociously, hit me behind the ear. Then I went at him, and instead of taking the minute's rest during the intermission we started fighting, hammer and tongs. This little encore created a world of excitement, but before we had been at it long his seconds and mine jumped in the ring between us and pulled us apart, and at last we went to our corners.

We had hardly been seated when the gong sounded again. I sprang at Mitchell like a tiger, not letting up one instant; and things were fast and furious. We had been boxing only about a minute of this third round when I caught him on the chin with a vicious right-hand punch, harder than I usually let loose in a fight because I like to protect my hands until time for the knock-out. However, it was timely enough and I saw I had him, for after receiving the blow he stiffened out straight, then fell forward, right on his face. I knew the fight was over, so turned my back, went to my corner, held out my hands to my seconds to have the gloves unlaced, and didn't even bother to turn around and watch him. It was not necessary. He was dead to the world and counted out.

Sometimes the general impression that I am a light tapper, a story started by some newspaper men who do not know the game, amuses me. Not that it worries me, for I am content to stand on my record; but it is wrong. The idea has gained ground, I suppose, because I did not waste my strength wildly and did not unloose punches with all I had until the critical moment. My hands have always been delicate; in fact they do not look stronger than a billiard player's (the lady who often takes my dictation says my hands are like a piano player's); and I had learned my lesson after breaking both right and left in my fights with Choinyski. The last punch I landed on Sullivan had this same result. It put him out – and my hand too.

So I rarely tried to put full force into a blow until I had my man where I wanted him and was ready to put over the finishing touch. I contented myself with jabbing and good hard jolts that would gradually weaken my opponent and manœuvre him into position. You will never find any man who ever fought me who will say I couldn't hit hard with either hand. It was just two years ago that Jeffries told me I had him licked at Coney Island before the ten rounds were fought. He confessed that when I sank one in the body with my right I hurt him a great deal, and when in the tenth round I landed on the jaw with my right hand I saw his eyes roll; and all this was when I was past my prime and 35 years old, and those blows did not have the old steam behind them.

Fitzsimmons, too, has talked with me, many times, and he has told me himself that I gave him the worst licking he ever had in his life, and he repeated this statement in St Louis one night to a theatre audience, and called me up and shook hands with me on the stage; an action which I thought very courteous and generous.

Furthermore, I have a picture in my memory of Peter Jackson in that steam-room, hugging his stomach and moaning; and if anyone thinks a light tap would put away the 212 pounds of the mighty Sullivan they ought to try it – but then it is easier to argue outside the ropes than to fight inside them.

Reservation of one's strength is all important, and I can best illustrate my method by a comparison with a very clever man in the baseball world – grand old Christy Mathewson. He would often let them hit his offerings when he had a safe lead, but would tighten up when runs counted.

Now in the Mitchell fight, as is evident from my description of it, I did not follow my usual system of keeping cool, although I was thinking pretty rapidly and craftily at that. But calm poise and self-control are indispensable in a bout with a bigger man, and this battle is the exception that proves the rule.

Mitchell certainly 'got my goat' that time, as I had so often gotten others'.

After the battle was over, Porter Ashe met Mitchell's trainer, Woods, and said: 'I thought you said Charley was going to get Jim mad and then lick him?'

'He did,' replied Woods; 'but he got him too damn mad!'

APPENDIX TO CHAPTER XII

It is interesting to note the following estimate of Corbett given by Mitchell after the fight just described and which appeared in a Florida newspaper.—R. G. A.*

MITCHELL'S TRIBUTE TO CORBETT
'THE GREATEST FIGHTER WHO EVER STOOD IN A RING'
– WAS DEFEATED FAIRLY

Jacksonville, Fla. Jan. 25. The scene in Mitchell's corner while the crowd was shouting over Corbett was in marked contrast. Jim Hall, with a bitter recollection of the day in New Orleans, when he opened his eyes to ask Mitchell, 'What round was it, Charley, when I was knocked out?' was gently wiping away the blood from the face of the man who ministered to him after his defeat by Fitzsimmons, and who had now undergone a more crushing defeat than had ever come home to Hall. 'Bat' Masterson, the picture of disappointment, stood beside him, and 'Pony' Moore, whose face throughout had almost been a mirror of the fight, busied himself in fanning and rubbing his badly beaten son-in-law. It was fully two minutes before Mitchell came to himself again, and he then said, to nobody in particular: 'It's all over, eh?'

* R. G. Anderson, editor of the first edition

'All over, Charlie,' was the response, and with a long-drawn sigh Mitchell subsided into silence. He left the ring not long after Corbett.

After the Englishman had returned to the hotel and got a good bath he talked freely of his encounter.

'It is all over now and it can't be helped,' he said. 'I only wish I had been a little longer. I shall never fight again. I have no complaints to make, and I am a great deal like the old saying: "I'd been all right except for the other dog". I bear no hard feeling and I can say that America has reason to be proud of the greatest fighter who ever stood in a ring. I don't care who goes against him, if he keeps his health he will never be beaten. I am satisfied that he can defeat me at any time.'

'How are you feeling, Charley?' asked a friend anxiously.

'I am in just as good shape at this moment as when I went into the ring,' replied Mitchell. 'I don't know how or when I got the punch that dazed me, but after it I did not know what I was doing. Corbett is the cleverest man I ever saw, and his style was a complete surprise to me.'

13

I am tried by Jury – I send a Letter to the Old Folks by Phonograph – They cross the 'Pond' with me and Dad learns to play Poker – Father James – The Old Drury Lane.

AFTER the fight the principals and all connected with it were arrested. The trial was set for a date about three months later, and Mitchell and I went back to Florida on the same train. We became very well acquainted before we reached Jacksonville, and I remember his telling me how he had been informed before the battle that I couldn't hit.

'My word!' he exclaimed, 'I never was so surprised in my life! Every time you hit me you hurt me.'

In turn I told Mitchell that I had always understood he was a very smart boxer. 'But,' I added, 'you are not as smart as I thought you were.'

'How's that?' he inquired.

'Why didn't you send word to me the day before the fight that you wouldn't fight unless I split the purse with you? I would have given you fifty per cent of that purse rather than lose you, I felt so sure I could lick you and you had me so mad.'

The Attorney-General prosecuted the case, and I sat with our lawyers and picked the jury myself. When a juror went on the stand, I would look at him and I could tell by the way he returned my glance whether he was for us or not. One of them, after he had been sworn in, deliberately looked over at me and laughed and winked! And that wink had a very different effect on me from Charley Mitchell's in the ring.

The jury was out but ten minutes and brought in a verdict of 'Not Guilty!' After the trial I met a couple of the jurors and they told me that the only reason they had remained out even that time was that they wanted to make it appear that they were really discussing the case. As a matter of fact, it was settled as soon as they reached the jury room.

One of the panel who was rejected was asked if he had ever seen Corbett or Mitchell. He replied in the negative.

'Have you ever heard of Corbett, the champion of the world, and Charley Mitchell, the champion of England?'

'No.'

'Didn't you ever read or hear of the prize-fight for the championship of the world, in New Orleans?'

He hadn't heard of that, either.

'Excused!' said the Court. Such is fame!

In 1894 my manager, Brady, booked me for a fall opening in the melodrama *Gentleman Jack*, at the famous Drury Lane Theatre, London, England. After the run in London we were also to tour England, Ireland, and Scotland.

My mother and father had never been in Ireland since they had left it about fifty years before, while they were still kids, and I remembered how often they had expressed a desire to see the old home before they died; that is, the old homes, I should say, for they had left from different ports and did not become acquainted until after they had settled in America.

My father had a brother in Ireland whom he had never seen, as the latter had been born after my father left. This brother, Father James Corbett, became a very famous priest in the days of the Land League in Ireland, and my father named me after him, intending to make a priest out of me too; but this he found impossible. He was naturally quite as anxious to see Father James, as he was to visit the old country, and now I thought up a plan to make the dream of the old folks come true.

It was about this time that phonographs were first put on the market, and I conceived the idea of talking into one and making a record of travelling instructions to send to my parents. You see, I felt that if Dad once had the money in his hand he would think it was too much to spend on a trip when he had such a large family and would stick it in the old stocking.

So I went into a phonograph place in New York and prepared this record. I talked slowly, just as if father were there, trying to put into my voice all the persuasion I possibly could so that he would be impressed. I told him how to get his ticket, what to do with his money on the train, and added little tips about travelling across the continent, giving the exact dates and all. Then the record was shipped to California, and as my letter directed, father took it to a phonograph store in San Francisco. The record was put on and the old gentleman and old lady, I was afterwards told, sat there in delight, drinking in the words of their boy! It was all very wonderful to them – in fact it would have seemed so to anybody – for this invention was a new thing in those years.

After listening to me as if I were actually present in the room, they were impressed with the seriousness of disregarding my instructions and wrote me that they would leave just as I had directed. About a week before we sailed they landed in New York and of course, as any boy would, I took them around and showed them the sights. They had a grand time, and so did I.

My mother had told me that she did not have any close relatives left in Ireland that she knew of, but on the boat that first brought her to America she had met a little English lady by the name of Miss Wilkinson and they had become great chums. After some years Miss Wilkinson went back to England. And all my mother would say, when she would talk about going over to the other side, was: 'I wonder if Miss Wilkinson is alive? Oh, if I could only see her!' Over and over she would repeat this, and for his part my father was just as excited over the thought of seeing for the first time his brother, the Reverend Father James.

144

Before I sailed I received a letter from Colonel Ochiltree, who was stopping at the Waldorf Hotel in New York, asking me to call on him as he had something of importance to tell me. When I went there he said that John W. Mackay, the father of the present Clarence Mackay and one of the owners of the Nevada Bank where I had worked as a kid, had read in the papers of my intended trip and wanted to see me before I left. So the colonel made an appointment with Mr Mackay and together we went to the latter's old apartment on Fifth Avenue. Now I hadn't seen Mr Mackay since the time when, on my way to New Orleans to fight Jake Kilrain, I had run into him as I was sprinting up and down by the railroad tracks and he had expressed that wish – that Kilrain would give me 'a damn good licking'!

During my call Mr Mackay said that in England 'they look on a pugilist as a pretty tough customer; and I want to give you some letters to some of my friends over there to show them that a man can be both a pugilist and a gentleman'.

He dictated about half a dozen letters to his secretary and handed them to me, then, after a couple of hours had passed very pleasantly, he wished me good luck and I was on my way.

I had a lot of fun with my father on the steamer going over. I told him not to look upon me as his son, but as a pal, and I coaxed him into the big card cabin of the boat and got him mixed up in some very lively poker games at a dollar limit. The highest stakes he had ever played for was ten cents in the little game of Pedro, which some call 'High Five', and that was only on very rare occasions. So now, no matter how good his hand was, he would bet his dollar, then, if someone raised him, he'd lay down the cards! 'That's too much money!' he would say and quit. If he had had a dozen aces, he'd have done the same.

So I had to play with the old man alone – and great sport it was. I could always tell by his face when he had a good hand; he'd grin all over, and I'd keep raising him! Before we reached the other side he had grown to be quite a plunger and would bet on a couple of deuces!

The voyage over, we arrived in London and went to the Victoria Hotel. The next day I noticed in several of the newspapers accounts of the arrival of the world's champion, many recording his experiences and even including little details of his biography. It was correctly stated that my father was Patrick Corbett of County Mayo, Ireland, and that my mother's maiden name was Katherine McDonald and that she came from Dublin. It made the old folks rather proud.

The first thing I did on reaching London was to telegraph the uncle for whom I had been named, to come up to see us as soon as possible. He wired in return that he would arrive at the hotel at a certain time, but I did not tell the others this news.

The hour for his arrival came – my father and mother wondered why I looked at my watch so often, for I was as impatient as a kid – and I left them lunching in the dining-room and went out into the lobby to wait my guest.

While I stood at the desk talking with the clerk, a little roly-poly old lady came up and very excitedly asked: 'Is James J. Corbett, the prize-fighter, here?'

'I'm James J. Corbett,' I said, before the clerk could speak.

'Oh!' she exclaimed. 'Tell me quick! Tell me quick! Was your mother Kate McDonald?'

'Yes,' I answered, 'that was my mother's maiden name. May I ask what is yours?'

'Mrs Catamore,' she said. (I cannot remember the exact spelling, for though I have won many prizes in the ring, I would never take one in a spelling match in the 'bushes'!) 'But your mother wouldn't know me by that name,' she added; 'she'd remember me as Miss Wilkinson. I went to America with her a long time ago – fifty years it is. . . .'

I have had big moments in my fights, but honestly I never had a bigger thrill than when that old lady told me her name, for she was the one person my mother had expressed a wish to visit, though she never dreamed of seeing her again in this world.

Well, I took her into the dining-room, which was pretty well crowded at this noon-hour, and said very quietly, as if it meant nothing in particular: 'Mother, Miss Wilkinson.'

For a second my mother looked at her as if someone had been brought back to her from the dead. Then she threw her arms around her and they both began to cry. I have described Miss Wilkinson as stout. Well, mother was also quite heavy for her height, and I could see people in the dining-room giggling at the sight of these two little roly-poly old ladies embracing each other and crying from joy; but to me it was one of the most pathetic things I had ever seen, and a lump came in my throat and I just had to leave the room.

As I walked out of the dining-room back to the office again, in walked a man in clerical clothes. I knew Father James had red hair like the newcomer's, so I walked up and took a chance.

'Father James?' I said.

'Yes,' he replied.

'I'm Jim,' I announced.

Of course he embraced me; and we chatted for a few minutes, then I took him over to the hall just outside of the dining-room. Having seen the people laughing at that other meeting, I determined to make this one less conspicuous. Excusing myself a moment, I returned to the dining-room and asked Dad to come out in the hall.

It was almost too much, for when he came with me to where the priest was waiting and I said 'Dad, I want to introduce you to your brother, Father James', they stood and looked at each other for a second in amazement, then embraced, and my father broke down completely. My uncle, of course, had more control, having been prepared for the meeting, but to my father it was too great a surprise.

I have been associated with the stage for many years and realize that, if anyone should cook up such incidents as these and put them in a play, people would laugh and say it could never happen – that there was too much coincidence. But life is far stranger than fiction or the stage; and I have never witnessed behind the footlights anything prettier than these two meetings, taking place within fifteen minutes of each other between people separated for so many years.

And I know in this practical commercial day it isn't considered fashionable to be sentimental, but I thank God I am Irish and *am* sentimental. The time of my mother's death I will never forget; and the only consolation I had that dark day was the thought of the happiness I had been lucky enough to be able to give her, on this trip abroad, before she left me. There were ten of us children and there was not one of those Irish boys and girls who wouldn't have done just as much, or more, than I did if they had had the money. We were a very united family, and I simply dwell on this because I am sometimes surprised and sorry to see how little families seem to hang together today.

147

The very next morning after these reunions, Mrs Catamore, whose husband was the scenic artist at the Henry Irving Theatre, took my mother and father, bag and baggage, out to their lovely home in the suburbs of London and made them stay with them the whole two months of the London visit.

Thinking it would please them I used to get theatre tickets for different shows in London, and they would promise faithfully to go. The money was wasted, for each night they would wind up at the Drury Lane to watch our play! My manager would come to me and say: 'Where did you send the folks tonight, Jim?'

'To the Empire Music Hall', or to 'The Savoy', or whatever theatre it happened to be, I would say.

'Well, they're not there,' I would be told. 'They're out in front, in the last row!'

I have heard many discussions as to whether Booth was or was not greater than Irving, but my father and mother could have decided it. James J. Corbett was the greatest actor of them all!

On our opening night at the Drury Lane Theatre, a gorgeous, gigantic, floral piece was handed over the footlights, and when I reached my dressing-room and looked at the card I read: 'With the compliments of Clarence H. Mackay.' Later in the evening Clarence Mackay came back to my dressing-room, with the Duke of Teck, introduced himself, and told me his father had cabled him from America to be sure and give 'Jimmie' Corbett a good time.

'Now, Mr Corbett,' said the boy, 'if you will just put yourself in my hands I'll give you a royal time.'

He did, making good his promise in many different ways: the most delightful of which was probably a supper at the Savoy Hotel, where an Hungarian band and Lois Fuller, the dancer, at that time the talk of America and Europe, entertained. Here too Mme Yvette Guilbert sang and recited, making her first appearance in London, and I appreciated it all as a very nice compliment to America and my profession.

14

A Gorgeous Poster – William McKinley – Tom Sharkey – The
Referee is thrown on top of me – Bob Fitzsimmons – Two
Governors and a Sheriff – Fitzsimmons's Nose is pulled in the
Lobby – We begin Training.

WHEN I returned to America and went on the road with the show
Brady got out a great poster, a magnificent affair twenty-four
feet long and picturing all the crowned heads of Europe in their
royal get-up.

There were the Czar of Russia, the Kaiser, the King of Italy,
and others, surrounding Queen Victoria on her throne, and, in
the centre of this group! he had me standing, chest out, and
shaking hands with Gladstone, thus implying, without exactly
stating so, that I had met all the monarchs of Europe and been
entertained by them, though I had never seen a single one of
these people, not even from the curb! Underneath the master-
piece was a flaming sentence: 'James J. Corbett, Champion of
the World, on His Return from His Triumphal Tour of
Europe!'

One day as Brady and I were seated in the smoker of a train
heading for a 'one-night stand', he informed me that 'the
crowned head poster' was going up in this town.

'I'm anxious to see it,' I replied, quite truthfully.

'So am I,' said Brady.

When we reached the town, we strolled around looking at all
the bill-boards in the place and at last ran across one with this
poster on it. Sure enough, there I was, surrounded by all the
big-wigs of Europe and giving the 'glad hand' to Mr Gladstone.
Two rubes happened along at the same time, and paused to gaze
at this gorgeous picture. 'I bet that fellow Corbett is a great
actor as well as a fighter,' one of them said, with an air of great
wisdom.

'What makes you think so?' the other asked.

Pointing up at the row of kings and queens, the first one
replied, very seriously: 'Why, look at the big company he
carries!'

On this tour we played Lima, Ohio, a one-night stand; and

William McKinley, who was then Governor, and the Presidential nominee on the Republican ticket, was slated to speak in the Town Hall as our opposition attraction! All day the street in front of the hotel was crowded with people, some anxious to see McKinley, and others, I was proud to hear, calling for the champion.

After dinner that night, Mr McKinley's secretary came to my room and asked if I would like to meet Mr McKinley.

'I would consider it a great honour,' I told him, and he replied: 'And he wants to meet you, too.' So he took me to Mr McKinley's room, presented me, and we sat there chatting for about half an hour, during which we could hear the crowd outside cheering for McKinley. Every once in a while someone would vary the cheers by shouting, 'What's the matter with Corbett?' and another roar would come up through the windows.

About 7.30, I rose to go to the theatre and was saying 'Goodbye' when Mr McKinley, who had to go to the Hall, took hold of me by the arm and said in his lovable way: 'They want to see you down there just as much as they do me. We'll go downstairs together.'

So, arm in arm, we descended the circular staircase of the old hotel, to the lobby, which was jammed with people. Two little newsboys, who didn't know that such a man as McKinley existed, but who wanted to see the *fighter* who licked John L. Sullivan, were wriggling their way through this crowd. As we appeared another great cheer was given, and louder than any that preceded it, because everybody thought it was a very nice thing for Mr McKinley to bring me with him. But the little newsboys didn't look at it that way, I guess, for one of them said to the other, so one of the actors in my company reported later: 'I tell you the tall guy is Corbett.'

'Yes; but who's the other feller that's got hold of his arm?'

The kid had a sure answer for this, too. 'Don't you know nuthin'?' he said. 'That's Con McVey, his sparring partner.'

There was another newsboy who made a hit with me about this time, and I have wondered what sort of a great man he became. One cold, snowy night, as I was leaving the stage door of the Williamsburg (Brooklyn) Theatre, he came up to me, a little red-haired kid with a very dirty face.

'Say, Jim,' he says – he wasn't fresh, just comical – 'give us a nickel, will yer? I only got one father and mother.'

This last remark struck me as a good line, so I gave him a quarter and he walked down to the ferry with me. I forget the rest of our conversation, but he was an extraordinary kid, one you would always remember. I do recall that as I was getting on the boat he asked me where I was going next (I believe it was on a Saturday night) and I told him I was going to open in Bridgeport, Connecticut, the following Monday.

'Gee! you travel around a lot!' was his only comment.

'Yes, I'm travelling all the time,' I replied.

I arrived in Bridgeport about six o'clock in the evening. As I stepped off the train a little kid with red hair came up to me.

'Don't you know me, Jim?'

'Who are you?'

'I'm the kid wot's got only one father and one mother.'

Well! You can imagine my amazement at seeing this kid so far from his beat!

'How in the world did you get here?' I asked him.

'Beat my way on the train,' he said, and as I didn't have the heart to shake him, I took him over to the hotel, where he had dinner with me; then I shipped him back to New York on the train, with orders to go home at once.

It was just before my meeting with McKinley that I had a rather funny encounter in the ring. In the summer of 1896 I had taken my wife for a pleasure trip, to Hot Springs, Ark., where we enjoyed the baths for three weeks, then started for California, stopping at several places *en route*. While I was in San Francisco Tom Sharkey, a sailor, was matched to fight a mediocre heavy-weight named Williams. A short time before this I had read an account of a bout between the former and my old friend, Joe Choinyski, and had gathered the impression that Sharkey was a fellow capable of taking a lot of punishment, but good only in a 'rough-house' fight. So I went out to see him fight this Williams. Although he defeated Williams, as a boxer he seemed to me to be very crude.

Nevertheless, the promoters of the club tried to induce me to sign up for a four-round go with Sharkey. I was not in very good condition; and as I hadn't been out home in a long time I was being wined and dined by all my friends. But the club people were confident that as champion and Californian I would draw a capacity house, and they offered me the first ten thousand received at the box office and a fifty-fifty split of all beyond the ten. It was good money and I accepted.

This time I didn't go out of the city to train, but stayed in town, going up to the Olympic Club to 'take a sweat' every day; which was all I did in the way of preparation for the bout, for I had never seen the time when, even though out of condition, I couldn't box four fast rounds, certainly fast enough to beat such an awkward fellow; and I had made up my mind not to exert myself by trying to knock him out, but merely to make a fool out of him for the short period, by my superior skill. That would give the audience enough show for its money.

Well, the night came and we appeared in the ring. He had a marvellous physique, being about 5 feet 8 inches tall, about one hundred and ninety in weight, and fully as powerful as Jeffries, but of different type – a short-coupled sort of chap with a squat, thick neck. When I started feinting at him, he mistook each feint for a lead, and he didn't know how to duck. Instead of rolling or swinging his head on his neck as on a pivot, he squatted down on his haunches, crooking his knees and popping up and down like a jumping-jack. He did this so constantly and looked so funny that the audience fairly screamed, and I was so weak with laughter I could hardly land.

I managed to get through the first round, however, feeling all the time as though I were boxing a burlesque, the sort I gave on the stage in my act this year with Norton, in 'The Ziegfeld Follies of 1924', and on the vaudeville circuit in the summer.

While I was sitting in my corner during the intermission, I got past the humour of the thing. I now thought less of my plan of making the bout simply an exhibition of boxing skill, and began to flirt with the idea of putting him out – he seemed so easy to hit and didn't know a thing in the world about boxing, or, for that matter, about fighting.

So with this idea in mind, I started up in the second, and after the tap of the gong hit him one terrible wallop in the eye, using a left-hand hook. His eye-socket bulged out immediately to the size of a baseball – I never saw such a swelling on a man's face nor any that ever rose quite so quickly. I had him dazed and tried my darndest to finish him in that round, and as it ended he was floundering all over the ring, very groggily, and actually started for my corner when his seconds rushed in and led him to his own.

When I sat down in my chair I knew I was not right. For the first time since that honeymoon bout in Salt Lake City, about eleven years before, I was absolutely tired out; so when we went up for the third round, Sharkey's seconds, not knowing I was tired, but thinking that since he had been so nearly finished in the second round he would surely be knocked out now – and with him their 'meal ticket' – told him to go out and wrestle with me, grab hold of me, and do anything he could, but never on any account to let go!

He took his lesson all right; and came at me in the third round, and pulled and pushed me all over, and even tried to shove me through the ropes; I looking all the time like one of these slender animal trainers in tights waltzing around the stage with a huge, clumsy bear. I only wish I had a motion-picture film of that bout; I think I could make a lot of money exhibiting it, for it was a riot, although it might have turned out a serious thing for me and proved a tragedy instead of a comedy, since I was champion of the world, with nothing to win except the money, and everything that goes with the championship to lose.

Mind you, all this time he was not hitting me at all, while all I was doing was just tying my arms around his neck and trying to prevent him from pushing me out into the audience. Towards the end of this round he threw me flat on my back, and while I was on the floor he threw the referee on top of me, right on my stomach. It happened that just before the fight I had eaten one of the French dinners for which San Francisco was noted in those days, and when the referee landed on my stomach I realized how many courses I had tried – shrimp salad, Swiss Gruyère, vanilla ice-cream, *vin rouge*, etc. etc., and instead of protesting to the referee all I thought of doing was calling for the steward, as one does on shipboard on high seas.

Meanwhile, all through this round I kept appealing to the referee, but the audience was making so much noise, booing, hissing, screaming, shouting, and laughing that he seemed to be afraid to assert his authority. I never heard such an uproar!

When I finally reached my corner after this third round, I was nauseated and was doing my best to keep control over my stomach muscles. If I had been in condition, I wouldn't have minded all the roughing he tried, for he was not landing, not even hitting at me – just pushing me around – and with my judgment of balance it would have been easy for me to offset everything he did.

When we came up for the fourth I could hardly realize that I, who had always kept in such fine condition, could be so exhausted without ever having been hit once in the fight. But there I was, wobbly inside, and all in.

He started the same tactics again, still doing little but wrestle and shove and push, once in a while, for variety, trying to throw me out of the ring. As I stood up with my arms around his neck, with a minute to go, I knew that if ever he threw me down again the champion of the world would not get up. Realizing the danger, I couldn't understand why Delaney, usually a quick thinker, did not jump in and claim 'Foul!' He had every justification. So I looked at him over Sharkey's shoulder and gave an appealing nod, trying to tell him to come to the rescue, when suddenly the Chief of Police jumped in the ring and stopped the fight, partly because of the extremely rough and foul tactics of Sharkey, more because he thought the great disorder of the audience would turn into a riot.

He allowed the referee to give his decision, which he gave all right – a draw – and yet I had not been hit once in the whole fight!

However, in a way it was a lucky thing for me. I could not leave my corner for fully half an hour, just reclined there, completely exhausted, shaking in the legs and very sick at my stomach. Although from many standpoints the bout was a joke, it was a lesson to me not to take any antagonist too lightly, above all not to take any chances in training, for though I had not done any serious dissipating, I had kept pretty late hours, abused my stomach, and taken only the lightest of exercise.

About this time Bob Fitzsimmons, who had been defeating everyone he fought, from middleweights to heavyweights all down the line, grew so big he could no longer make the middleweight limit; though there are some sporting editors to this day who mistakenly believe he was still within the lighter class. A challenge to me was issued by him, to fight for the championship, a $10,000 side-bet and the largest purse offered. With Brady, who was still my manager, I met Fitzsimmons and his manager in the *New York Herald* building, but it seemed that Fitzsimmons hadn't been able to scare up the $10,000. Still, we made the match and arranged for the $10,000 to be put up in instalments, Fitz feeling sure he would be able to get the money on the strength of the match.

The biggest offer was made by a promoter named Dan Stuart, who at once started to build a big arena in Dallas, Texas; and everything was breezing along nicely, Fitzsimmons training at Corpus Christi, Texas, I in San Antonio, when we had trouble from an unexpected quarter.

Before Stuart had sent in his offer for the fight, he had seen his political connections and also the Governor, who assured him that everything was all right and to go ahead. But after the promoter had spent a fortune on the big arena, and interest in the fight had been worked up to the highest pitch, the Governor, just as a grand-stand play (I can't read it as anything else) came out and declared we could not fight in Texas. We did not object at all to a man doing his duty as he saw it, but we wished he had only seen this duty a little sooner, and *before* we had wasted so much money in our preparations.

At a loss for a place in which to fight, and all our plans upset, we were relieved to receive an offer from Hot Springs, Arkansas, and it was settled that the fight should take place there. Fitzsimmons continued working out at Corpus Christi, but I went right into Hot Springs itself to train.

Unlike the Governor of Texas, the Chief Executive of Arkansas came out flat-footed right at the start and said we could not fight in his State, but the local authorities of Hot Springs insisted the Governor had no such power. Relying on this assurance, I got a concession to erect an arena in the centre of the local racing-grounds, and arranged to build some stands with my own capital.

The time drew near for the fight, and, hearing that Fitzsimmons was on his way to Hot Springs, the Governor sent a couple of deputies from Little Rock down to meet him as he came over the state line into Arkansas, and the sheriff and a few deputies from Hot Springs also went down. As Fitz reached the line, the sheriff of Hot Springs said: 'If you want to fight Corbett, come with me. If you want to go into the arms of the Governor and don't want to fight, go with those fellows.'

Fitzsimmons foolishly took the latter course and went to Little Rock with the Governor's men; and the sheriff returned to Hot Springs and reported to me. Well, we made a test case of it, secured a hearing in Little Rock, but the decision was against us. The fight could not be held.

I was so disgusted with Fitzsimmons's dunderheadedness in going to Little Rock with the Governor's deputies, and so angry at being chased around the country from state to state, that I publicly announced my retirement from the ring and handed over the championship to Peter Maher, the Irish champion. This, of course, I had really no right to do, for you cannot *hand* a championship to a man; he has to win that with his own hands in the ring. To settle the dispute, Fitzsimmons and Maher were matched to fight for the championship, and Fitzsimmons won.

Meanwhile Fitzsimmons and I were roasting each other in newspaper interviews, the reporters of course exaggerating whatever we said and working up very bitter feeling between us. They even went so far as to declare that Fitzsimmons had threatened to punch Corbett the first time he met him on the street; while Corbett was aching for a chance to pull Fitzsimmons's nose! All quite reminiscent of the old Choinyski days.

The climax came when we hit Philadelphia, at the same time, and while the bitterness was at its height. I was stopping at Green's Hotel, Fitzsimmons at another place near by, and one evening as I was sitting in the dining-room my brother Joe, who was travelling with me at that time, rushed in, looking worried. 'What do you make out of that?' he exclaimed.

I glanced out of the door and there was Fitz at the desk.

'He's arranging for a room,' said Joe.

Now this changing of hotels and coming down to where I was staying seemed to me looking for trouble on Fitzsimmons's part, and at once I adopted my old policy of being the aggressor when an unavoidable row was ahead. Jumping up from the table, I walked over to the desk, bent over Fitzsimmons's shoulder, and said the first sarcastic thing that came in my head:

'Here, you can't register by just making your mark. Joe, take the pen and write Mr Fitzsimmons's name. He doesn't know how to.'

156

Naturally enough, Fitz blew up, and though I cannot recall the exact dialogue, it had pepper enough, and I wound up with:

'When you come down here, under the circumstances you show you're inviting trouble. There's been a lot of talk in the paper, about punching faces and pulling noses and all that; and it's time someone had his nose pulled at least.'

With which defi, I grabbed hold of his nose and twisted it so it hurt.

As you can imagine, there was a lot of excitement in that lobby, and all the bystanders were hugging themselves, expecting a free show. And, as usual, my thoughtful friends seized me by the arms and, again as usual, not a soul thought of doing the same for the other man. He could have 'knocked me stiff' right then and there.

Brother Joe came to, however, and, though a lighter man, ran up behind Fitz and pinioned his arms. Fitz tried to jerk away, but couldn't at first, and they wrestled all over the lobby, my good friends, about ten in all, still sitting on me.

At last Fitz managed to break from Joe's clutch, and he grew madder than ever when he saw that it was my brother who had held him, and struck at him, but a lot of bystanders had crowded between and the blow was blocked. Then what must Fitz do but step in the dining-room, seize a castor from the table, and hurl it, pepper, salt, vinegar, oil and cayenne and tabasco, as red as his hair, at Joe – Joe who had simply held him, when it was I who had twisted his nose. Joe ducked and the salad-dressing splattered the wall. Then the manager came in and pacified us, and the incident was closed.

The public, quite reasonably, refused to recognize Fitzsimmons as champ because of his victory over Maher, and I decided I would again try for a meeting in some place where the law would not interfere. We finally hit on Carson City, Nevada, and the same Dan Stuart of Dallas, Texas, was chosen as promoter. For the first time in the history of boxing it was arranged that moving pictures should be taken of a fight, and for this reason, if no other, it was sure to be an historic affair.

15

FITZSIMMONS and I both trained in Carson City, though on
opposite sides of the town. Billy Delaney still acted as my trainer
and he suggested our taking on as sparring partner Gus Ruhlin,
the Akron heavyweight. Before these arrangements were made,
however, I received a note from De Witt Van Court, still the
instructor at the Los Angeles Athletic Club and one of the best
boxing teachers in the country, telling me of a fellow, a 'comer',
who was big and strong and a good man to 'rough it with'. I
wrote Van Court, telling him to send his man on.

He came and boyishly presented his letter of introduction,
from which I then learned his name – James J. Jeffries it was –
and he was added to our training force. At first I gave him the
job of rubbing me down. I had four rubbers, one for each limb;
he had a leg, and that was all he attended to, but one day I thought
I would try him out with the gloves.

I found him, as Van Court had said, a big, strong fellow (he
weighed about two twenty) with a hefty left and very willing,
but he didn't know the simplest fundamental of the game.
Without intending to hurt him I hit him a short uppercut with
my right, but with little force behind it, as I thought, and he fell
helpless in my arms.

But I liked him and tried to teach him something and continued the bouts, although often he gave me so little to do that
in despair I used to back him in a corner, promise not to strike a
blow, then order him to work his way out. He had so little
instinct for the game at this stage of his career, that even with
this advantage he stayed cornered. Simply by ducking, blocking,
and holding his arms, I kept him there.

There was one quality he had, however, which soon came to
light and impressed me greatly – his work on the road. I had
always considered myself as good as any pugilist that ever lived
in this part of training and tried to do with him as I had with the
rest of my handlers, start off on a dog trot, then spring and run

them off their feet. But it didn't work – there I was trotting along mile after mile and this big young fellow was always right at my heels, politely enough never trying to pass me, but always right there. When I came within a couple of hundred yards of the camp, I started my sprint, and thought I would leave him flat. When we breezed in, the distance between us was the same. And day after day, no matter how fast or slow I went, there was this dogged fellow, right at my heels. I began to wonder if after all Jeff might not amount to something.

The next arrival at the camp was Brady, who brought with him a famous trainer, later a still more famous referee – Charley White. He had trained Fitzsimmons for two of his contests, and Brady thought he might be able to give me many valuable pointers.

It was an unlucky move, however, for it started dissension in my camp, for the first time since I had been a 'pro.' Billy Delaney's nose was immediately put out of joint and he regarded the bringing of White as a personal insult aimed at him by Brady. No matter what I did to smooth matters over, I was misunderstood.

The jealousy grew almost unbearable. If one had said it was foul to hit below the belt, the other would have sworn it was foul to hit above; if Charley called Peter Jackson a negro, Delaney would have sworn Peter was pure white. If I happened to converse with one a few seconds longer than I had with the other, the latter would think that I had told something of great value in those few seconds which I had concealed from him; and he would nurse an awful grouch. This was the only time that I was really unhappy during my preparations for a fight.

Another feud was under way before long, innocently started by my brother Harry, when he sent on from the Coast a beautiful Scotch collie; one of the most intelligent dogs I have ever seen. Harry was fond of him, but knowing that I liked dogs too thought it would be a good chance to get him out in the open. It was, for I had him with me constantly and for a while even allowed him to sleep in my room.

But when Brady arrived he not only brought White but my old mascot, mongrel Ned. As soon as Ned caught sight of the collie, a terrific battle was started and we had a hard time separating the two. However, we thought they would get used to each other after a few days. We were wrong. They sulked and were as jealous of each other as were the two trainers. At night we had to confine Ned to the hall of the house, which was warmed by a stove, while I still kept the collie in my room, since he was quite valuable and belonged to my brother.

But one stormy evening, on my return from town where we had driven to see a show, I stumbled over something on the mat outside of my door that looked like a bundle, covered with snow. It stirred, barked, then jumped up and licked my hand.

Such devotion was too much for me. Next day the collie was shipped back to Harry, and the old mongrel stayed on with me. He lived for a year or two after that, and died at my father's home. Dad had him stuffed and that old dog stood in the parlour, as big as life, in a glass case, until Dad himself died.

Fitz and I were training in real earnest now, and as the day for the fight drew nearer, and the interest more intense, the clans began to gather.

Some of the people from the east spoke of a little newsboy who had beaten his way out from New York, and who was supporting himself by selling New York newspapers at a dollar apiece, and by polishing shoes at a half-dollar a shine. Naturally, such enthusiasm and financial enterprise aroused my curiosity, and I was hoping the kid would come out our way.

I had had a pavilion constructed back of the house and in this I used to punch the bag, skip rope, box, and wrestle before the crowd which each afternoon came out from town to see me. There were no seats, and some of them would stand, others sit on the ground.

One afternoon I noticed a youngster in the front row of the standees. He had red hair, a bundle of papers under his arm, and a bootblack's outfit slung over his shoulder. During a rest spell I looked over at him and decided that this must be the industrious kid I had been told of. Catching my eye, he looked up, gave a familiar grin, and said:

'Hello, Jim!'

'Hello!' I returned, 'are you the kid who has the nerve to charge a dollar a throw for a New York paper?'

'Sure,' said he, 'don't yuh remember me, Jim?'

'By Jove, I ought to; that red hair and those freckles are familiar. Where did I see you before?'

'In Williamsburg when you played at de teaytre. Dat's where yuh saw me first. De next time wuz at Bridgeport.'

160

'Williamsburg?' I repeated, 'over in Brooklyn, you mean?'

'Yep,' he said, 'I'm de kid wot's got only one father and mother.'

So we had a happy little reunion and he stayed to dinner with me, becoming as great a favourite with my trainers as he had been downtown.

All champions and ex-champs too receive lots of letters, rabbits' feet, 'good luck' coins, and other souvenirs that are supposed to help a man win; and I had my share. The one that I prized most was a letter from the students of Yale College, signed by many names which have since become famous.

When playing in New Haven, where I was booked frequently, I had always gone around to the gym to box with the boys, among them Tom Shevlin, perhaps the greatest, certainly one of the greatest, football players Yale ever turned out. He was a wonderfully built fellow and boxed very well for an amateur, though I do not believe, as some sports writers have said, that he would ever have had the same success in the ring, had he taken up boxing professionally, that he had on the gridiron.

With the letter came a Yale flag which the boys asked me to carry into the fight. This I did, placing it in my corner, the first time, I believe, a college pennant was ever carried into the ring by a 'pro'.

This was the first time too that articles describing preparations for a fight, actually signed by one of the principals, ever appeared in a newspaper.

This I had arranged for, a few months previous, when interviewed by a reporter during my engagement in Chicago, with my second play, *The Naval Cadet*.

During the conversation the young fellow apologized for his 'greenness', saying that he had been but a short time on the paper, and that he didn't know much about interviewing champions, but he had to make a stab at it, for the managing editor had given him the assignment.

'So you're just a kid reporter?' I said, sizing him up.

'Yes, sir,' he replied with a modesty I liked; and suddenly an idea struck me.

'Well,' I said, 'if you'll do what I tell you, you'll make a hit with your boss, and maybe get a raise.'

'What do you mean?' he asked, his eyes lighting up.

'All you'll have to do,' I explained, 'is to go back now and tell your editor that for $5,000 you can get Jim Corbett to give out from his training quarters the only signed statements about his training and the fight.'

The boy rushed out, and returned the next evening, telling me that he had 'made a hit' with his boss. Conditions were tentatively agreed on, and a few weeks after that I signed the contract in Kansas City. The Hearst string of papers followed the idea through by approaching Fitzsimmons, too, and taking him on. It is a common practice today, but it was pioneer work then.

However, the five thousand never touched my hands, for a few days before the fight I gave my brother Harry an order on the *San Francisco Examiner* for the full sum, and adding eleven thousand more, told him to bet it all on me.

About six days before the big one, I was out taking a stroll, not for stiff exercise but for relaxation and fresh air, and I suggested to Delaney, Brady, and Judge Lawlor, my old friend of the Choinyski days, who had come on to visit me, that we go by the arena. It was a big one for the time, holding about 25,000 people, and I thought I'd like to look it over before the fight.

Just then Delaney spied a group of five men with a big dog dusting along about half a mile down the road.

'I think that's Fitz,' said he, 'and he's headed this way.'

Judge Lawlor seemed to grow a little nervous over some idea of trouble and the unwelcome publicity he might get. 'Come on, Jim,' he begged, 'let's hurry up. We don't want you two boys to meet now, here in the road.'

'That's all right,' I replied, seeing a chance I had all along wanted, 'let's mosey along till he catches up. I want to see if he thinks he can really whip me.'

Still the Judge objected, but I assured him I would avoid real trouble, that I only fought when I was to be paid for it. I only wanted to feel out this fellow's nerve, I added, and he consented to wait.

We slackened our pace, hardly moving at all, and just as we reached the arena Fitzsimmons and his crew breezed alongside.

He came up and clapped me on the shoulder, saying 'Hello, Jim' cheerfully enough.

Sometimes, as I tell this story, many years after the event, I have to smile and almost feel like apologizing for my unchivalrous treatment of Bob that day when all the time in my heart I respected him as a great fighter; however, there was nothing really so personal in it all, just the old strategy which I have found as effective as many punches. So when he put out his hand I refused it, growling out curtly: 'I'll shake hands with you when I meet you in the ring next Wednesday.'

Then as he looked at me in amazement and stammered and stuttered, I jerked my shoulder towards the huge dog he had with him and added:

'You'd better bring that fellow along with you, too. You'll need him!'

At that he turned and walked off, quite embarrassed.

I turned to the Judge and Delaney.

'Come on, I've found out what I wanted,' I told them. 'That fellow *doesn't* think he can lick me.'

The work in training eased up as the last days came, but the interest increased as the time grew short. Every train brought new arrivals and instead of hundreds we now had thousands of strangers in Carson City.

Then the day of the fight dawned, the hours crept by, and we came to the arena.

It was a magnificent sight, all those twenty-odd thousand of people in the seats climbing up the arena and with all those snow-capped mountains for a background. In the throng I recognized many famous citizens and picturesque characters, and was amused to see that 'One-eyed Connolly', the most picturesque of them all, was not among the missing. No matter where he happened to be – and he was in a lot of places – or how distant the fight, he would ride the brakes, beating and stealing his way, across a continent if necessary, to show up at the arena in time for hostilities. He was a very capable and versatile gentleman with unusual ways of earning a living, one of which I often laugh over. I knew him to work this in Havana at the Willard-Johnson fight, where he had arrived from the far West, 'broke', as usual, that is with just a dollar in his pocket.

Immediately on his arrival he went into a fruit store, planked down his dollar, and ordered that amount's worth of bananas (yes, they had them in those days) to be sent up to an hotel, a fashionable one whose name he had heard of. Now a dollar would buy all the bananas on the island, but the Cuban merchant took the order, and the room number which Connolly gave, promising to send up the fruit *pronto*.

As he started to write down the order, the Cuban heard his customer angrily cursing and turned around – to look into a big pit on the right side of Connolly's face, where an eye had been.

'Lock the doors!' said Connolly, getting down on all-fours, and searching the floor, 'that glass eye of mine's worth five thousand dollars. I had it made in Paris and it can't be replaced.'

The Cuban of course frantically joined in the hunt, and after looking around for a while, Connolly told him:

'I'll give you five hundred dollars if you find it and bring it to the hotel.' Then he left.

He had no sooner gone than another Americano gentleman entered and asked to see some bananas. Yes, they still had them, so he inquired for grapefruit. Suddenly, as the merchant was attending to the order, the newcomer made an exclamation, stooped down and came up with something in his palm.

'What's this?' he asked.

'It's mine,' said the merchant, in Spanish which I cannot quote.

'Nix,' said the other, 'I found it.'

'It's mine,' said the merchant, ' I own the store.'

Well, they had a long argument, with many gestures from the Cuban, until finally the Americano gentleman asked what he'd give for it, and he kept the Cuban raising until he had offered one hundred dollars for this glass eye.

He accepted and, pocketing the money, left. There was quite a commotion in the hotel when the excited merchant with the huge bunch of bananas over one shoulder, and the glass eye in his hand, was told that no Señor One-eye Connolly was stopping there.

You see, Señor One-eye Connolly had no less than six or seven of these glass eyes, all for jobs of this sort, and at that very moment he and the other Americano gentleman were in a café, spending the hundred dollars.

Last but not least, my father had come for the first time to see me in a professional fight, and with him were my brothers Harry, Joe, and Frank, none of whom had seen me in the ring since the old Choinyski days.

All this time Judge Lawlor and I, still in 'cit' clothes, were standing in the race-track, and after looking over the crowd, and learning that I was a 10 to 7 favourite, also that Fitz had arrived and was dressed, although the fight was not to come off for an hour and a half, I suddenly decided I'd get away from the place for a while.

'Come on, Judge,' I said to my companion, 'let's take a walk. I'm thinking too much about the scrap.'

So we walked around twenty minutes or so, chatting about other things; then I returned and went to my dressing-room, changed my clothes; and shortly after orders came for the principals to enter, and with Billy Delaney, White, Brady, and the rest of my crew, I made for the ring. Fitz came along a moment later, and I was very much surprised to see that his wife, formerly Rose Julian, sister of his manager, was going to act as one of his seconds. She did a good job of it too, and from then on to the finish was very conspicuous, shouting at me and encouraging Bob.

The preliminaries were over quickly, nothing of any importance occurring. I shook hands with Fitz, thinking what a peculiar-looking figure he was, with his red hair, freckles, and bald front, knock-knees, and shambling gait. But he had a fine chest, neck, and shoulders – from the waist up a splendid-looking fighter, but not promising from the waist down.

Our weights were, 172 for Fitzsimmons, 180 for me, which may surprise some people to-day, particularly my old friend Bob Edgren, a remarkable man in track and field athletics, but not always 'wise' to things going on in the ring. Fitz in his prime always weighed about eleven pounds more than Edgren and others have claimed. Louis Hausman, his time-keeper, verified this statement once in my presence.

'They're all wrong,' he said. 'Why, I weighed Fitz myself, Jim, the day he fought you, and he scaled a shade over 172.'

Being a little heavier than my opponent, and figuring after the meeting on the road that I had the greater confidence, at the tap of the gong I went after him, maintaining, though, all my coolness and using all the science I possessed. Left-hand jabs marked his face up pretty well during the first two rounds, and soon Fitz began to swing rather wildly for him, which was encouraging, for he was usually accurate. He was missing most of the time, and meanwhile I was driving home these left-hand

jabs, switching them from body to head, and occasionally varying with my right to the body. Of course his bad marksmanship
was due to my speed. I was here, there, everywhere. As Peter
Jackson had said, it was like boxing a ghost. Almost every time
he would set himself to hit me with one of those famous punches
that had put so many good men out, he'd lose his target;
actually, a few of his misses were by ten-foot margins, and he
looked as foolish as had Sullivan at New Orleans.

When he did land, he had had to hit so quickly that he lost
much of his force and I wasn't hurt.

Five rounds went by, and I found I had accomplished this
much: I had bothered him by cutting his face to ribbons, jolted
him pretty badly, and he was rather tired.

In the sixth I landed a stiff left hook and knocked him down.
As he crouched there, in a daze, he clutched my legs with his
arms. The referee, George Siler, for some reason was not counting, which he should have done, and I told him to make Fitz let
go. As I spoke, Fitz released his clutch, and the referee, rather
late, did begin to count.

'You're counting slow,' I told him, and he pushed me with
his left hand and ordered me to 'Step back!'

Meantime Bob's wife, Rose, was begging and pleading with
Bob to get up. And finally, as the referee reached his slow 'Nine',
Bob did get up.

I don't like to squeal, but Fitzsimmons was on the ground, as
you can reckon from the foregoing description, fully fifteen
seconds. I have never spoken of this incident before, and feeling
I had him at my mercy, I didn't complain then.

As he rose, he wrapped both his arms around his head in a
bewildered, instinctive sort of way, and my supporters and
seconds yelled at me to finish him. But I saw no opening for
reaching a vital spot at the moment, so I started feinting to draw
him out of his cover. The gong sounded and he escaped.

For the seven rounds following I punched him at will. He
certainly took an awful licking and was dead game about it too.
By now the fight seemed so easy that I began to look at the
audience, in clinches, over Fitz's shoulder.

Every once in a while I would see my father. The dear old
man was sitting there, looking intently at me, uttering not a
word; just thoughtfully scratching his chin. He never ceased this

motion. Then on the other side I caught glimpses of a big, blonde, and very excited woman, her hair loose, hat jammed down over one ear, the blood from Fitz spattering her own face, and she, meanwhile, yelling at me things that were not at all flattering either to my skill as a fighter or my conduct as a gentleman. The lady was constantly urging Fitz to 'Hit him in the slats, Bob, hit him in the slats!'

In the fourteenth round, I found that Fitz, who had been swinging pretty wildly in the earlier rounds, was now worse than an amateur, just taking desperate chances. Then I knew I had him, for no fighter ever lived who had hit so accurately and in such naturally correct form as Fitzsimmons, that is, in his previous fights. He could uncork short, snappy punches loaded with dynamite from almost any angle. And to see him flailing away so blindly at me convinced me that he was bewildered and panicky over the fact that he couldn't time me at all and I was out-smarting him. Like all fighters, even the great ones, now that he felt that he was meeting a man who really had it 'on' him, he had forgotten all it had taken so many years and so many and painful battles to learn, and was fighting like a kid, just trying 'to pull a home-run' in the ninth inning. 'One good punch,' said I to myself, 'will settle him now.'

All at once he began to swing so hard that when he missed he spun around as though on a pivot. Several times he did this, and I jumped so far out of his way that I couldn't reach him when he came back to his original position.

At last I figured on staying in line the next time he turned that fool trick and decided, instead of jumping back, just to pull my head a bit back. Then when he pivoted around I'd have my right ready and shoot over the blow that would end it all. It was a grand idea and on it the championship was to depend.

To tempt him into the trick I thrust out my head, and he started his old vicious right, but as I had planned, just at the beginning of the swing I pulled my head back sufficiently to be out of reach.

As one does when getting off to a wrong start, he pulled his punch and started again for my head. Again I jerked my head aside, and this time, seeing he was going to miss once more, again he pulled his punch. Now a man with the natural fighting instinct that Fitzsimmons possessed will never let any arm be idle, so as my head flew back and he checked his right, he let his idle left try something, just started it haphazard and landed on the pit of the stomach. Quicker than all this takes to tell, I sank to my knees. I was conscious of everything that went on, the silence of the crowd, the agony on the faces of my seconds, the waiting Fitzsimmons, but my body was like that of a man stricken with paralysis.

I could hear the referee counting and grew desperate. He came to 'Eight' and I reached for the rope to try and pull myself to my feet. I missed it, and fell on my face. I was nearer the ropes, and reached for them again. 'Ten.' I was out!

No longer the champion of the world.

We were fighting in a very high altitude, 7,000 feet above the level of the sea, and the air was so light that it took a longer time than usual to get the air back into my lungs. As soon as they began to function again, I became a raging madman, wild over having lost the championship without sustaining an injury of any kind, and without one drop of blood or mark or bruise anywhere on me. I rushed at Fitzsimmons and he ran out of the ring, and when the referee came to award him the fight, he had to stand him on a chair in a private box to hold up his gloved hand as signal to the crowd of his victory.

Over here I rushed too, the crowd trying to hold me back, for they thought I intended to hit him. But I shouted: 'I only want to shake his hand', and they let me go.

Reaching the box, I reached over the edge and grasped his hand, but did not congratulate him at all; only said, very angrily: 'You'll have to fight me again.'

This doesn't sound so very pretty to me now, but I am trying to tell all events as they happened, those that reflect discredit as well as those on the other side of the ledger.

Fitz shook his head.

'I'll never fight you again, Jim,' he said. 'You gave me a bloody good lickin'.'

I looked at his battered face and knew that this was true.

'You'll *have* to fight me again,' I repeated, growing desperate, 'or I'll lick you every time I meet you on the street!'

'Jim,' he replied, 'if you ever hit me I'll shoot you,' and he edged away.

16

The Ex-champ drowns his Sorrows in ⸺ – My Rubber
becomes Champion – What the Sports Writers pronounced a
'Fake'! – Another Bout with Sharkey – Am I Slipping?

I WENT back in better style than is usually the lot of a defeated
man, for the *San Francisco Examiner*, which had a special train
for me, expecting it to bear me home still the champion, treated
me very nicely and did not let my loss of the title affect their
attentions in any way. Fitzsimmons was taken to his training
quarters and was unable to leave town for three days after my
departure.

Dad took my defeat to heart, though, and it *was* pretty hard
for him, especially as he thought he had brought me bad luck by
attending this fight, the first of mine he had ever seen. But he
managed to keep a stiff upper lip, and when he saw others of our
neighbourhood beginning to whine out their disappointment,
he reproved them and made light of the affair, acting as if
nothing of any real importance had occurred, though he really
thought it was the saddest event in history.

As soon as I reached the old home I went right to my room,
for I had taken things pretty seriously too, and not being as
plucky as Dad didn't want to talk even to my wife or sisters who
I felt would start in pitying me. This I would have hated worse
than anything in the world, so about six o'clock I tumbled into
bed. The family stayed in the adjoining room, holding the usual
post-mortem, of course; and some of them actually wept. About
midnight they were surprised to hear me call for my wife.

'Jim must be pretty bad,' one of them said, 'I guess he's
calling for a doctor.'

So my wife came to the door.

'What is it?' she said.

'I'd appreciate it if you'd get me a quart of ice-cream,' I
replied, and when the folks heard this news they fairly shouted
with relief and amusement, at the thought of an ex-champ drown-
ing his sorrows in ice-cream instead of wine. As a matter of fact,
ice-cream has always played a prominent part in my life, as you
can readily believe, if you haven't skipped in reading this story.

When I recovered from my disgust sufficiently to look at the reports, I was puzzled and astonished to read of something revolutionary and new — a solar plexus blow. 'So that's what defeated me,' I said to my folks. 'Very fine! But let me tell you something. It was just an ordinary left-hand hook for the stomach.'

But the sporting writers seemed to fancy the term and it became boxing history.

Which makes me think — I do not want to seem to reflect on Fitz's victory in my account of it. He did have a lucky break that time on the floor, and the stomach blow called by the fancy name was just a chance delivery; but Bob was a game fellow and of champion calibre. Any man that had courage enough to take such a beating as he received and admitted, and whose fighting instinct kept him going so long in the face of defeat and prompted him to deliver that last telling blow, *is* a man! In fact, he was in my opinion one of the greatest of all the fighters who have worn the crown, not what you might call a really clever boxer, but a born fighter, with a terrific kick in his punch from any angle, and one who knew all the tricks of the game and was as wise as a fox. I do not believe he could have defeated Jeffries in his prime or that remarkable negro, Peter Jackson, but he would have given each a run for his money and might have defeated them. Certainly no man ever had so much T.N.T. left in his fist when tired and groggy.

However, I was so disgusted with myself at losing a fight, after so badly out-pointing the other man, that I bade goodbye to Delaney and my trainers and left San Francisco, with Mrs Corbett, for New York, and for twelve months did everything I could to induce Fitz to meet me again, but without success. This young fellow, Jeffries, by the way, started in fighting the same year, under Delaney's management, and became quite successful.

In the meantime, Tom Sharkey too was climbing up the ladder and finally he and Jeffries were matched for a bout, which Jeff won. Then, to avoid me, Fitz took on Jeffries, thinking he had 'something soft'. The fight came off at Coney Island, and I acted as second for Jeff, at his and Delaney's invitation, and saw our man knock Bob out in eight rounds.

So the wheel turns. This young fellow who a year before had

been considered good enough only to rub one leg of the champion was himself now champion of the world!

In 1900, Fitz failing me, I arranged a second bout with Sharkey. This is one of the most bitterly discussed fights of the last thirty years, and certainly was the bitterest for me, for the sports writers called it 'a fake', when – but I'm getting ahead. To go back – the afternoon of the fight I received a night letter from my brother Joe telling me that Sharkey was a strong, rugged fellow. In it he gave this caution:

'You're getting older, Jim. Don't do any unnecessary footwork. Save yourself all you can because he has more than ordinary endurance.'

All this, I decided, was sensible advice, and realizing I was a kid no longer, resolved to follow it. So, in the very first round, instead of jumping ten feet away, I just pulled my head out of danger a little, and ducked and shifted, rather than call on my legs as much as in my former battles. Of course, to vary my style and puzzle Sharkey, I would fall back on leg-work every once in a while, but I reduced it about fifty per cent.

In the second round I saw that Sharkey was anxious to use his right. So I feinted at him, he 'bit', and let the old 'haymaker' go. I saw the blow coming and according to my plan, instead of using the usual footwork, drew my head aside a little, but not far enough – the old judgment of distance seemed to have gone – and it landed on my chin, and I fell flat on my face.

All I could see was the stage revolving. In a few seconds I was up, dazed, but realizing where I was. Knowing that the best thing to do when a fellow begins swinging these haymakers, which was all that Sharkey did, is not to get in range of them but to bore in close, so that the blows just whistle around your neck and head, I called on all my reserve and dove in. To the amazement of the crowd, I began slugging him clean across the ring and had the best of the round. But just the same I came to my corner a bit hazy and the seconds had to work hard to freshen me up.

With the gong's tap for the third, I found my head clear once more, but when I tried a little side-step discovered that my ankle had gone lame. This accident had occurred when Sharkey knocked me down in the second, but I had not then been aware of it. So now I had to give up all footwork and stand still, a condition which first led the newspaper men to think the fight was 'fixed', that I was not half trying. I'm sorry I couldn't have made a speech from the ring-side, saying: 'Ladies and Gentlemen and Fellow citizens: I have sustained an accident, and cannot fight with my usual skill – and so on' – bow – applause – 'I thank you for your kind attention.' It would have been pretty, but the fight game is not made that way. Besides, it would have told Sharkey my condition. As it was, he didn't know of the sprain and just thought I *chose* to stand still. When I came from my corner each round, I'd just walk up to him, bore right into him, and force him to slug with me, and had the best of it at that.

But with each round the pain of my ankle increased; it was getting wellnigh unbearable and I had hard work to conceal it. In the intermission I told my seconds about my condition, and we were in a quandary. But each time I'd wind up with: 'Well, I'll try another round', and I'd get up, still bluffing Sharkey. He didn't know what to make of this change in my usual style.

Now Sharkey and I had agreed not to hit in the clinches, a condition which would have been in my favour if I had not had this accident, for I always could make him look pretty shabby, boxing. But Sharkey did not like the pace at which we had slugged any too well himself, and in the ninth or tenth round (I forget which) he started to punch me as we clinched and to rough me a little.

I welcomed this as a way out of my difficulty, for I thought the referee would call 'Foul' if Sharkey continued these tactics. If Kelly should fail to take notice, I felt I would have to quit anyway before long. But one of my seconds must have lost his head through his very desire to save me further agony, for he didn't wait for the referee and jumped in the ring, protesting against Sharkey's blows and hitting in the clinches.

He meant all right, but I lost the fight right then, for Honest John Kelly, the referee, cried: 'You lose!'

Not having seen my second – Con McVey it was – in the ring, for he was behind my back, I thought at first that Kelly was addressing Sharkey. To make sure, I asked:

'Who loses?'

'Aw! *you* lose,' he exclaimed, 'what's the matter with you?' and, turning me around, he pointed out Con standing there in the ring.

Then, of course, I knew it was all up. I had lost the fight and in addition to that the papers tried to make me lose my reputation, declaring next day that the fight was 'fixed', and that I had agreed to lose it. That story has been repeated for twenty-four years.

I think perhaps the hardest blow came from my old friend, Bill Naughton, who had managed Peter Jackson, and later became a sporting editor, one of the best, I think, that ever lived. His statements were really a left-handed compliment to me, after all, and showed that I had not only fooled slow-thinking Sharkey, but also wise Naughton as well. He said the fight had been 'rehearsed blow for blow'. Now I have been on the stage but never really had known how good I was before. After that I felt I could give my friend Maurice Barrymore points.

For several weeks after the fight I limped and, being disgusted, formed the habit of answering, when people asked the cause of the accident:

'Well, it was this way: After the fight I stood upon a chair to make a speech, and the chair toppled over and I sprained my ankle.' Every time someone inquired about my injury I gave this explanation. But the sarcasm then was entirely wasted, and it is almost useless now to try and catch up with a lie. Twenty-four years is a pretty good head-start.

However, perhaps I should have been worrying about something else. When a champ or ex-champ is put in the position of having to make excuses; when he is accused of 'fixing' a fight, no matter how honourable he may be, something is wrong. He cannot be the man he was. Was I on Time's toboggan? I didn't think so. Didn't I have all my old-time skill? Hadn't I out-pointed Fitzsimmons and Sharkey by many miles? Yes – but — However, there were no *buts* in my mind. I was as good as I ever was.

17

'Corbett's' on Broadway – Six Old Actors – I try to stage a
Come-back and Fred Stone acts as my Sparring Partner – Gus
Ruhlin – The Blows used in Boxing – W. A. Brady and Delaney
are in Jeffries's Camp – I return to the Ring and face Jeffries –
I see Electric Lights – Then Stars.

ANYWAY, I was not going back in the financial game; and I
opened a café at Broadway and Thirty-fourth Street where Saks's
store now stands, and across the way from the old Manhattan
Theatre where Minnie Maddern Fiske was then playing. This
theatre has since gone the way of so many, and part of Gimbel's
store stands on the spot.

It was a clean, orderly place that I ran and I tried to keep it
always on a high level. Consequently we had, usually, only the
best sort of patronage. This was in the centre of the Rialto then
and many of the leading actors of the day dropped in when they
were playing on the Big Lane. Maurice Barrymore, father of
Jack, Lionel, and Ethel, and an old friend of mine, was a frequent
visitor; and it was here that he stood when they had to take him
away – that last time before he died.

Come to think of it, I have had the misfortune to be present
when six famous old stars lost their reason; and these memories
hurt, for, though I have met all sorts of people from Presidents
to pickpockets, the actors have always been my greatest friends.
A kindlier set I never met. Their hearts and their purses are ever
open, and they are never uncharitable in their judgments of
others.

Back in '91 it was, that W. J. Scanlon, the best Irish comedian
of those years, met me on Broadway one day. Perhaps I was
tactless, but I couldn't believe the report I had heard, that he was
losing his mind, and I said to him, thinking it all a great joke:
'What's all this talk about your going crazy?'

Immediately poor Scanlon flew into a rage, and pointing to
all the people passing by, exclaimed: 'Why, Jim, I'm feeding all
these people! Yes, I'm feeding them all, and now they turn
on me.'

I soothed him for a while, and as soon as he was calm bade

him 'Goodbye'. A short time afterwards, he had to be taken to Bloomingdale.

About this time too I met Johnny Page, another comedian of the day, then with *Beauty and the Beast* in Chicago. I thought it strange that he wasn't at the theatre, for his show was on, and I said: 'Johnny, aren't you working tonight?'

He looked very frightened at the question, and his lips began to quiver. I repeated the question, and finally he answered:

'I'm going over to see you play.'

And I was not billed at all that week.

A few days later I read that he too had been taken away.

One of the best-known vaudeville teams of thirty years ago was that of Conroy and Fox. Little Johnny Fox was with me the night I demanded $10,000 to fight Peter Jackson. About the time of the Sharkey fight I lent him $100, and he immediately went into bankruptcy, listing this as a liability! Not long after this, he came into my café and wanted to borrow two hundred more.

'Why, Johnny,' I said, 'you borrowed a hundred not long ago, and have gone into bankruptcy and listed it as a liability. That's strange. Aren't you getting a bit mixed up in your affairs?'

At this question he started to cry, and I made up my mind that he was out of his mind. A week later they had to take him away too.

Then there was Bert Leslie, the slang comedian, a most lovable man. I played pool with him at the Lambs' one night, he laughing and kidding in his familiar way. It was his last rational hour.

Maurice Barrymore was probably the handsomest actor that ever graced our stage. He had fine flashing eyes, and a wonderful voice into which he could put volumes of feeling. He had been amateur boxing champion of England, when a young man, and he loved the game and idolized boxing champions.

One night he dropped in the café, slapped me on the back, and cried: 'Hello, Jim!' seeming his usual cheerful self, I thought.

Then after I had responded to his greeting, he pulled up a chair and sat down with me. Suddenly thinking of a poem he had often recited, and wanting a copy of it, I said:

'Barry, would you mind giving me a copy of that poem you recite – the one about the clouds?'

175

'Did you like that?' he inquired, looking at me rather excitedly, I thought.

'Yes,' I replied, 'I thought it was beautiful.'

Immediately he stood up and started to recite it, with his fine rounded voice and magnificent gestures. It was always a treat to listen to him. But just as he said: 'The big cloud said to the little cloud' (I forget the exact lines, but they were sad) he started to cry.

I got up, pulled him down into his chair, and remonstrated with him:

'Barry,' I said, 'you're too big a man to get up and recite in a place like this before a lot of strangers.'

But he wouldn't listen to me, and insisted on getting up again and reciting it through to the finish.

'Don't do it,' I urged. 'There are two newspaper men over there, and it might get in the papers.'

I thought this argument might stop him, but it had a very different effect. Rising, he walked over to the two reporters and began ripping it into them, with a magnificent flow of language. He seemed to remember every grievance he had ever had against any paper in this country or England and was taking it out on these two fellows, and I never heard a man more eloquent. Only, instead of talking to just two, he appeared to be addressing a big audience. Finally I got him into another room and again implored him to keep quiet, when, wheeling suddenly, and seizing the lapel of my coat, he exclaimed:

'Jim, I'm a greater man than Shakespeare!'

Now I knew he hadn't been drinking, and that by nature he was one of the most modest men that ever walked the stage. So I felt it must be all up with poor Barry. At once I sent a message over to the old Lambs Club, and dear old Digby Bell, a great pal of Barrymore's, came over and took him to his room. That was the last night he was ever seen on the streets.

While I was training for the Sullivan fight, in Asbury Park, in '92, Harry Kernell, of the Kernell Brothers, a favourite vaudeville team on the big-time variety circuit, came out to see me. It was after dinner when he drove up; and seeing him coming I went out on the porch to greet him. Without saying anything that a man would naturally say on meeting a friend he hadn't seen for a long time, he seized me and dragged me to a secluded corner of the porch and began telling a long string of jokes without any points – an endless succession of them.

Feeling chilly, I excused myself and went in to get a jacket, but when I returned, Kernell was driving away in the buggy.

Without thinking of the significance of my words, I said jokingly to Brady: 'That fellow must be crazy!'

This was repeated to him, and one night a few months later, when he was appearing at Tony Pastor's, now the Olympic Burlesque Theatre, in the Tammany Hall Building on Fourteenth Street, he couldn't remember his lines. Suddenly he spoke up and told the audience: 'Jim Corbett says I am crazy, but I'm not.'

They led him off the stage and he too went up the road that the others of my poor friends had taken.

Meeting Mrs Kernell one day, I asked her when she was going to see Harry. Agreeing on a day, we went up together to visit him and also poor Billy Scanlon.

Kernell had been there some six months then, but he recognized us, kissed his wife, and shook my hand very heartily.

'How are you getting on?' I asked him.

'Fine,' he answered. 'They gave an entertainment for the poor "loonies" here last night, and asked me to appear.'

'And did you?' I asked.

'Why, of course; and a lady came out and introduced me as "Harry Kernell, the greatest Irish comedian in the world". You should have heard the applause! You never heard such an ovation!'

All of a sudden the look on his face changed from the fixed stare that such people have to a saner expression, and he seemed startled. He looked at his wife. He looked at me, then around the room, and I could tell that for the time being he realized where he was. All at once he laid his head on his wife's shoulder and cried as though his heart would break. And we all cried. I couldn't help it.

Then just as suddenly as the other change had come, his sobs stopped, and he whispered cunningly:

'Don't let them know I was crying – they'd put me out of here. You see that fellow out there? That's So-and-so; he's crazy. . . .' He was off again.

To calm him, his wife asked: 'What did you do at the entertainment, Harry?'

G

'Oh, the old stuff,' he replied, 'song and dance,' then off he started – to show us his new steps. He had been one of the best eccentric steppers we had in those days, but his wife told me, as she left, that never had he danced quite so well as he did that afternoon on the floor of that asylum.

I had been out of the ring and running this café between four and five years, also appearing on the stage very frequently, when I made up my mind that I could whip Jeffries and regain the championship. With this determination in mind, I started in exercising at Wood's Gymnasium on Twenty-eighth Street, just off Fifth Avenue. My principal companion and sparring partner was Fred Stone, who was a fine athlete, as anyone who has seen his stunts on the stage can well believe. He could also box very well; in fact, I have never met a man in my life who could do so many things expertly. He was the only one who knew of my trips to Wood's and we kept it all a dark secret, for I was anxious to find out if I couldn't bring myself back into condition. That would warrant my challenging Jeffries; but I didn't want anyone to learn of my plans. After one year I felt that I had reached this stage, and meeting Brady one day, I said:

'Bill, why don't you get Jeffries to fight me? He's giving Sharkey and all these fellows a chance.'

Knowing nothing of my secret work, Billy was shocked.

'Why, Jim,' he exclaimed, '*you* can't fight any more. Jeffries is liable to kill you!'

'Perhaps,' I returned, 'but we'd get some money for it.'

Just as I made this remark to Brady, who should walk in but Jeffries – everyone seemed to come to my place those days – and Brady repeated to him what I had said. Jeffries stood there with his head bent down, partly because he was never much of a talker, and partly because he still felt the old respect for me that one would for his old boxing instructor. So I spoke up.

'You ought to give me a fight, Jeff. It doesn't make any difference who wins, it's just a business proposition. We'd draw a big house.'

Brady added his arguments, and they promised that Jeff's next fight would be with me. Then they left to go over to the Manhattan Theatre.

I had made the acquaintance of a little newspaper man by the name of Smith, and running across him just then I asked:

'Smith, how would you like to make a hundred dollars in two minutes?'

'Fine,' he replied, then waited for the proposition.

'This is how it's done,' I explained. 'Jeff's over in the Manhattan, and he has just promised me the next fight. You run over and ask him if the story's true; and if you print his acceptance in the paper, the one hundred is yours.'

Well, he ran across the street, and came back and reported in quick time. Jeffries had said 'Yes'.

'Now get busy,' I told Smith. And he did, the papers coming out next day with 'Jeffries and Corbett to Fight' in big headlines, for it was a surprise, I being an old timer and four years out of the ring.

The date was set for October 1901. Meanwhile Jeffries found out in some way (not through Stone, of course, but probably a gym attendant) that I had been exercising for the year previous; and, having figured when they made the match that I would not be in condition to put up much of a fight, his manager got excited and saw Brady.

As the result of this meeting Brady came to me.

'They won't let us wait until October. They want it to be set for August.'

I laughed.

'Well, this is one time you're not so smart,' I said. 'I'll fight Jeffries next week if you like. I'm ready any minute.'

The Jeffries crowd, not wanting to allow me any more time, hustled the match, setting it forward to August, at Coney Island. I trained at Lakewood, never working harder in my life. I was nearly thirty-five, hadn't had a fight in years, and wanted to make up all I could for these handicaps. As I had gone at things reasonably, I had gradually worked myself up to a point where now I could begin real strenuous training, and to this grind, when I reached Lakewood, I settled down.

And I did go at it, neglecting nothing that might bring me victory once more, though there was not so much fun in the business of training as there once had been. Twenty-one years of boxing – that is the length of time I had been in the game – bring a different viewpoint. It is not that I had it so much easier in my earlier training periods, but then I had the spirit of youth and sheer delight in exercise. And I guess too there was the feeling that always goes with the man climbing up and destined for the top, a sort of wind of hope and confidence and prophetic feeling that makes him breeze along through all the hardship. It was quite different now. I had been at the top and fallen. I was old for a boxer, middle-aged for a business man, and I was trying to climb back. Of course, I myself felt that I had a splendid chance, in fact, that I really would win. Still, there wasn't quite the old bracing atmosphere around our camp.

Feeling the need of a pretty tough sparring partner, I thought of 'Gus' Ruhlin, then considered one of the strongest heavyweights and the one whom I had come so near to hiring at Carson City. I offered him a hundred per week, and he accepted. But there was an odd condition that went with his acceptance. At the last minute Madden, his manager, came to me and declared we must box 'in private'.

'You see, Jim,' he explained, 'you're a damsight better boxer than Gus and would show him up. It won't do him any good as a drawing card.'

To make everybody happy I agreed and we decided on a plan. I would box in private all right, but I'd make him (Ruhlin) sweat for the concession. This was practical too, for I had been out of the game so long that I needed a few hard fights under my belt. In ordinary sparring you do not get thumped and hurt, and therefore hardened, as you do in a real go. And I determined to force Ruhlin, who stood 6 feet 2 inches, weighed 220 pounds, and was quite tough, to give me the nearest thing to a real fight any sparring partner ever gave to a champion or challenger.

For three weeks we kept at it, with everybody out of the room and Madden standing outside the door on which he would pound to call 'Time!' We went for each other for all we were worth, and as the place was only about twelve feet square, I had less opportunity for footwork than in the usual ring; which was precisely what I wanted – to be forced to fight at close quarters.

Poor Ruhlin was game enough, but he grew so discouraged that twice he threw down his gloves in disgust, exclaiming: 'I'll never make a fighter.'

Somehow he couldn't hit me, no matter how close in I went; and he knew little about the knack of clinching, and balance, and 'riding blows', as we say in the ring, which is simply the act of swinging your head and shoulders to the right with your opponent's right, to the left with his left and so avoiding altogether, or at least dissipating half the force of the attack.

And it is always knack and judgment that make the good boxer, for the weapons are few – two arms, two legs, and a body, and of course a head. Even the blows it is possible to use are but few: right and left for the head, the same for the body, left-hand hook for head or body, right and left uppercuts, wild swings with either hand, and a few short punches, perhaps, in the breakaway. That is about all, barring the foul 'rabbit' and 'kidney' punch. All told there cannot be more than twenty.

Still, the star pitcher has even fewer tricks in his bag – an in-and out-curve, a drop, a slow ball and a fast one with a hop on it, and perhaps a few freak shots such as 'the spitter'. The pitcher is successful because he knows how to assort these cleverly and outguess the batter. So the varying and assortment of the really small number of blows known to the game, the knowledge when to use each and how to time it, with a little knack in the clinches, balance, and proper footwork are what make the good boxer. Of course, courage and condition have to be thrown in; and, as I have tried to show in this story, ability mentally to dominate the other man will top it off nicely.

Finally I did get in what I considered to be excellent physical condition. And I see now no reason why any man of thirty-five to thirty-eight, if he will, cannot keep in almost as good shape as he was ten years earlier. However, 'almost', like 'but', is mighty for so little a word. And it does mean that, as a three-year-old will make better time on the track than he ever will at five, so, after thirty, a man's muscles begin to set, and though he may make a show of speed, the old burst is not usually there.

Still, there are exceptions to every rule; and I determined to be an exception with a capital E.

As the day approached the odds settled at three to one, everyone figuring Jeffries had a walk-over, because of my age and my long absence from the ring; and many, feeling so confident that he would put me out in four rounds, placed bets on that basis, though at the better odds of two to one. There was another handicap too, Jeff's engagement of Brady as manager, with Delaney as chief trainer.

It was an odd thing to confront these two old friends in the enemy's camp and supporting the fighter whom I had originally taught, and to spare whom I used to have to pull all my blows. I don't know just how Jeff felt at the time, but I know Brady figured I had little chance, for he was back of one of those two to one four-round bets. However, I felt almost as supremely confident as I had when I entered the ring against Sullivan. The disadvantages I have cited above I have dwelt on rather in the light of memory; I was inclined to discount them then, actually forgetting all about them, as my training went on, I felt so fine. And so I at last found myself in the ring.

And in some ways I was right, for when the fight started and Jeff came on rushing me, as was good strategy, for it was the only way for him to fight – to let his weight and strength tell – I far out-pointed him. I was in and out, and everywhere, these first rounds, feinting, side-stepping with all my old skill. Never before had I such marvellous judgment, such accurate timing.

There was not one thing that I had ever done before in a fight that I didn't do that night and do well. People at the ring-side began to wonder at it.

In the second Jeffries landed a terrific left hook in my side. I grabbed hold of him at once, and as I did so I could feel my spine quiver. The feeling was new to me; it had the effect of a cramp, but in a second it was gone; and I danced away as light as before. Then I started jabbing him with my best left hooks, and landed so many that the audience went wild with excitement. They hadn't expected this from an old-timer.

About the fourth Jeffries slipped in another terrific left to my body, and again my spine quivered and the feeling of cramp such as comes over a swimmer made me shiver for a second. But I just smiled, clinched, took my time, then broke away as cleverly as before, and when I started dancing around in my old style, the blow seemed to have left no ill effects. Right away I was delighted, for I knew that if I hadn't been in good condition those two blows would have left me in considerable distress. So I must be in the pink and grew more confident than ever that I was to win that fight.

As the rounds went on, the audience, as many told me afterwards, grew resigned to losing their wagers placed on Jeffries. It was worth it, they thought, seeing me win my old championship back. They were with me almost to a man, and in the tenth round they rose and cheered me till the walls rang, and as I went to the corner I felt no fatigue, no hurt of any kind.

Meanwhile, I had been working out in my head a punch that I thought would fool and perhaps finish Jeffries, and had waited for ten rounds for an opportunity to try it when this opportunity came.

I had built up carefully for it, by pretending that each time we clinched and I held him in, my hands on his forearms, that I was afraid he would sneak over a punch as we were breaking away. To further this idea, as we broke I would let my hands slip down his forearms, and just before we were clean would stand for the fraction of a second holding his arms out full length, while his chin was a little up in the air.

I repeated this manœuvre each time we clinched during the ten rounds, precisely in this way. But in the tenth, as I was holding by the hand his left arm fully extended, and his chin was up, I suddenly let go of his wrist, closed my fist swiftly, and clipped him on the chin. I saw his eyes roll; then, to protect himself, he dove at me, wrapping both arms around my body. The audience didn't realize he was dazed, simply thought he was trying to tire me with his great weight, but I saw his eyes.

He recovered and weathered the round; and several others followed, at a terrific pace, I hitting, side-stepping, jabbing, and hooking rights and lefts to his body; he never landing on my face, but every once in a while sending that heavy fist to the body.

As 'time' for the sixteenth period was called, I figured to myself that the fight was sure to last the scheduled twenty-five rounds. I had won on points each one of the sixteen already fought, and couldn't lose the match except through robbery; so I decided to relax a little until the twenty-fourth, when I would rush over to his corner and slug on to the finish, breaking my hands, and everything else if necessary, in the effort to put him out.

Now this was not madness, for I was fully able to out-slug the heaviest for two rounds, but would have been out-slugged in time, because of his superior weight, if I had tried that method for too long, or too soon. Then, too, even if I should not succeed in a knock-out, just to have him groggy at the end of the twenty-fifth would be a nice topping-off after so far out-pointing him and giving such an exhibition of boxing science. It would be quite dramatic, I thought.

With this programme in mind, on I went, relaxing a great deal, although still pulling enough 'stunts' to show the crowd that I had a fine margin on points. Some thought I was tiring, and said so afterwards, but I never felt better in any fight than I did all through this, nor ever fought, I think, with rarer judgment than I did that night – that is, up to the twenty-third. And I was fighting the champion, too, a chap of twenty-six, one of the toughest men that ever entered a ring.

My hands knew all right that he was as hard as a rock; and his punch would hurt even when he struck a glancing blow. Sometimes, when he hit at my ribs, I would swerve and turn my back. I accomplished my purpose, but his fist as it slid along my back or arm, with half its force gone would make a deep impression on me. Only I was so fit that the effect didn't last. After all, gameness is so much a matter of condition.

However, we were talking of the twenty-third. I still think of it. While I was resting in my chair after the *twenty-second*, I began to plan what I would do when champion again. My handlers were cautioning me to be careful, as I had the fight now, but I had made up my mind to slug the last and make a whirl-wind finish and not play safe. Well, I had settled that; and not listening to my seconds, I sat there puzzling over the choice of a road manager, planning out a new play, and I was actually deciding what size type I would use on the big posters that would proclaim me CHAMPION OF THE WORLD AGAIN!

These vivid pictures were still unreeling in my mind as the gong sounded for the twenty-third.

We came to the centre, I with one round left before my final charge. We began hostilities and Brady and Delaney kept yelling to Jeffries, as they had ever since the sixteenth: 'The only way you can win, Jeff, is by a knock-out', an encouraging admission, I thought, that they had already lost. And as he had done ever since the middle of the fight, Jeff was trying to rough me round, swinging madly, and missing me most of the time by as big gaps as had Sullivan and Fitz. So I just relaxed once more and danced here and there, often letting my hands lie idle at my side. My ankles were so springy that even while I fell back on all this footwork, I was not tiring my legs. And all the while I was still seeing in my mind's eye those wonderful posters and electric lights and waiting for the twenty-fourth.

The *next* thing I saw was not the electric lights but a hand holding smelling-salts under my nose!

I was in my corner, sprawled out on a chair.

A cousin of mine, Tom Corbett, whom I hadn't seen for years, was bending over me, kissing me on the cheek.

The crowds were standing up on the chairs cheering.

It sounded like music in my ears.

So I straightened myself to get up and allow the referee to hold up my hand in token of victory, but somehow felt a little hazy in the head. I saw my seconds look at me peculiarly and I turned to George Considine.

'What is it?' I asked, sort of groggily, I guess.

'Jim,' he said sadly, 'you were knocked out.'

And from that day to this I don't remember ever being hit.

I don't remember being on the ground at all.

All my memory calls up is, my answering the gong, relaxing a little as planned, and dancing around – and – seeing those posters and my name over some theatre in electric lights!

Finally I took the dose, went over to Jeff and shook hands with him, and when, a little later, he came to my dressing-room, I couldn't help saying, although I shouldn't have: 'Jeff, you're the luckiest man in the world to win tonight.' He didn't answer; just stood in front of me, like a big boy, with his head hanging down.

Now Jeff and I have been friends since he was just good enough to act as rubber for one of my legs, later while he was champ, and also when he was down and out. That friendship has continued for many years, and among a thousand and one things we have talked about this fight. He has often told me I had him licked in the tenth round; had him licked worse than I realized myself. The body punches hurt him terribly, he said, and he had given up all hope, except of a lucky blow. Finally, against his expectation he had landed it, and he admitted that as I had said he was the luckiest man in the world.

I have tried to figure out what really happened in that fatal twenty-third, and from what he told me and what I have gathered from those in the ring, this is the story:

I started to jump back from one of his wild swings and was nearer the ropes than I thought. Hitting these hard, I was bounced back as he was swinging his left. Into that fist I bumped. They tell me he hit me with such force that I flew up into the air, my neck struck the lower rope, and I was dead to the world. George Considine ran over to throw water on me, and Jeffries was so excited that he started kicking at him to keep him off.

That was all there was to it – and enough! I have seen my name in electric lights since in my shows, but not as champion of the world. It was a costly lesson – and not as an alibi, but to drive it home as a lesson to all men who fight or undertake any job in life, I am going to add that my age, after all, made only one difference. I had trained well, was in good shape, and had my old-time skill. But if I had fought Jeffries when I was twenty-five or twenty-six, and coming up the ladder, with all the conditions quite the same as that night, the blows and breaks falling just as they fell then, I would never have sat in my corner figuring on any future. I would have been concerned only with the present; attended to the job in hand; and would have thought only of the fight. So all my faculties would have been alert and instinctively I would have known just how far I was from those ropes, and would have gauged the back-step properly, or have side-stepped, or something. In the end it was my own fault; but I lost to a very great fighter. They don't come any gamer than Jeff.

18

I try it again – The Cleverness of Kid McCoy – The most Scientific Fight ever fought – On Refereeing.

I HAD to go twice more to the well. This last encounter had brought me back into public esteem so much that when I entered Rector's, Martin's, or any places on Broadway, the diners would applaud, and frequently cheer me, an unusual tribute for a defeated man. I believe that I was more popular then than I ever had been as champion. Soon there were discussions about the possibility of my fighting McCoy, who was considered a wonderfully scientific fighter, having won over Choinyski, Dan Creedon, Gus Ruhlin, and the famous Tommy Ryan, breezing through his scraps and usually winning hands down.

So, flushed with what I considered my success even in defeat, I must take on McCoy for twenty-five rounds in the Madison Square Garden.

About two days before the fight a rumour that McCoy was going to lay down was heard on all sides. I was given this information as gospel truth by several supposed to be 'in the know'. However, I, who should have been 'in the know', knew nothing about it; and I replied each time that certainly McCoy would gain more by winning from Corbett than by training with any crooked gamblers.

Still the stories wouldn't down. Even Harry telegraphed me from the Coast that he had heard the story. I wired back, telling him to pay no attention to any such reports, and above all not to consider that I had a cinch. McCoy was clever, and the rumour was probably some trick of his to get me to let up in my training so that he could catch me out of condition.

The night came, we went to the Garden, and the fight was on. The first round, I think, was one of the most scientific ever fought by two men. Such feinting and fiddling, footwork and speed, had never before been seen, I am sure, in the ring. Each was trying to draw the other out, and feinting, or trying to fool your man into a lead when he is not ready, is one of the finest points of boxing (a lost art these days). McCoy was simply wonderful, and there was not one blow landed by either in the three minutes.

In this round I was quite cautious, because of the rumours, wanting to be sure of everything I did. McCoy might be planning something, but he was doing his best then; and certainly he would want to make a good showing at the start and not have it said he didn't hit Corbett *once* in the whole fight.

In the second we loosened up a little, and before long I hit McCoy on the jaw and dazed him; but though the punch took effect, he slipped away and dashed around the ring so fast that with all the speed I possessed I couldn't lay another glove on him during the remainder of that round.

187

This disgruntled the audience. It should not be, but always when two scientific men meet the results are unsatisfactory to the average onlooker. He wants slugging, and blood, and when one of the well-matched men in the ring is trying to make the other do something, the other too frequently off-sets him. It all takes time, and the audience, not understanding the finer points of the game, and not being able to see the two brains working, grows uneasy. A match between a slugger and a scientific man pleases them more, for it is far more spectacular, the one jabbing and tapping, ducking and cleverly getting away, doing all the things that look pretty from outside, and the other floundering after him all over the ring.

Such a combination is what makes a fight between Tendler and Leonard such a hit. Lew is a slugger, Benny an artist, as good, probably, as any that ever entered the ring and one of the few present-day champions of whom this can be said. At that he would have his work cut out for him if the competition were as keen as when Kid Lavigne, Frank Erne, Joe Gans, and Kid McPartland fought it out among themselves.

At last the gallery birds began to complain, then the ring-siders, but of one thing I am sure, I never fought more carefully or tried harder than in this fight with McCoy. I was doing my darnedest all through.

In the fifth or sixth, I can't remember just which, I saw my chance and started slugging for a few seconds or so. I say slugging, but it was pretty scientific slugging, and I knew I had my man. Up to this round we had feinted and fiddled and dashed around the ring, I out-pointing McCoy a little, but not much. I had landed a few hard blows and furthermore had accomplished one very important thing – I had drawn him out several times against his will. And remember that when two skilful men meet, and one finally begins to draw the other out, the end is in sight. The one thus drawn out is not defeated at the moment, or in that round, or maybe for several rounds, but he will be in the end. Having done this several times, you make your opponent lose his morale.

That's what happened to McCoy. He lost his, though he stood up for five rounds. Then suddenly he went to pieces, threw all science to the winds and fought like a crazy man. As soon as I saw him swinging 'haymakers', I knew he was in worse shape morally than Fitzsimmons had been when doing the same thing, for McCoy was far more clever than Fitz, and therefore was more demoralized than he had been. At once I got inside the range of his swings and centred my attack on his stomach. I had had pretty reliable information that he hadn't been training any too well, and the stomach is the spot most vulnerable under such conditions. Some lefts and rights to this spot had the famous Kid all crumpled up; one more I sank in, then he flopped to his knees, all doubled up. In a neutral corner I was waiting, ready to put all the strength in a knock-out blow the minute he rose, when Charley White stepped up to me, tapped me on the shoulder, and said: 'You win!'

Immediately there was an uproar of disappointment simply because White had not counted McCoy out. And stories began to come out in the papers, a few days later, intimating that the fight was a fake. This accusation hurt me more than anything that had ever been said about me or done to me in my life, for I certainly saw no evidence of McCoy's reported endeavours to 'lay down'; and he fought very hard in that fight. And I knew I gave to the public the best that was in me. Ever since I started in boxing it had been one of my aims, in addition to making something of myself, to elevate the sport; and I believe I have a host of supporters who will substantiate me in that claim. I had bluffed my opponents sometimes, but it was beyond me ever to descend to *fixing a fight*.

All of which shows, I suppose, what a difficult job the referee has. Charley White saw that McCoy had been severely punished and had not the ghost of a chance after that last attack, and to save him unnecessary punishment, awarded the fight to me.

It would have been a good thing if the referee who officiated at the Dundee-Criqui battle in 1923 had possessed some of this spirit, and had saved Criqui, the little Frenchman who proved his bravery in the ring that night and before that, in the Great War. That was one of the most brutal exhibitions I ever saw. But you can't argue about it; the crowd wants blood and the thrill of the kill.

I know what it is from experience, for by request I tried refereeing one night in Providence, while I was playing there. In advance, I told the crowd from the stage that it wasn't a pleasant job, since I had my ideas of how fights should be conducted and these ideas didn't always run with those of the audience. I added that if I saw one man being hopelessly beaten I would stop the bout and award the victory to the other man. They all applauded – and seemed to approve – at the time.

In the seventh round this very thing happened – one man sadly outclassed the other, and the other was bleeding and groggy. Moreover, the first man was so tired that he wasn't able to put his opponent out; all he could do was to hit the injured fellow on the jaw as the latter was floundering around the ring, and inflict more pain without any decisive results. The leader had his arm set for another one of these blows, when I grabbed his arm and said: 'You win!'

What must the winner do but fall in a faint, right there in the ring! The seconds carried him to his corner, when the defeated man, coming to for a little, and seeing the other unconscious, wanted to carry on with the fight, bleeding and groggy as he was. And it was funny – there was the fellow who had won the fight being brought to with smelling-salts in his corner.

There is no need of describing the uproar that followed; but I tried to quiet it by explaining that the fainting man had not fallen through his opponent's blows, but through fatigue. He had relaxed too suddenly after his violent exertion and so had flopped. If his heart had failed, and the coroner had been called in, my decision would have been right just the same. He was the victor quite as much as would have been a sprinter who had reached the tape ahead of his rivals and then dropped dead.

This incident, though not a usual one, of course, still shows the difficulty of refereeing honestly and at the same time satisfying the crowd.

It takes manliness to make good fight referees as well as to turn out good umpires for the diamond.

Further, I think one man is enough. I do not like this method of having three men in the ring, now prescribed by law in the State of New York. There is opportunity for distributing the blame when there are three, and more of a chance for 'fixing'. No one feels the responsibility as much as a single man who alone faces the great crowd and feels that his reputation is at stake.

This McCoy fight was my next to last. I was to have one more before the curtain would fall. And I had determined that it would be my last, for I was getting old.

19

As one may guess, the next fight, which I have spoken of in the
last chapter, and which I had determined would be my farewell
bow, was with Jeffries.

Could I win this time? After my victory in the McCoy fight,
and my clear out-pointing of Jeffries at Coney Island, I felt that
I could, even at thirty-eight, for I would be that by the time I
met him, as it had taken two years to get Jeffries' consent to fight
me again.

And it was a dangerous job at that age, with Jeff ten years
younger, but I felt all the old confidence. I can be champion
once more, I said, then I'll retire, and either hand it over to
another, or let the young hopefuls fight it out among themselves.
It was sound reasoning and admirably planned.

There was some discussion about details when we met at the
Delavan Hotel, on Broadway and Forty-first Street, New York,
to arrange the fight; the chief argument arising over bandages,
which I had used on my hands ever since '97 or '98.

'No, you can't have any bandages,' Jeff said, shaking his head.
'You've got to fight without them.'

He seemed pretty set about it, and he was champion and could
have had his way, but I tried to argue him out of the idea.

'Why, Jeff,' I said, 'what are you talking about? You know
that in all the fights nowadays the principals use bandages.'

'Nope,' he said, 'you can't use 'em. Fitz used 'em in his last
fight with me. He dipped 'em in plaster of Paris the night before,
and they were just like cement. You ought to have lamped my
face when I was through.'

That is just what Fitz had done, and when people speak of
the rumour of Dempsey's use of plaster of Paris at Toledo, the
trick was not as new as they thought. Whether this last Jack
tried it or not, I do not know, but if he did Willard was not
smart to let him get away with it. There's nothing new under
the sun, they say. And that goes for the prize-ring, too.

Finally the argument was settled by my agreement to have the bandages wrapped on my hands in the ring, an arrangement I gladly suggested, since I have always wanted to win my fights fairly and with the use of such mental strategy as I have before described.

A great deal of dickering with fight promoters followed, that fine sportsman, Jimmy Coffroth, now connected with the Tia Juana race-track in Mexico, making the best offer. The Yosemite Club in my old home town was selected as the place.

In the bargaining between Coffroth and the principals, the former put over a 'shrewd one' on me, and quite legitimately. Jeff and I had agreed to fight on a sixty-five thirty-five basis, but in skirmishing around I learned that the biggest house they had ever had in San Francisco was $34,000, and promptly I insisted that my percentage be based on this sum. Jeffries accepted a calculation on the actual receipts.

I thought I was shrewd, but found that I wasn't, for two weeks before the fight the receipts had already reached $40,000. Naturally I hollered and threatened to withdraw unless they changed my contract to read thirty-five or sixty-five per cent of the actual receipts instead of the same proportion of $34,000.

Coffroth just laughed when I put up my argument.

'Jim,' said he, 'you know you wouldn't break your word with the public. You asked to have your percentage based on the $34,000 when you thought that was a top figure. Now you want it changed. I know you're going to fight, for all you say.'

He was right; and I took the dose, also learning another lesson. I fought to a $64,000 house and all I got by my wonderful generalship on which I prided myself was a percentage of about half that sum!

During the negotiations for the match I was playing in vaudeville, doing a monologue, and arranged my booking so as to finish my tour in San Francisco about three months before the fight, thus allowing myself sufficient time for training.

I was not unhappy during this period. Rather I was quite cheerful. I felt no fear of the results of the fight; was as popular as I ever had been; my work on the stage was wholesome and congenial; and I had made many friends, among them – but here I must tell about one of the best of all – Mike McGrath of Salem.

I was playing at Lynn, Massachusetts, a week's stand those

times, and on the opening night was stopped by an old Irishman at the stage door.

'Mr Corbett,' he said, 'ye don't know me, but I was a cousin of yer father's. Me and the ould woman went to school wid him in Ballenrobe. Wud it be askin' ye too much now to stop around an' see the old woman? She's that crippled with rheumatiz she can't walk.'

'Of course. I'd be delighted,' I said; and round we went, the next afternoon, to a poor little room, but one made cheerful by these dear Irish people who reminded me so much of my old home, long since broken up.

We had a good chat, the two old people and I, and I repeated the visits while I was in Lynn, noticing that on each occasion they had a great deal to say about some Mike McGrath, a great friend of theirs.

'Oh, if McGrath cud see us now!' it was, or 'What a trate it wud be if McGrath cud only shake yer hand.'

'Who is McGrath – and where does he live?' I finally inquired.

'Over in Salem – just a bit of a way,' said the old man, jerking his hand over his shoulder, then he added: 'And he wint to school wid yer father; and ivery time we see him he ashks: "Have ye met the man that whipped Sullivan?"'

Now it happened that the White Steamer Auto Company had asked me to ride out in their new model as a sort of publicity stunt. I hadn't accepted, but with a new idea in mind I telephoned the manager to bring around his car, and I would take the ride he had wanted.

When we were seated, I said to him: 'How long will it take this car to get to Salem?'

'About an hour,' he told me. 'We'll go, Mr Corbett, if you want to.'

'Yes,' I said, 'I've an old friend over there.'

I had gotten McGrath's address from the old people, and when we reached Salem inquired for the street. We were directed there, only to find it a little alley in the poorest district, full of tenements, tin cans, and goats.

Looking up the alley, the driver shook his head.

'I can't make that, Mr Corbett. We'll ruin our tyres.'

'You wanted me to drive out in your car,' I roared. 'Now if

it's any good it can negotiate that alley. Drive ahead and blow that old horn like the devil.'

So, tooting the horn, we drove up the little alley, thousands of people, it seemed to me, sticking their heads out of the windows.

We found the number all right and a poor little place it was, but it had a neat little patch of grass a bandanna handkerchief could cover; and a little old man about five feet high, with all the map of old Ireland on his face, was watering the plot with a dinky watering-pot.

He gave one look at the wonderful car, then went on with his work. He wasn't going to show that he was impressed.

And he refused to show it when I came to the gate, dressed up pretty well, as I usually was those days, and asked:

'Does Mr McGrath live here?'

'It is poshible,' said he, 'but who is ut that wants to speak wid him?'

'A friend from Athlone,' said I.

He nodded, gave me a suspicious glance, then went on with his work.

'Are you a Mayo man?' I then threw at him, and he almost dropped the watering-pot when he heard the question.

'I am that. Are you?' he asked, looking up at me, then cunningly he shook his head and turned to his flowers again.

'Did you ever hear of the Corbetts?' I went on. 'The Corbetts of Ballenrobe?'

Immediately he looked up at the sky, as if he were seeing angels and began: 'Oh, the Corbetts – sure. There was tin uv thim – there was John – and James – an'...' He named them all over but one as he stood there looking up at the sky.

'Haven't you forgotten one?' I said. 'Wasn't there a Pat Corbett?'

His face shone.

'Sure – Pat!' And he smiled kind of shyly, the way old Irish do. 'Why, whin the bhoys wud see me comin' round the corner, they wud say – "Pat Corbett'll be here in a minute", we wuz that thick when we was bhoys.'

Then he stopped and looked at me in bewilderment, and came nearer, the water from the pot pouring down his old trousers.

'But who is it askin'?' he said. 'Did ye know Pat Corbett?'

I grinned. 'My name's James Corbett,' I said.

194

'Sure and ye couldn't be "Scientific Jim"?' he inquired, putting it that way, you see, to save himself being caught in a bad guess.

'I am,' I said and honestly I was proud that day to own it, 'and I've come all the way from Lynn to shake your hand.'

The ice was all broken then.

'Shake the two uv them,' he said, holding his old hands out, the tears pouring down his face.

Yes, we Irish are sentimental and I hope to Heaven we never change.

Our tour at its end, I wound up in San Francisco, and was given a wonderful welcome. I never saw so many flowers on one stage in my life. I noticed one piece decorated with the letters of the Olympic Club and more of the Irish came to my eyes, for it had come from my old pals at the club where I had spent some of the happiest days of my life.

There was another similar piece, too, with the letters Y.C. on it, a compliment from the Yosemite Club where I was to fight. However, for the time being I had forgotten this fact, and as I was looking at the displays after the show, asked: 'What does that stand for?'

'Vot does vot stand for, Mister Corbett,' said a stage-hand, standing near by. He was a Swede.

'What do these letters mean?' I repeated. 'Y.C.'

He gave me his answer in all seriousness.

'Vy, Yim Corbett!' he said.

20

My Last Fight

FATE seemed to take a fancy to placing my old friends in the enemy's camp. Not that I regarded it as ominous at all – but again Delaney was training Jeff – at Oakland this time – and he knew my ways so thoroughly! However, with me in my quarters at Croll's in Alameda, where I started hard work after closing at the Orpheum, I had two pretty good boys, 'Yank' Kenny and a clever amateur, Sam Barger of the Olympic Club; so I didn't worry about my handlers.

My condition was already pretty fair in spite of my thirty-seven years, as I had been in the habit of going to some gym in every city where I showed, to play handball or box, and had done some road work each day to keep myself fit. And I had also been very careful about my diet and had cut down on my smoking.

An outdoor ring was set up and here I did practically all my boxing – a new stunt in those days, although my friends Deschamps and Carpentier consider it their invention. When I was over at Manhasset, Long Island, in 1920, they took great delight in showing me their outdoor ring, and asked what I thought of it.

'Very good,' I replied. 'I used to box that way before you were born.'

The two French boys showed me another invention of which they were very proud too – a rib in the palm of the glove to aid in clenching. But it happened to have been invented by me in 1891 when I was training for Sullivan.

Never had I trained so hard as I did for this last bout. Among my daily stunts was shadow-boxing for a full hour without a second's pause, a demand on one's strength and will-power which would prove pretty hard on present-day boxers.

One thing did puzzle me, although it did not seem any more ominous to me at first than the fact of my old friends being in Jeffries's camp. I was boxing one day with 'Yank' Kenny, who was strong and weighed 225 pounds. He was as slow as a truck-horse, and I had boxed with him hundreds of times before this period, and never had he been able to put a glove on me, unless I wished it. Now, however, every day or so, slow as he was, he would hit me right in the face and the punch had steam behind it. I couldn't understand this and put it down to sheer luck. Still, it troubled me enough to keep me figuring it out for a couple of months; and each day during that time, he would land on me at least once with one of those awful punches.

One evening, as I was sitting after dinner and talking with my wife, I confessed to her that Kenny was hitting me now and then in spite of my defence, and I was almost ashamed to admit it even to her.

'Dear,' I added, 'that fellow shouldn't be able to reach me with a horse-whip. I don't understand it.'

'Maybe it's your eyes, Jim,' she replied; but I couldn't agree.

She persisted. 'I notice, Jim,' she argued, 'that when you read the papers you squint. Probably you need glasses.'

This gave me food for thought.

Things went along pretty well as the day approached. My brother Tom was with me most of the time, and thousands of my old friends from the city came out and watched me at my stunts. During the last few weeks, however, Tom began to grow pessimistic. Often, to take my mind off the coming battle, I would ask him to go walking, but I found I had to cheer him up.

'You're almost thirty-eight,' he would say. 'Do you really think you can stand it?'

I told him that I had never felt better in my life; and, barring a little anxiety about the Kenny incident, it was true.

'If anything does happen, and it looks as if you're going to be licked,' Tom finally blurted out, 'I'm going to do something to stop it.'

'Tom,' I said, very sternly, 'this is to be my last fight. If you see me getting whipped, let me take it. You'd break my heart if you tried anything to save me. I want to pass out of the pictures taking my licking.'

He promised not to interfere.

About a week before the fight, Tommy Ryan, the ex-middle-weight champion, and one of the greatest fighters for his weight that ever lived, came over to my quarters. He had had a quarrel with Jeffries and offered his services to me, saying:

'Jim, I don't want a cent for it, win or lose, but I'd like to be one of your seconds in this fight. I'd like to be in your corner when you lick this fellow.'

Naturally I accepted and considered his coming a great help, he knew so much about fighting and was on to all of Jeffries's ways, having taught him many himself, among them Jeff's peculiar crouching position.

We spent much time discussing Jeffries's blows, particularly that left-hand hook for the body which was the only thing that had worried me in the first fight, and which was his worst weapon.

Incidentally, I might mention that Ryan, who had been in Jeffries's corner that night at Coney Island, told me that Jeff had been in luck to pull the fight out of the fire.

The first afternoon of Ryan's stay, we put on the gloves, and ordering everyone to leave the room, argued pro and con about Jeff's different blows and tried to devise a means of defence. I don't know that it was at all significant, but this was the first time since my younger days that I had listened to any fighter telling me how to fight. Before, I had always relied on my own judgment and intuition. Still, all he said seemed well reasoned out and scientifically correct and I determined to consider his advice.

The blow that worried me was shot over in a deceiving way, in somewhat the manner of a clever baseball pitcher. There was a sort of hook with the left and at the same time a slight uppercut to it. Ryan showed me how, by putting my hand at a certain part of my side, I could catch this blow in my hand, as he said, every time. I tried it on Ryan and he tried it on me until we had this defence down perfectly; and I was much relieved, because this left hand that Jeff would slip in every once in a while had been the only one of Jeffries's stunts that I was afraid of.

On the morning of the fight, we took the boat to Alameda and by a strange coincidence found Jeffries among the passengers, with Delaney, Van Court, and many others that I knew. It was like an Old Home Week. Jeffries too was a Californian, and in the main his friends were mine, as mine were his. Van Court, by the way, whose brother had originally sent Jeff to me at Carson City, often handled men in the ring, and had been asked to act in this fight; but he refused to second anyone against me.

Being older and more staid now, or because we were among friends, I didn't try any of my old ring-poker and mental strategy. I just chatted pleasantly with all the boys, and each of us fighters shook hands and wished each other good luck! As we did this, I found Jeffries actually trembling, he was so nervous.

At nine I went to the Yosemite and at once entered my dressing-room. At ten o'clock I was dressed, had been rubbed down, and was ready to enter the ring, Jeffries having agreed to go in first.

Word came that he had started, and I took some valuables I had with me, and some money, and handed them to an old friend of mine named McKenzie, saying:

'Jack, I'm going in this ring feeling too good.'

'Feeling too good?' he repeated, in surprise.

'Yes,' I answered. 'I'm not nervous enough – too cool. I don't seem worried in any way, and that's the reason I'm afraid something's going to happen.'

It was true, too. I could not work up any excitement at all over the fight, and as I left him I repeated:

'I'll fall down and break an ankle or something. I don't like this feeling so fine. Something is sure to break.'

Then I walked up the aisle and found Jeffries in front of me. Such a big back I thought I had never seen in my life. It seemed like a man-mountain or a big elephant leading a parade. He looked so big that it struck me as funny, and I began to laugh.

We went up through the ropes, and I expected him to come over and shake hands with me. It was the custom for the champion to do this, but he overlooked it, and stood with his back to me talking with Delaney. I had pulled none of the 'old stuff', and, perhaps a little late, thought it was time to begin to work on his nerves a little. So I walked over to him, and said: 'Hello, Jeff', slapping him on his back.

He replied very nervously, and shook hands, again trembling, doubtless because he was thinking of the punishment he had received in the Coney Island battle, when I had out-fought him for twenty-three rounds – and this was to go only twenty.

He didn't grow any easier as we went through the preliminaries. When the photographer asked us to pose for a flashlight and chalked a line for us to toe, he couldn't find the line. His foot was several inches over and when one of the camera men asked him again to toe the line, he fumbled around so that I said to him, as one would to a small boy: 'There, Jeff, get it back on the line.' At that he couldn't manage it and I had to bend over and push his foot back!

For the second flash they wanted us to pose in fighting attitude, so after fixing his toes I had to bend his arms in position.

'Now stay that way!' I ordered him, then got into the picture myself. And all the time I knew that I should have had a little of this nervousness myself.

The day before the fight, in telling Harry not to bet on the rounds, since he would get bigger results by wagering on the result, Jeff being the favourite, I had prophesied something about the fight:

'There is only one way Jeffries can fight me,' I had declared, 'and I know just as well as he how he will fight. If he boxes, he will be out-pointed and he can't afford to try that game. So he'll tear into me from the tap of the gong, using that left if he can, but chiefly roughing me, pushing me, and bearing down on me to tire me out, taking all the advantage he can of his strength and youth.'

These advantages he certainly had, as could be seen by anyone who wanted to compare us as we stood there, both 6 feet $1\frac{1}{2}$ inches in height, but I weighing one hundred and eighty, forty-eight pounds heavier and ten years younger. Those shoulders and back and chest were convincing enough matched against my slenderness. But I wasn't worrying. It all struck me as funny.

Sure enough, as the gong sounded, Jeffries came from his corner running, as though he were in a hundred-yard race, and, as you will remember, he was good at running. At once he tore away with his feared left hook and in the clinches began to maul me and rough me around. But though he was in prime condition and very fast for a man of his size, I skipped out of the way with ease, not yet bothering to try the little defence that Ryan and I had planned; and for the greater part of the first round Jeffries just tumbled all around that ring after me.

When we came up for the second, I decided to save my legs, and try our trick against the left-hand hook. One started; I saw it coming, and I put my hand down, as Ryan and I had planned, to catch the blow and muffle it in my glove. But it was not in the right place – and I took full in the side one of the most terrific body blows I had ever received since the Jackson fight. I sank to the floor, feeling as though all my ribs had been broken; and there I lay.

I knew I couldn't get up in the ten seconds, but the time-keeper was an old, old friend of mine and I thought he might have mercy. I tried to catch his eye, and if ever a man told another without speaking: 'It's all up with me if you don't give me a good long count', I did then. I guess it was really the longest and most deliberate ten ever given to a man in the ring; and Eddie Grainey, the referee, whom I had known since we were boys, and who had handled Choinyski in the old fight on the barge, ordered Jeffries to step back, not only the required ten feet but clear to his corner. And as soon as Jeff was out of ear-shot, he leaned down and whispered to me between counts:

'Get up, Jim, then fall down and take another ten.'

At the 'Nine' – about seventeen seconds must have gone by – I felt I couldn't humiliate any further these old pals who were trying so desperately to give me another chance; and I managed somehow to get up. Jeffries came at me like a lion, I grabbed hold of his arms and the gong sounded.

I got to my corner and sat there, not telling a soul how badly hurt I was or that I thought I had broken my ribs. My seconds looked pretty sad, as they worked away, fanning me, rubbing a damp sponge over me, and trying to freshen me up as much as they could. And things did look bad for me. 'Why didn't I stop it,' I thought to myself, then: 'I guess she (my wife) was right. The old eye and timing aren't there any more.'

I got up for the next round, but couldn't take the straight position that I usually assumed, and tried a crouch like Jeffries. By bending over with my stomach in I found some relief. I also covered my ribs with my right arm, not even lifting it for some time; and I know it both amused and puzzled the old-timers to see me, not erect and supple as I usually was, but locked up in that crouch. They thought it was some new dodge of mine.

I also found that I couldn't pull my head back to avoid a blow, because the motion wrenched so badly the muscles of my hurt side, almost seeming to tear them out. So I was forced to bore into Jeffries – that way I didn't feel the pain quite so much.

Robbed of my footwork and not able to duck, I was knocked down about five times in the first five rounds. I was also hit on the head many times, but one thing I still had left, the old knack of riding the blows. When he hit with his right I would let my head sway with the blow; when he swung to the left, my head would go with his left, so accurately timed that instead of colliding with his fist I would rob it of half its force, and he couldn't hit me squarely, and never found my jaw.

I was in terrible agony, though, but didn't 'let on' to my friends, just sat between rounds saying never a word, and wondering if there was any way out. I couldn't seem to think of, or plan, a thing. I was hitting, of course, fighting close in, as I said, to save my side, but there was no steam behind my blows. I couldn't put my body behind them, since every time I moved at the waist the pain was overpowering.

Still Jeff kept rushing me and trying his darnedest to put me out; so I started to laugh at him and to talk him out of it. I told him what a poor fighter he was, called him an awful excuse for a champion, and told him he 'couldn't put me out in a thousand years', when all the time I wanted him to do it and quickly, to end the misery. But of course I couldn't let up and quit. Pride kept me going.

A strange thing happened when we came out from our corners in the seventh. Instead of making his usual bull-rush, the proper thing for him to do, he stopped and looked at me. As soon as he did that, I realized it could mean but one thing. No man who has his opponent almost out will stop his attack, unless he is pretty well tired himself. So all at once, I called on that last reserve of which I have so often spoken, and started hitting, hitting him right and left, with everything I had. I was landing at will and he was so tired that his hands were hanging at his side. He couldn't lift them. It was no use, there was no strength in my blows. I might as well have been slapping him.

The crowd, however, did not perceive this. When I went to my corner, they seemed to have gone mad and the building rocked with their roar. They had visions of my winning the championship back. But I didn't. No, there was no way out, I said to myself. My plan of battle was all right, for, just as I had told Harry, Jeff, who, great champion as he was, was no champion because of any boxing ability, but because he was so heavy, a natural left-hander, and the fastest man for his weight I ever saw, had hauled and mauled me around with his superior weight. And I had carried him along for seven or eight rounds as I had prophesied so that he felt the effect of those 230 pounds going so fast. To quote myself exactly I had said: 'If I don't get crippled, after the eighth I'll be just as big as Jeffries is and I wouldn't be surprised if I beat him out.' But the thing that had thrown the monkey wrench in the works was that left-hand hook or my defence against it. I cursed myself out for trying another's advice – and for the first time in my life. Listening to others was what had done it – or else my failing eyesight. But there were only a few seconds of the intermission left. I must pull myself together – for the last charge.

Tommy Ryan was crying with joy as he worked over me. 'You've got him licked, Jim,' he said, 'you've got him licked.'

So I had him fooled, too.

I pulled his ear down near me and whispered: 'Tommy, don't get your hopes up; I've been all through since the second. I think a couple of ribs are gone and I've no strength left – just making a flash.'

The gong sounded and again I managed to conceal my weariness and pain and tore in. Still Jeffries couldn't use his arms, but he had gotten on to the fact that I couldn't hurt him, that I had no force in my blows. This confidence kept him on his feet.

In the ninth or tenth – I don't know which and would rather tell it as I remember it than look up the records – Jeffries came to again. He had gathered some strength as I was rushing him, and he struck out. It was another terrific blow – and it landed this time – in the stomach.

I doubled up on the floor.

I don't know so much about what happened afterwards – I started to get up – but Ryan says that just as I was staggering to my feet, Harry forgot all about his promise, and his hat sailed in the ring.

I heard the 'You win!' so near and clear for the last time in my life.

But it was to Jeffries that Grainey spoke.

Like the pitcher that goes too often to the well, the boxer who goes too often to the ring is broken.

Pulling myself together I walked over to Jeffries, as he stood in his corner.

'Jeff,' I told him, 'this is my last fight. I'm never going to try it again. You're a wonderful man; and I've nothing but admiration for you. Good luck.'

I kept my promise. I never fought again.

21

IN my shows we always like to ring down the curtain with a laugh; and I did with a vengeance, on my ring career. For the next night, though feeling pretty rocky, I didn't want to give in and went with some friends to a restaurant where Jeff happened to be sitting celebrating. You should have heard the laugh as I entered – I don't blame them – for I looked so cocky. I had to crook my shoulder because of my side and also wore a big lump on my head from Jeff's blows, so that my new derby wouldn't sit tight. Like an old Bowery tough's, it just perched on the side of my head. However, I was far from feeling so swagger. It was sad to feel out of it, but I had had my day, and was determined to go on with my other work, that on the stage, and do as well as I could to round out prosperously an honourable career.

So the champions come and go. I have seen many a one climb to the top, then fall, strive futilely to climb back, then pass out of the picture. I have heard too each in his day hailed as the greatest of the line, in the most foolish of arguments. It can never be decided really which was supreme since few of the discussed wearers of the crown can be matched with each other at their prime; and so many now lie six feet under.

Still, I feel I can size them up fairly, though some of my newspaper friends think little of me as a prophet. This legend, I believe, is due to two causes: my backing of Jeffries in his fight with Johnson – a stand I had to take despite my doubts, as I was his second – and also to my old custom of coming out in the local papers, when on the road, and hailing the unknown local boy as a coming champion – merely a joke and a publicity trick for my shows. Dempsey I prophesied would knock out Carpentier in four rounds, also Firpo in four (I nearly lost that) and have so called the turn in many bouts, and trained up fighters like Gus Ruhlin whom I taught to defeat with a straight left Sharkey who had previously beaten him in one round.

However, enough of this! It is sufficient to remember that

there are only three reasons for a man becoming champion – he has something that the other fellows haven't, or has it to a greater degree, or else has a better assortment than the other men of his time.

John L. Sullivan had 200 pounds 'in the pink', a magnificent physique, considerable speed for a slugger, ferocious fighting spirit, and a punch as terrific as any man ever uncorked.

Fitzsimmons – Herculean strength from the waist up, and the rare ability to hit with either hand, accurately, from any angle, at long range or close in.

Jeffries – 230 pounds, speed for that size, ox-like strength, a good punch in his right, and a terrific one in his left – if he hadn't been a natural left-hander, he would never have been champion.

Johnson – his blocking and little short punches at close range – in short, his defence, which made up for his light hitting and which no slogger could ever break through.

Willard, those 6 feet 6 inches and 250 poundage – that 'let's him out', as they say.

As for Jackson (never champion, since Sullivan wouldn't give him a chance, but great he was – perhaps the very greatest) – he had range, height, reach, sufficient weight, and the most beautiful of builds. He could box with the cleverest or slug toe to toe with the heaviest hitter, as he chose; and he was equipped with the keenest intelligence.

And such success as I have had was due to boxing science, footwork, speed, and the faculty of out-guessing them, all of which offset my lightness. Then too I had ambition, took care of myself, thought things out and had the ability to dominate the other man. That is the whole of my secret.

And Dempsey, the last?

Fairly quick, with a good punch in each hand, he came up simply through natural fighting spirit, in this being as great as any man I have seen. He is not a clever boxer, showing flashes perhaps in training quarters, but rarely in the ring, the 'weaving' motion of his so often talked about being nothing but the swing of the body as he lets his punches go. Nor does he know much of footwork, nor how to cover and stall when dazed and in trouble, and his punch is not as hard as one thinks. Six times he felled Willard, and up Jess got; five times Firpo in the same round, only to have the latter get up and put him through the ropes.

But, like all champions, he has enough. It is a hard road to the top and he stands there – now. But he will fall – in the dust – like all the others; and a new man will be hailed as the greatest of them all, perhaps some boy now fighting in the back lots of one of our little villages.

It is fun while it lasts, although the strange thing about it all is, that when one is actually at one's best, as I was at New Orleans, one does not realize it. When one does realize it, then starts the decline. But that there was more real genuine fun in the old days of the late eighties and nineties I thoroughly believe, because the sport was not so tainted with commercialism. Then the competition was keener, battles more frequent, and there were not such long waits between the defendings of titles, while the loser frequently got little or nothing for all his work and pains, fighting for sheer love of the game.

But my hat is off to anyone who reaches the top, today, or at any time for that matter. It will always be a struggle – make no mistake about that, taking ambition and courage and will-power as well as clean living to win. It is for these things that the prize-ring, with all the brutality and faults that go with it, still is of importance in life.

But – I must not preach – and I do not fight any more, except in life, where I still have battles. To use an old expression of mine, I have not 'taken a real punch' at anyone in many a year.

I came near it once some time after my retirement, on the Long Island Ferry, when Fritz Williams, the actor, and my old friend, had been threatened by three plug-uglies while he was escorting his wife home from the theatre. Looking down the boat he spied me and waved casually as though nothing were the matter, calling out so the whole boat-load could hear:

'Hello, Jim Corbett! Going my way?'

The three plug-uglies faded out of the picture.

Such is reputation that persists long after a man has gone. I think old Mark Twain, dear old Mark, another good friend of mine, put it nicely one night not long before he died. I had not known him before, but seeing him in a crowd at a benefit I introduced myself to him.

'I've always admired you, Mr Twain,' I said, 'though I've

206

never met you before. I want to shake your hand. My name's Jim Corbett.'

Putting his dear old white head down on my shoulder, he held up his hand.

'Don't hit me, Jim,' he said with a smile.

No, I'm not hitting anyone any more, except in my good-natured act on the stage. The roar of the crowd is no longer for me. I am one of them.

(Signed)

JIM CORBETT.